THE DIGITAL
WORKPLACE

THE DIGITAL WORKPLACE

Designing Groupware Platforms

Charles E. Grantham

with Larry D. Nichols

VNR VAN NOSTRAND REINHOLD
New York

Copyright © 1993 by Van Nostrand Reinhold

Library of Congress Catalog Card Number 92-46201
ISBN 0-442-01123-7

I(T)P   Van Nostrand Reinhold is a division of International Thomson Publishing. ITP logo is a trademark under license.

Printed in the United States of America

Van Nostrand Reinhold
115 Fifth Avenue
New York, NY 10003

International Thomson Publishing
Berkshire House
168-173 High Holborn
London WC1V7AA, England

Thomas Nelson Australia
102 Dodds Street
South Melbourne 3205
Victoria, Australia

Nelson Canada
1120 Birchmount Road
Scarborough, Ontario
M1K 5G4, Canada

16 15 14 13 12 11 10 9 8 7 6 5 4 3 2 1

Library of Congress Cataloging in Publication Data

Grantham, Charles E.
    The digital workplace : designing groupware platforms / by
Charles E. Grantham with Larry D. Nichols.
       p. cm.
    Includes bibliographical references and index.
    ISBN 0-442-01123-7
    1. Communication in organizations—Data processing. 2. Work
groups—Data processing. 3. Customer service—Data processing.
4. Management information systems. 5. Information resources
management. 6. Organizational change. I. Nichols, Larry D.
II. Title.
HD30.3.G73   1993
651.8—dc20

92-46201
CIP

To the memory of Jean Marie Arp

And to Joan Nichols

CONTENTS

Preface

This book is meant to help managers and executives make better decisions and take effective action when they are faced with integrating advanced communication technologies into their core business operations. It is intended to provide understandable, practical advice and tools to accomplish this technology diffusion process.

Introduction of technologies into large, complex organizations creates a change in the process of communicating among people; a change in the heart of the connection between work and a change in the structure of the organization, especially in information intensive industries. The relationship among technology, teamwork, and business processes as they relate to the service of customers forms the central thrust of this book. Our work with business managers consistently points to a lack of ways to think about technology introduction. We find that guidelines for managing this process is the key factor in the effective use of computers and telecommunications.

The driving technology of change is software, as it controls and shapes communication among workers; software which paints a picture of organizational functioning; and lastly, software which moulds the way information is presented to workers and customers alike. The subject area of the book is how to effectively design, develop, and implement these new software platforms that integrate work teams and distributed organizations.

The major contribution of the book is in providing access to bodies of knowledge and experience in separate disciplines to an audience of business managers. Further, it provides a distinctive structured thinking framework for readers to apply in their day-to-day management activities. In synopsis, the book provides:

- Focus on integration of technology diffusion and organizational change
- Develops a perspective of "social factors" as a design strategy
- Adds the dimension of dynamics to structural analysis of organizations
- Builds upon the metaphor of visual data analysis as a management tool
- Offers practical guidance for increasing executive capabilities

The tone of the book is somewhat academic and we hope that will not put off the more professional business audience. We hope that the additional references and technical language will act as a guide to further investigation of the many issues we raise in these pages. Readers are encouraged to go beyond what we have written, check the original sources of our thinking, and expand your own thinking by taking our material and modifying it to meet your unique needs.

This book has taken the better part of two years to complete and as it goes to press we are aware it is incomplete because the world continues to change. When we began this venture, our primary focus was to provide accessibility to a set of diverse literatures, disciplines and traditions of managing the changing workplace and technology diffusion. As we reach this point, we are struck by the pervasive magnitude of organizational changes over the globe. We truly do believe that a new way of working is emerging, especially in the symbolic analysts jobs that Robert Reich, the Secretary of Labor, talks about.

This new way of working is the birth of *The Digital Workplace*. This book is intended to make that birth a natural one—one filled with hope and promise. We wish you, the reader, a good journey through the territory we have mapped out here. This new way of working has begun to influence workgroup, company, and even national work processes and structures. This book is intended to help that influence be a positive improvement over old ways—to help move work knowledge towards work understanding.

Acknowledgments

There are many people to acknowledge for this book. In the early days, as the ideas were maturing, we were influenced and coached by our consulting partners, Eric Lloyd and Barney Barnett. As time went on and a larger and larger audience was exposed to our thinking, our difficulties in expressing complex ideas succinctly increased. So we acknowledge the clients and graduate students who endured countless iterations of our attempt to communicate our ideas clearly.

Of note are the many colleagues who acted as reviewers and critics. Dr. Brad Hesse, American Institutes for Research; Ms. Cynthia Lewis; Dr. Kate Ehrlich, Sun Microsystems; Dr. Hans Brunner, US West Advanced Technology; Professor Shumpei Kumon, GLOCOM; Adam Peake, Institute for Network Design; and Susan Stefanac and Barry Warren Polley, Association for Software Design. Our special thanks to Susan Kinney, University of Georgia, who with great diligence went through large portions of the manuscript, not once but twice and to Professor Victoria Marsick, Columbia Teachers College, who encouraged us strongly to move quickly and get our ideas into print.

Our families were especially patient with our absence. Their support was critical for us to stay the course as our efforts turned from joy to work and back to joy again. To them, we promise we won't say "Someone ought to write a book about that" for at least six months. Also to Zak the Wonder Dog who kept Charlie's feet warm while writing.

The faculty and staff of the University of San Francisco were very supportive of this effort. Acting Dean Robin Pratt and Associate Director Bonnie Blystone who saw fit to let Charlie experiment with telecommuting were very helpful in letting us live out what we were writing about. A sincere thanks to Karen Cobb who edited large portions of the manuscript and kept things organized.

And of course, the marvelous team at Van Nostrand Reinhold who coached us along and bore with us in the rough spots: Larry Press who was the person who encouraged us to embark upon the project and held us to a high standard of clarity with our writing; Dianne Littwin for her encouragement and shared enthusiasm; and Risa Cohen for cheering us on, and making sure everything was gone through just one more time to make sure. Without them, we would still be writing and rewriting.

Also, we would like to express our sincere appreciation to the AT & T foundation for their financial support. Their help has allowed us to take our ideas and present them to colleagues in Europe, who are living out the process of becoming a Digital Workplace.

Lastly, sincere appreciation to all those who we haven't mentioned by name. There are very few people that we deal with who can't enjoy some credit for this work. To all those people we are grateful and give credit for the helpful thinking you will find in this book, and from all of them, we withhold any blame for errors, omissions, and unhelpful thinking.

THE DIGITAL
WORKPLACE

1

Introduction

THE PURPOSE OF THIS BOOK

This book is about organizational change. Specifically, this book deals with organizational change that occurs as new communications technologies are introduced into the workplace. Although organizational change and technology diffusion are usually treated as separate topics of research and analysis, the purpose of this book is to integrate these two streams of thought. We believe that this integration has not taken place because:

1. The theories underlying organizational and technology design are too complex to hold in the mind at once without some overarching cognitive construct
2. Lack of role clarity between technologists and general management resulting in an absence of responsibility for managing the change process
3. A general lack of ability to confront organizational re-structuring

This first chapter presents a general cognitive model used to counter the first barrier to integration of organizational and technological design. The book follows the Enneagram model of a nine stage process in completing a task. This model, borrowed from the work of John Bennett, has been adapted for use in various fields, such as manufacturing, psychology, and strategic planning. We have chosen this model because, over many years in consulting with software developers and in organizational development projects, we have found it useful.

So why write a book about organizational change and technology? The short answer is that many trends in the business world are combining to create a need to

1

increase decision-making effectiveness. Global competitiveness and the spread of a radically different business climate are the two major drivers of this need.

Organizational change and technology use are typically seen as separate activities by corporate executives.[1] However, every major change in culture has been associated with the adoption of a new technology. The invention of gunpowder gave rise to modern warfare and, some would argue, the rise of the nation state. Later, the printing press spread knowledge to the masses and a mercantile class arose.[2] We feel that not only must these events (organizational change and technology introduction) be thought of as parts of one event, but also that each will fall short of its purpose without a thoughtful process of accommodating the other. This book is about how to provide that accommodation.

Efficiency and Effectiveness

Decisions must be made about what technologies to use to increase business effectiveness. Decisions must be made about how best to organize workgroups to promote improvement in individual, organizational, and business effectiveness. Business leaders who develop methods of continuously increasing their decision-making effectiveness will be successful; others will not. There is an important distinction between decision-making efficiency (the purview of economists) and effectiveness. Making decisions quickly is not necessarily effective. By effective, we mean decisions that link today's action to tomorrow's productive result. Put another way, making the right decision—grounded in the purpose of the organization—is effective decision making. One key strategic advantage in the information age is decision *effectiveness*.

TECHNOLOGY DIFFUSION CREATES CHANGE

Changes in technologies are inextricably linked to changes in organizational process and, often, to structures as well. Communication technology, for example, has altered the way in which people interact in the workplace, which, in turn, has changed the nature of working relationships. We have all experienced this with the introduction of personal computers ten years ago and, more recently, the ubiquitous facsimile machine and electronic mail. We feel that an elevation of the understanding of technology diffusion and organizational change is essential.

The aim of this book is to place in the hands of business managers an understandable, practical, and accessible set of models and procedures to assist them in managing organizational change. The book's premise is that if managers have understandable models and practical guidelines, they will increase the effectiveness of their decision making. We posit a general model called the Enneagram for managing the change process. This model is a mental map of the steps, and a sequencing of the action, which managers must go through to successfully manage any organizational change. Our belief is that introduction of new technologies is creating a climate ripe for the fundamental restructuring of business enterprise, especially in Europe and the United States. For example, at this writing, legislation is pending in the U.S. Congress to create a national coordinating authority for the emergence trend of "telework." Many firms are moving business operations to parts of the world where labor is cheaper and integrating their operations through use of technology.

THE FUTURE OF WORK

Information technologies are creating new forces in our environment, forces that promote formation of new organizations. For example, key workers can—and do—live hundreds of miles from their employer's location and only travel to "the office" once or twice a month. The old centralized, formal bureaucracy is crumbling. Even "bigness" is under attack. Small, independent workgroups are linking up from all over the landscape. One firm, The Networking Institute in Boston, specializes in training managers how to link their small enterprises together. They report success in efforts ranging from connecting metal-working firms in Ohio to large operations of aircraft manufacture in California and Taiwan.

Economic pressures, environmental concerns, and congested transportation arteries have made consideration of alternative ways to work an imperative. Telecommuting is growing as one of the best alternatives to more traditional patterns of work in businesses throughout the world. Now, telecommunications technologies are starting to combine in ways that allow groups of people separated by great distance and working at different times to work in a collaborative fashion.

Computers, and more specifically programs on the computers, shape the form of information; telecommunication provides the pipeline to move information; education becomes the content of highest value; entertainment influences the style of human-to-human communication, making it enjoyable and less formal. Tremendous increases in computer power and integration of technologies into "multimedia" and "telepresence" are eliminating the distances between people. We are beginning to see that there is great potential in the phrase, "Move information, not people."

There is a new electronic workplace growing up around us. Its most visible manifestation is telecommuting. People are working at home, or in a community center, two or three days a week. Current estimates are that two percent of the white-collar workforce in large metropolitan areas are presently telecommuting and this is projected to increase to 10 percent of the white-collar workforce by the end of the decade.[3] LINK Resources, a market research firm, estimates the number of home-based telecommuters in the United States at 5.5 million, or 4.4 percent of the entire workforce—an increase of 250 percent in the past four years.

This change in how we work together is a complex process of change. It is helping the environment by cutting down pollution and saving energy. There are even reports that telecommuting is good for lowering stress levels of harried office workers. However, the real issue is productivity.[4] Productivity is the compelling issue in America and any new workplace needs to be evaluated as an advancement of worker productivity at both individual and work unit levels.

Precise figures are difficult to come by, but some preliminary studies have shown as much as 16 percent increases in productivity for certain tasks through telecommuting.[5] Companies with effective telecommuting programs are experiencing enough of a gain that they are not talking about it too much, as they see their work process as a strategic advantage.

The Potential

Large organizations are rethinking the values of bigness as they hear more about the flexibility needed in the marketplace and as the quality movement cries for business to lower the barriers between organizations as a means of integrating suppliers, producers, and customers. Some organizations are restructuring themselves into independent business units. In some cases, these independent units are actually the precursors of autonomous business units.[6]

In the future, work units will be formed where, and as, needed by an electronic coming together of workers via a centralized broker to perform specific, issue-oriented tasks, and then dispersing again. An increasingly ubiquitous information technology is furthering this process. The spread of Integrated Services Digital Network (ISDN)[7] technology will allow the development of community work centers, where independent workers go and plug into the virtual workplace. Increased bandwidth can help spur this movement along, much the same way the placement of highways helped increase suburban growth. ISDN is just the most visible form of electronic highway. Other forms, such as use of cable television for telephone traffic, or power cables for data transmission, may enter the competition in early 1993.[8]

However, a major barrier exists to the realization of this vision. Our current economic infrastructure, based on the man-as-machine model, assumes that the organization has the power to withhold salary and benefits. If, for a moment, we take a view suggested by Handy in his *Age of Unreason*, and turn the world upside down, we can envision a quite different scenario. A scenario driven by scarcity of workers, not work. A scenario driven by increased global interconnectivity, where work moves to the worker willing to do it.

What if the market continues to demand productivity increases, and people start to have more choice in where and for whom to work, even on an hour-by-hour basis? We don't believe this will be true for all occupations. Current estimates show that this way of working could be applicable to approximately 20–30 percent of the current workforce.[9] These new, emergent ways of working highlight two major issues for employees: pensions and health insurance.

Under current conditions, the loyal employee puts in time toward a pension. And companies have learned how to make quite a bit of money on the pension fund. But what if the pension went with the person through a portable pension? Then, the company has some new issues, and so does the employee. Pension plans are emerging to address this "portability" issue. For example, college professors contribute to a plan that transcends any particular university. It is quite normal in this career path for faculty members to work at several universities over their lifetime. Contributions made by faculty and their employers are credited to a central account, which is the combined source of their retirement annuities. We believe this issue of portability of pensions will be a major public policy question in the 1990s.

The second problem deals with health insurance for people working in such a fashion. Right now there are no quick answers to this issue. The trend is towards increasing the amount of payment made by employees toward their health plan as the percentage paid by employers decreases. We believe this problem of individual-based, affordable health insurance is tied to the larger issue currently being debated in the United States about nationalized health insurance. We would point to Canadian and Scandinavian examples as models that would enable a transition in the United States to this new way of working. For the present, we find that individuals are negotiating contracts with employers on a case-by-case basis to maintain an equitable position vis-a-vis the more traditional office worker.

Employees have learned a bitter lesson about corporate loyalty. The current move toward "downsizing" has been a shock for most workers affected. In a very large number of instances, employees have seen senior officers grow rich while laying off workers. They now know they work for themselves.

We believe that this shift away from employee-company mutual loyalty will grow in the 1990s as American business learns to adapt to new processes of getting work done.[10] Technology is giving workers, and soon communities, the democracy that business and government have conspired to deny them. Soon, companies will have to "market" their working conditions along with their products. We are already beginning to see this in specific pockets of the new "symbolic analysts." Areas like Silicon Valley in California and the famous Route 128 area of Massachusetts are reporting problems in obtaining and retaining these highly skilled workers, unless a significant effort is made to address their concerns about environment, pollution, traffic congestion, and education.

Communities are becoming communities of choice. People pick living locations because of climate, access to recreation, and the community ambiance. Access to work and schools becomes secondary. The *future of work* is really a reversal of a 350-year trend. Work and home are coming back together. There is a change in urban form occurring as communities are being reconstructed on a new model. For example, in California, entire communities are designed around the use of technology to substitute for travel.

Employees will want even more in the way of education and training for themselves and their children. Neighborhood work centers are constructed as an integral part of housing developments and combine educational, work, and day care functions.[11] The U.S. government is looking for ways to deliver higher-quality education through technology infrastructure that would link homes, schools, libraries, and government service centers.

Although the major impact of this trend is felt first by highly skilled workers, the return to community is a process that very quickly spreads to service occupations and in-person services. In our own research with telecommuters in public sector jobs, we note that they span all job categories from attorney to administrative clerk. Business in these community centers also benefits greatly as they also restore declining areas.[12]

Barriers to Change

But middle management is not a quick friend of these alternative ways of working. Separating workers and managers in both time and space creates problems. Recent surveys show managers fear situations where knowledge workers can't be seen directly.

"How do we know they are working if we can't see them?" is the refrain often reported. The utility of a middle manager who translates company direction into specific work instruction obviously becomes useless overhead because workers do not need to be that closely supervised. At the heart of management's fear is a realization that the work processes and structure that promoted the growth of a middle management layer are no longer relevant in a continuous information environment.[13] Scheduling, coordinating, planning, and tracking are increasingly being embedded in network functions. When Local Area Networks arrive in the workplace, "productivity" is the issue of concern. But, when Electronic Data Interchange becomes the maturing technology, issues of business sustainability move to the forefront because the unique identity of the business firm is blurred when the boundaries between different firms disappear. Workers themselves begin to serve as their own managers.

Workers demand ever more say in *how work gets done*—spurred on by the quality movement, a more diverse workforce, and their own increased mobility. For example, the movement towards "self-managing work teams" is a popular response to this idea in production industries.[14] The most successful way to support the movement toward the distributed work environment is through education, policy analysis, and research aimed at understanding workgroup productivity. Not all work tasks can be adequately supported in the telework environment. In general, tasks that can be separated as discrete units from an overall workflow are prime candidates for telecommuting. Tasks that require individual concentration (such as computer programming), report writing, and most forms of paper processing are very amenable to telecommuting. Group planning, negotiation activities, and strategic decision making are not well suited to this electronic environment. If it's something you can do in your own cubicle at work, you can probably do it more effectively in a home work center, where fewer distractions allow you to increase productivity significantly.

Just what type of work is getting done in these new workgroups? The work is the type that Reich has called "symbolic analysis." It is the information-intensive task that involves problem identifying, problem solving, and strategic brokering, or linking problems and solutions. Typically, people have such job titles as scientists, engineers, public relations experts, lawyers, accountants, and consultants. Their core work tasks are those that require individual concentration and are part of a larger workflow.

History of Technology Changes

Technology has been affecting organizations for a long time. We have had telephones in business for almost 100 years, computers for 40, and personal computers for 15. The basic trend that we focus on in this book is the shift from mainframe computing—and the organizational structures and systems that flow from it—to the paradigm in which network computing becomes dominant. The corresponding cultural shift is seen in erosion of company loyalty, questions about empowerment, and other cultural issues.

From a historical perspective, computing has gone through five distinct stages. We can describe each of these stages with a distinct purpose, principle, and root metaphor. The first stage came in the mid-1950s. The purpose of computers during this time was to solve existing scientific and engineering problems faster. Processing complex numerical calculations was the focus of computers. The principle for computer engineers was that the machine was preeminent. The application of computer power was almost mystical and the root metaphor was *the back room*. Wizards worked in the back room and practiced an art of engineering.

The second phase spanned the mid-1950s to about 1967. Computer use was primarily to centralize business data resources. The data-processing industry was born. Routine business operations, such as payrolls and invoice processing, became computerized. Control became the principle as computer engineers fanned out through the business and began centralizing processing power and strengthening middle management. The root metaphor was *the data processing center*. Business data processing was internal to the center; users saw only the input and output. You dropped off your card deck, and came back the next morning to see if your program "ran."

The next stage of computer use was the longest stage and carried us well into the late 1970s and ended with the appearance of the minicomputer. This was the frontier stage, characterized by an explosion of computer power. Everything, without question, was subject to automation. Computer professionals became "the keepers of the corporate database," which was jealously guarded. *The warehouse* became the metaphor of the period. Each business department had its own wizard who could talk to the keepers of the database.

The 1980s was the decade of the neighborhood mechanic. Information resource centers sprang up all over the business with their own "supermini" computers and localized databases. A struggle for power was under way and continues today. Specialties grew up and control moved from the center to the periphery as "information community developers" became the norm. Each manager had a local guru who had responsibility for departmental-level data. The root metaphors changed again and computing power came from *The Neighborhood Garage*. Conducting business without computers became very difficult to visualize.

The stage we find ourselves in now is the development of applications tools that allow many people to tailor computer power to their needs. Computer professionals are seen as business team members. The key question is "tell me how to drive this computer." *Partnership* is the central image. Computer science[15] emerges and assists in designing core business processes to take advantage of technology's capabilities.

Our speculation? The next stage will be the "democratization of computers," as computing power moves from under the desk to the laptop. It is already moving to finger tips of workers. *Hunters and farmers* become metaphors for seeing computer users. Some people take the tools to the field; others stay home with them. The advent of portable, affordable computers is another manifestation of this development. Hunters carry their tools with them. Farmers leave them at a central location that they return to on a regular basis. Business process and computer design merge. In fact, they become very interactive as new technologies are developed to meet the needs of changing work patterns.

The full 350-year cycle is nearing completion. Before the onset of mercantilism, people worked at home selling their output at the village market. With the rise of capitalism, people moved to town to work with others for companies creating output (i.e., products) under the control of agents of supervision. Now we are moving back to people working at home, selling their output in an omnipresent global market.

THE PLAN OF THIS BOOK

This book is designed to be unique in several respects. When you review the current management literature on the topics of technology diffusion and organizational change, you find little cross-referencing, and limited, if any, integration of concepts. Our own practical work in the field as organizational design consultants for over 15 years has shown that both a conceptual and *practical* integration is required for success in managing these change processes. Therefore, we offer you four threads of thought and action:

1. Focus on integration of technology diffusion with organizational change
2. Develop a perspective of "social factors" as an organizational design strategy
3. Add the dimension of dynamics to structural analysis of organizations
4. Create a symbol of visual data analysis as a management tool.

As you go through the book, you should constantly refer to these four central themes. Ask yourself, "How does this material fit into the four central themes?" These themes are the context of the book.

The plan of this book follows the outline of a series of management-development seminars we have put together over the past few years. Each chapter is a distillation of a separate two-day training seminar. The plan that runs through the series is that individual capability needs to be built first, then team effectiveness, business process, and—finally—installation of systems that promote continual improvement. The purpose of using a central map of the process organizational change (i.e., the Enneagram) is to provide a reliable map of linking organizational change and technology diffusion. As you will see, the Enneagram is a highly reliable model for this process and its use forces a consideration of all factors necessary for effective management of changing business processes.

The Enneagram Model: History and Applications

The Enneagram model depicted in Figure 1-1 comes from a tradition of Sufi mysticism. "The word *Enneagram* stems from the Greek *ennea,* meaning 'nine,' and *grammos,* meaning 'points.' It is a nine-pointed star diagram that can be used to map the process of any event from its inception through all the stages of that event's progress in the material world."[16] It is often called a nine-term system. There is a logic behind the choice of a nine-term system to represent completion of a creative process—bringing an idea to fruition. Other term systems, used throughout the book, also have significance. For example, a three-term system represents dialectical change; four-term systems represent rational order; five-terms, uniqueness; six-terms, structural stability; and seven-terms, the process of transformation. Nine terms, in Bennett's schema, are the minimum necessary for creation.[17]

The Enneagram provides us with a conceptual model of *process.* We are

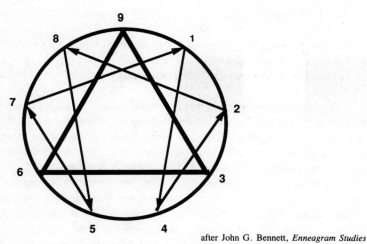

after John G. Bennett, *Enneagram Studies*

Figure 1-1. *The Enneagram Model*

concerned here with providing a reliable model of thinking that has proven itself useful in organizational development practice. The Enneagram is a *map* of the organizational change process. There certainly are others, such as McWhinney's use of different "pathways of change."[18] We have found the Enneagram to be very reliable in application in numerous settings.

The history of the Enneagram can be traced back as far as the oral history of the Sumerians and the legend of Gilgamesh. The Enneagram has been used in several contexts. Personality analysis, project planning, and experimental designs are among the better-known applications. The Enneagram entered Western intellectual circles through the teaching of G. I. Gurdjieff in the 1920s. The tradition was carried on by his students—the most notable being John G. Bennett. The most lucid explanation of the enneagram is contained in Bennett's *Enneagram Studies* of 1983. Our application of the model to organizational design (particularly that associated with technology) represents an extension of the model to new fields of practice.

Difference Between the Thinking and Doing Processes

The enneagram is, as we quoted, a map of a process. In this book, we will apply it to the process of organizational change. As with any systemic analysis, you first carefully bound the problem. There are several system principles that underlie the construction of the Enneagram model, as adapted from J. G. Bennett.[19,20] The basic principles of enneagram operation are:

1. Every process that moves from inception to completion undergoes deviation from the planned path due to environmental disturbances.

2. Only with an externally constructed feedback system can the process be maintained on course.
3. Certain points in the process can be identified where application of environmental feedback is most effective.
4. This feedback process itself requires adjustment and more feedback.

To fully understand the Enneagram it is easiest to break it down into its constituent parts. Figure 1-2 is a diagram of the Enneagram's inner pattern of the triad. The points that correspond to points 9, 3, and 6 are the dynamism of the process as mapped by the Enneagram. They are the points where corrective feedback can be introduced to the process under study. As an example, consider an airplane flight.

A good pilot understands that there are certain times where course alignment and correction can be most effective. Point 9 represents planning the flight path before takeoff. This feedback initiates a process of mapping the desired results (flight path) to the environment as known (weather conditions, other air traffic). After the flight has commenced, it is typical to conduct a midcourse correction (Point 3) to adjust to unforeseen condition in the process such as changes in weather, air currents, etc. This may also represent a point of no return. Halfway there, and you need to make a decision to continue or turn back with ample fuel supplies. The final correction point comes just before landing when detailed course changes are made on approach (Point 6). This is the final opportunity to make a last-minute adjustment before completing the flight.

The second constituent parts of the Enneagram represent the movement of the process through the steps labeled Points 1 through 9 in linear order. That is, the Enneagram depicts a process that moves from step 1 to 2 and so on, in order, until step 9. Step 9 then represents the beginning of the next iteration of the cycle. In our example, information from the last flight updates the pilot for planning the next flight, perhaps a return route.

The unusual-looking pattern of lines inside the circle is called the hexad (or six

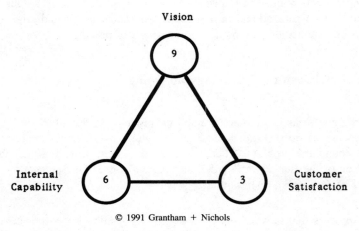

© 1991 Grantham + Nichols

Figure 1-2. *The Tri-Gram: Sources for Correction*

points). This is an internal pattern that is distinct from how the process occurs. These lines represent the pattern of *thinking* about the process. So we have a basic distinction:

Outer Process	Points 1, 2, 3, 4, 5, 6, 7, 8, 9	in order	How the process occurs
Inner Process	Points 1, 4, 2, 8, 5, 7	in order	How we think about the process

The outer process is linear in nature, a way of thinking that most of us are comfortable with. However, the inner process is *systemic* in nature and unfamiliar. When we plan to do something, we usually move from an image of the product, to the process necessary for construction, and finally a consideration of what tools will be needed. That is, what we want to do, how do we do it, and lastly, what do we need to do it?

However, when we actually do the task, we move in a different order. We collect the tools, complete the process, and then admire the results. The Enneagram is a way to capture in pictorial, visual form the essence of the distinction between thinking about something and doing it. Let's try a practical application of the Enneagram to the organizational change process.

Application of the Enneagram

Irmis Popoff (1978) was a student of the Gurdjiffean school. One of the examples he uses to illustrate application of the Enneagram is "the repair of an object." One could take the perspective that much of the organizational design work is, in essence, repairing an object. That is, we have an organization that is seen as deviating significantly from its desired direction, condition, or attainment. The organization is

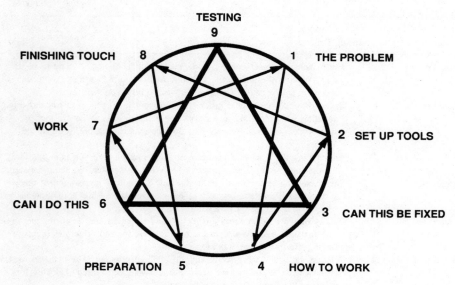

Figure 1-3. *The Enneagram: The Popoff Model*

off its intended flight plan, in the terms of our previous example. When we apply the Enneagram map to the process of repairing an object, we get the Enneagram shown in Figure 1-3.

Now let's trace the two separate processes of doing and thinking. The actual implementation of the repair process is linear and follows the pattern 1, 2, 3, 4, 5, 6, 7, 8, 9. Table 1-1 delineates that process and specifies the key questions the manager should be asking at each point.

The essential requirement for problem solution is the right pattern of action. For maximum effectiveness of action, you need good design—that is, planning the actions and how to carry them out. That would be, in our example, thinking through what

Table 1-1   The Doing Process[21]

Step/Point 1.	The problem—what is malfunctioning.	What is wrong?
Step/Point 2.	Bringing together all the tools you need to repair the object. All necessary tools so you won't have to interrupt the process to get tools you need.	What do I need to fix it?
Step/Point 3.	Reconsidering whether the problem is solvable.	Can this be Fixed?
Step/Point 4.	Viewing the problem and tools you can see how the repair must proceed.	What Do I do, in What Order?
Step/Point 5.	Preparing the work site. Possibly taking things apart to fix it.	Are things in worse condition than I thought?
Step/Point 6.	Committing to the work.	Can we really do this?
Step/Point 7.	The actual work—doing the repair. Combining all previous steps. Merging theory and practice.	How are we doing?
Step/Point 8.	Finish work. Cleaning up details and polishing. This is where the object can be made better than it was originally.	How can we make it better?
Step/Point 9.	Testing.	Does this meet our original repair goal?

Table 1-2   The Planning Process[22]

Step/Point 1-4.	The reason the object doesn't work must be understood first. The manager asks: What is the underlying systemic malfunction? Getting beyond the symptom to the cause. Looking forward to how you will fix it.
Step/Point 4-2.	Once you understand what process is necessary for repair, you can move to deciding what tools are necessary. The manager asks: Who are the stakeholders and what capabilities do I need? Looking backward in the process.
Step/Point 2-8.	Anticipating the final touches necessary and making sure you have the tools for that task, also. The manager asks: What is the plan? Looking forward.
Step/Point 8-5.	The finishing touches won't be useful unless adequate preparation of the work surface has been done correctly. The manager asks: What commitments are necessary? Looking backward.
Step/Point 5-7.	Quality of work depends on quality of the foundation laid down for the work. The manager asks: What are the purpose, vision, and principles involved? Laying the foundation. Looking forward.
Step/Point 7-1.	Relating the actual work to the initially defined problem. The manager asks: How will we know that we accomplished what we wanted? Looking forward a final time.

you are going to do: the why, how, and what. Applying this planning process to repairing an object yields a different set of steps. Table 1-2 illustrates these planning steps.

A useful way of testing your understanding of the conceptual map the Enneagram represents is to apply it to a process you are very familiar with. The most common teaching example is that of preparing and serving a meal. When a cook enters a kitchen, he or she has a purpose in mind. In the case of cooking, it is to sustain the life-force of people who consume the food. This purpose starts the process and corresponds to Point 9 of the Enneagram—it is what comes before any activity starts. Point 1 on the diagram signifies the kitchen ready for work. All the tools, utensils, and equipment are assembled and ready for use.

Beginning work in the kitchen is represented by Point 2. Food now comes into the process to be acted upon by peeling, cutting, or whatever preparation is needed; this is Point 3 of the Enneagram. Next, Point 4 (the actual preparation) takes place and is followed by Point 5, the actual cooking. Point 6 represents a state of readiness for people to consume the meal. If there were no hunger, it would not be necessary to continue the process. Point 7 is serving the meal and Point 8 the act of eating. This completes the "doing" part of the Enneagram and seems fairly straightforward.

However, if you try to jump from Point 3 (raw food) directly to Point 8 (eating), something would be missing: the preparing, cooking, and serving of the meal. Admittedly, this is a simple example, but it can be placed in the context of a manager saying "Let's computerize the accounting function" and jumping right to implementation (eating). Obviously, some important steps have been left out.

Now look at the "thinking" part of the use of the Enneagram in this example. In Point 1 (ready to work), we must look forward to Point 4 (preparing the food). If potatoes are to be served, we first need to think about whether they are to be boiled, fried, or baked. This decision has implications for what work actually occurs (Point 5) and how the food will be served (Point 7) and eaten (Point 8). We think analogies can be drawn that apply to business enterprises.[23]

THE FORCES CREATING CHANGE: VISION, CUSTOMERS, AND ABILITIES

Figure 1-2 illustrates where corrective forces can come into play, and you can see that organizational change is also driven by consideration of factors external to the business. This gives us a way of viewing the corrective forces that must be put into place to ensure a proper result from a planned intervention. In the cases we are discussing here, these intervention processes revolve around the introduction of new technologies or technologically-driven new processes to improve organizational effectiveness.

When you map a normal business process to the Enneagram, Points 9, 3, and 6 correspond to direction and strategy, customer satisfaction, and internal functioning capability. That is, direction and strategy need to be clear and articulated, customer satisfaction must drive the product and process under consideration, and effort must be expended to continuously improve capability. This introductory chapter itself represents Point 9, where we define purpose and determine what is not working right now.

Clearly, in our opinion, what is not working now is business attempts to improve by technology alone—a new systems, a new vendor, better machinery; or by organizational change methods alone—a new charismatic leader, a new vocabulary, or constant restructuring.

First we must ask ourselves why businesses are not effective before we can proceed to know how to go about fixing them. It is our opinion that the *why* rests basically on problems of communication within the organization. Therefore the next chapter focuses on communication processes as a foundation for integrating technology with organizational improvement.

A NOTE TO READERS: THE PATTERN THAT CONNECTS

Before continuing, let's step back and take a look at the overall pattern of this book, which follows the map of the Enneagram. Each chapter corresponds to a point of the Enneagram process. Figure 1-4 relates each chapter topic to the Enneagram.

Chapter 1 centers on Purpose: Why do you need to plan for technology introduction? We hope to make clear in the following chapters that lack of planning for the organizational change that always comes with new technologies leads to an ineffective organization. On the up side, if appropriate planning and interventions are put in place, a business enterprise can yield benefits both in efficiencies of operation and increased ability to respond to changing market conditions.

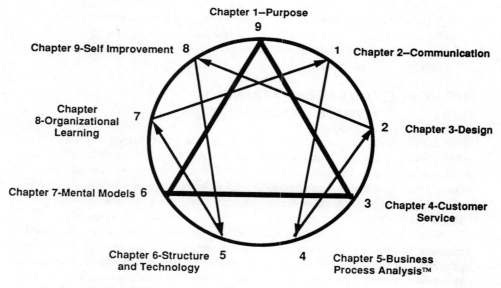

Figure 1-4. *The Enneagram Model and the Plan of the Book*

Our next chapter is about interpersonal communication. We believe that interpersonal communication is the cornerstone of healthy organizations. Without good communication among all team members, you cannot expect any organizational intervention to improve the business. Things are only made worse. Technologies that mediate communication, such as computer networks, are especially sensitive to this process. Once clear communication processes are in place, the cost to change the business for whatever reason is reduced because of the lack of redundancies, a focus on priorities, and smooth coordination between organizational members.

Chapter 3 is about our method of designing organizational processes. We believe that you always get what you design. No design, no results. Just as an architect designs a building before construction starts, we feel that you need to design the process of introducing a new technology. Failure in design, or complete lack of it, often yields an unexpected result. Some very strong leaders seem to have the intuitive ability to "design on the fly"; however, this is a rare talent, and we would not suggest that the future viability of a business be entrusted to an assumption that this skill resides in any one leader.

Chapter 4 of the book relates to Point 3 of the Enneagram: corrective input from customers. The intent of Chapter 4 is to provide readers with a proven organizational intervention process that we have found ensures necessary and sufficient input. More and more customers are being drawn into the actual conceptualization, engineering, and production process of technologies. Companies can not afford to build the wrong product—they seldom get a second chance. Proper use of customer input reduces design time, decreases reworking and increases customer satisfaction.

Chapter 5 (Point 4 on our process map) is concerned with making more effective use of your resources—the "how to work" of the Enneagram. We suggest here that taking a careful look at how you produce, market, and support your product is a good business strategy. What often gets in the way is that this takes time and energy. The Japanese have become absolute masters of reengineering business process and have shown the rest of the world that the effort is worth the investment.[24] Your internal organizational processes need to reflect the true requirements of your market conditions and customers. Wasted effort subtracts directly from the bottom line and can put you into a noncompetitive position.

Chapter 6 (Point 5) focuses on the core idea of integrating technology and organizational structure. This is the point of the developmental process where things always appear to get worse before they get better. As it happens, it also is the point where most interventions fail, due to a lack of will by organizational members. It appears to be the most difficult step for most executives who move forward with a developmental plan. This is the step where "the rubber meets the road." This chapter is the most extensive of the entire book because of our belief that this is what is missing in today's world. *Integrating technology diffusion and organizational change is what needs to happen.*

Chapter 7 (Point 6) begins the process of building capability by looking at additional conceptual models that can be used by business managers—taking the larger view. In other words, the previous chapters have led us to identify need, design prototypes, reengineer business process and find ways to use technology to help us become more effective. But all that cannot occur unless you have the right tools. The first step in building this tool kit is to obtain new ways of conceptualizing your business. The purpose of this chapter is to provide the reader with some of these new conceptual tools. Without them, managers continue to use what is available, even if the tools have outlived their usefulness.

Chapter 8 (Point 7) is about organizational learning processes and how these can be enhanced with technology. This follows from the acquisition of new ways of thinking. How can these techniques be put into practice? Putting the ideas to work begins the organizational restructuring process. More than just putting a new facade on the enterprise, fundamental reorganization is required to develop a true learning organization. Chapter 8 traces the development of this idea through examples of current application and a vision for what can be expected in the near future.

In conclusion, Chapter 9 (Point 8) returns to a theme of finishing touches by explicating the need for managers to constantly engage in a process of self-development. To have a business fundamentally change and improve requires that individuals in the business fundamentally alter their perspectives. This can not be done except through self-development. *Continuous individual improvement is the cornerstone of all successful organizational interventions.*

Each chapter in this book is built around the same pattern. First, we outline basic dimensions of theory from technology diffusion and organizational design literature. Next we delineate new conceptual models that can be used as practical guidelines for management action and conclude with case studies of these models. Not all chapters contain case studies. We have selected key studies to illustrate practical examples taken from our own experience.

NOTES

1. We return to this theme later in Chapter 8 (The Learning Organization), where we note the lack of integration of human resource management into the strategic planning process of technology-centered organizations.
2. The classic analysis of the correlation of these trends is Max Weber's *Economy and Society* (1978), Roth and Wittich, eds.
3. Institute for the Study of Distributed Work, University of San Francisco, Technical Report 01-91.
4. Some reports indicate that productivity does not increase with use of information technologies. The evidence is mixed in our opinion and depends to some extent on the level of analysis at which you approach the organization. Chapter 5 discusses this issue in some detail.
5. Earl Powell (1993), "Productivity and Telecommuters in the Public Sector," Master's Thesis, University of San Francisco.
6. See W. Kiechel, "The Organization that Learns," *Fortune,* March 12, 1990, pp. 133–136. Also, Roger Kemp, "Cities in the Year 2000: The Forces of Change," *The Futurist,* Sept–Oct 1990, pp. 13–15.
7. Integrated Services Digital Network (ISDN) is the next step in the evolution of the telecommunications system, especially in the United States. However, some would question whether this development is really necessary. The argument is basically centered on bandwidth requirements for residences. The secondary issue is a matter of public policy (i.e., how do you regulate these new services?).

8. There are many legislative efforts under way at this writing to permit this. U.S. Senate Bill 1200 cosponsored by Albert Gore D-TN and Conrad Burns R-MT is one example.

9. Robert Reich (1992), *The Work of Nations*. Reich uses the concept of the "symbolic analysts" as a new job category. He notes that it is difficult to make accurate translations from old job categories to these new concepts. We would not argue this trend for extractive and manufacturing jobs. These jobs are in decline in relative numbers and appear to be migrating to lower-wage areas of the developing world. The question then arises, "What do all these displaced workers do?" It is for these new jobs that these trends will hold in the United States.

10. See Lester Thorow (1992), *Head to Head: The Coming Battle Among Japan, Europe and America*. New York: William Morrow.

11. Synergy Planning, Fairfax, VA, has produced a report analyzing the urban planning implications of this movement. See also testimony of Mr. Edward Risse in support of HR 5082, July 29, 1992.

12. Personal conversation with Director of Economic Development, Santa Cruz, CA.

13. The skills that once characterized middle management are outmoded; not the function.

14. See, for example, C. C. Manz and H. P. Sims, "Self-Management as a Substitute for Leadership: A Social Learning Theory Perspective," *Academy of Management Review*, July 1980, pp. 361–67. Also, G. P. Lathan and C. A. Frayne, "Self-Management Training for Increased Job Attendance," *Journal of Applied Psychology*, June 1989, pp. 411–16.

15. It is interesting to note as a phenomenon of the sociology of work that names for new disciplines seem to emerge to legitimize new forms of work.

16. Excerpted from Helen Palmer (1988), *The Enneagram: The Definitive Guide to the Ancient System for Understanding Yourself and the Others in Your Life*, Harper and Row: San Francisco. Additional references to the use of the enneagram can be found in the list of references.

17. J. G. Bennett (1983), *Enneagram Studies*. We would invite the interested reader to consult the Bennett references for more detail. It is not our intention, nor purpose, in this book to provide an extended defense of Bennett's moral philosophy. We have found its application very useful in managing the process of organizational change.

18. See Will McWhinney (1992), *Paths of Change*, Beverly Hills: Sage.

19. These principles can also be interpreted as "cybernetic" system-design elements. Feedback loops, attenuation, and amplification of signals provide system analogs. The interested reader should consult the work of Stafford Beer and Barry Clemson (1984), *Cybernetics: A New Management Tool*.

20. Ibid.

21. Adapted from Popoff, 1978.

22. op. cit.

23. A useful exercise is to take another example of a simple process and trace out the planning and action implications, using this model. We merely offer it as an example to help the reader connect with the utility of using a reliable roadmap in the technology-introduction process.

24. Thurow, op. cit.

REFERENCES

Bennett, John G. (1983) *Enneagram Studies*. York Beach, ME: Weiser.

Clemson, Barry (1984) *Cybernetics: A New Tool for Management*. Turnbridge Wells, UK: Abacus Press.

Handy, Charles (1990) *The Age of Unreason*. Cambridge, MA: Harvard Business School.

McWhinney, Will (1992) *Paths of Change*. Beverly Hills, CA: Sage.

Palmer, Helen (1988) *The Enneagram: The Definitive Guide to the Ancient System for Understanding Yourself and Others in Your Life*. San Francisco: Harper and Row.

Popoff, Irmis B. (1978) *The Enneagramma of the Man of Unity*. New York: Wesier.

Reich, Robert (1992) *The Work of Nations*. Vintage: New York.

Riso, Don R. (1990) *Understanding the Enneagram*. Boston: Houghton–Mifflin.

Thorow, Lester (1992) *Head to Head: The Coming Battle Among Japan, Europe and America*. New York: William Morrow.

2

Communication: The Matrix of Interaction

This chapter is about human communication. Communication binds people together in the workplace and allows them to work in a collaborative fashion. Dysfunctional communication processes also lie at the heart of most problems in the workplace. Therefore, we believe the first step in any technology development process, or organizational change, is establishing clear communication.

Step 1 of the Enneagram is definition of the problem. We are defining the basic organizational change challenge as one of communication. Looking ahead (in our planning process), we see Step 4 of the Enneagram, how to work. We know that before we can figure out exactly how we will facilitate the change process, we need a profound understanding of the basic process under study—*communication*. A major focus of this book is the application of computers (and communications technologies) to enhancing group work—in this case, how to use technology to improve the effectiveness of communication between members of the group. As you will see later in this chapter, when technology is applied without an adequate understanding of the interpersonal communication process, disaster results. It is our belief therefore that if you intend to design and implement workgroup improvement, you *must* begin from a strong theoretical base of communication processes.

Throughout the chapter, we offer numerous examples of why good communication is a basis for effective organizational design or intervention. We also include a number of models of thinking about communication that you can use to test the adequacy of your particular technology or organizational design.

19

PLAN OF THE CHAPTER

This chapter builds on both the theoretical and applied work we have done in improving communications in workgroups. Communication theory is key to the development of new software to enhance workgroup effectiveness. This chapter reviews the major theoretical approaches; traces out the development of practical solutions to team effectiveness; and links technology, teams, and business results. The chapter concludes with a detailed case study of a new communication technology gone wrong.

Teams, Technology, and Business Process

Before we begin a discussion of communication theory and application, let's step back and look at exactly how interpersonal communication affects business. Figure 2-1 depicts the relationship of Teams, Technology, and Business Process. The first point is that these elements are related in a systemic fashion. That is, they must be considered as a whole and with a realization that they all affect each other.

The flow of information moves from left to right in the diagram. Please note, however, that business results are the ultimate outcome and the primary reason for improving the communication process or using technology to enhance it. Unless any of these interventions impacts business results in a positive fashion, they are of little use.[1] Business results, in turn, flow from customers. Profit and market share do not vary in a vacuum. They are related to customer satisfaction. The integration of teamwork, technology, and business process is necessary to improve customer satisfaction and hence, business results. Practical, measurable business results form the context of organizational change.

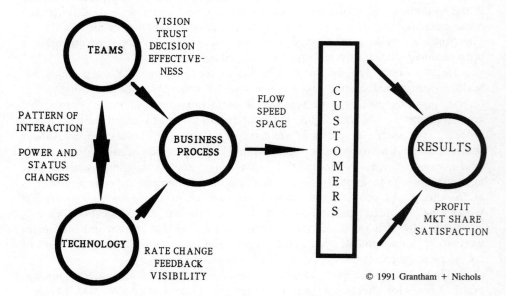

© 1991 Grantham + Nichols

Figure 2-1. Teams, Technology, and Business Process

Teams and technology go hand in hand. They interact with one another and jointly affect the shape of business process. Johansen and his colleagues at the Institute for the Future have conducted multiyear studies to clarify this point.[2] The question which seems to elude most technologists (and organizational development practitioners) is how do we characterize the communication process which is changed. As shown in Figure 2-1, we believe that articulation of vision, building trust, and decision effectiveness are very good indicators of the extent to which a team, rather than a work group is in place. Groups of workers are not *teams*. Teams operate on a different level of energy. Teams share vision, have mutual trust, and make joint decisions—not necessarily the case with work groups. In a similar vein, business process can be described in terms of temporal and spatial flow, pace and information flow. You can look at a process and ask: How does information move around? How fast does it move? Where does it go? These are the three defining characteristics of information flow that describe a business process.

Technology is characterized by how fast it changes, how it provides feedback, and how visible it is. Technology alters time and space with respect to business process. Technology can speed things up, or slow them down;[3] it also removes the need for people to physically be in the same location in order to work together. We have all seen this happen with personal computer networks, the facsimile machine, and now with the approach of the interactive video revolution.

Technology and teamwork interact. Each seems to be simultaneously cause and effect. Do secretaries change the way they work because they now have PCs, or do they obtain PCs because they are changing the way they work? Again, we see that these relationships are not linear and causal in nature; they are systemic. Certainly, we know that technology affects teamwork. Our observation is that this interaction is most effectively traced by observing the patterns of interactions among team members. How often do they talk and to whom? What do they talk about? Who is connected with whom in the group? These are the indicators of team functioning most directly impacted by communication—and supported by a technological system. Finally, power and status relationships among team members are changed by the use of technology. For example, those in the workgroup who know how to master a specific software package that is key to production have their relative status increased in the workgroup because of their technological expertise.

There are specific tactics useful to effect organizational change within these elements. Figure 2-2 illustrates how specific intervention tactics may be used to focus on the different parts of the model of teamwork, technology, and business process. We will return to each of these in later chapters. At this time, it is important to realize that there is a relationship of the problem at hand (Enneagram, Point 1) to the way in which we do the work (Point 4). Figure 2-1 shows the relationship of the various factors relating technology to communication processes. Figure 2-2 is a graphic depiction of how these elements relate to specific tactics for intervention in the organizational process. Chapter 5 will explore business process analysis, and Chapter 6, the fit between technology and structure. We will return to team development issues in Chapters 7 and 8.

Now that we have a model of the system, we can move forward to examining

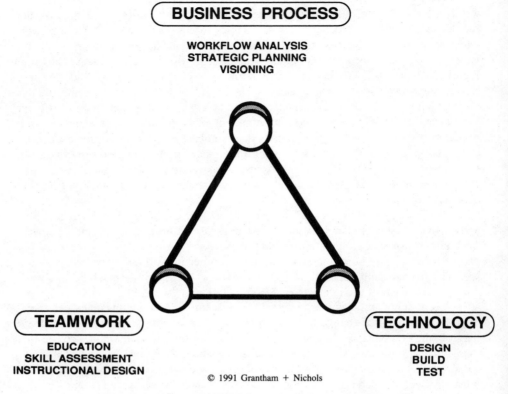

Figure 2-2. *Intervention Tactics for Improving the Relationships
Among Business Process, Technology, and Teamwork*

the basic principles of human communication. Communication is more than a mere process of information flow between team members. Communication is a *process*. In Chapter 1, we saw how trends towards globalization, a shrinking of space and time differences, and the integration of home and workplace are combining to move information, not people. But what is this moving of information?

In our view, there is a continuum of change from raw data towards wisdom. Data becomes information, information becomes intelligence, intelligence changes to knowledge, and knowledge into wisdom. The underlying dimension of this continuum is an increasing degree of organizational context. Context becomes larger as we move from smaller to larger work units. Communication as a *process,* then, occurs in ever-larger degrees of human organization and, by so doing, changes its nature qualitatively. Communication between two people is different in nature from communication between a political leader and citizens. Figure 2-3 portrays this pattern in relationship.

The point of Figure 2-3 is to provide you with a context within which you can

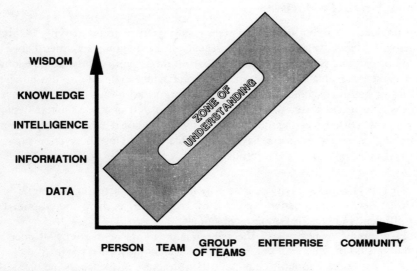

Figure 2-3. *Communication and Human Organization*

begin to interpret what is going on in an organization. Later, you will see that there are specific communication technologies that seem to correlate with differing levels in workgroups.[4] So, carefully think through the level of organizational analysis, and context, at which you are operating. *Intervention strategies at an enterprise level are considerably different from those of workgroup level.* Different kinds of communication occur at different levels of an organization. Therefore, the first orientation point on the communication map is to identify the level of organization you are working with. What are the boundaries to the group? Who is included, who is not?

COMMUNICATION AND GROUP WORK[5]

The use of computers to enhance workgroup productivity has increased at a dramatic rate since the introduction of data processing systems in the work place. The latest of these efforts has been labeled *Computer-Supported Cooperative Work* (CSCW), and aims to augment workgroups through communications enhancement.[6] The focus on group process rather than individual tasks distinguishes CSCW from the more traditional office automation efforts. However, because CSCW is used in so many different ways in the computer industry, it is difficult to define precisely. Applications ranging from electronic mail packages to multiuser database programs and calendaring facilities now claim to support group work activities. Despite the confusion about what work activities are actually enhanced, the basic idea of developing software to facilitate intra- and intergroup communications is a logical extension of current product offerings. Because many professionals work in groups, their productivity depends on their ability to work together and boost each other's skill and knowledge.

Defining Group Productivity

Group productivity refers to the end state resulting from group activity. A group's productivity is judged relative to what is created rather than group activities themselves. The unit of measurement depends on the goals of the group. A software-development group might be evaluated on the speed of producing applications, the number of problems or bugs detected in the released product, or the software's performance. At a more sophisticated level, the unit could be the speed or rate of internal process improvement. Differences in group productivity can be noted even when the members are working on similar tasks and have comparable talent. This observation suggests a number of questions about group productivity:

1. In what ways is productivity governed by the task(s) confronting a group?
2. To what extent is productivity affected by group size? Is there some optimal size for efficient and effective group interaction?
3. Does a group's cohesiveness affect the quality of its productivity? Under what conditions do pressures for conformity enhance and/or reduce productivity?
4. In what ways does a group's communication structure influence its members' style of interaction? Can the communication structure foster a high level of performance in a group?

We will address each of these topics, with an emphasis on the last point.

Factors Affecting Group Productivity

Group Tasks

Understanding group productivity requires an analysis of the task to be completed. The nature of an individual task affects group performance as each task fits in with other group tasks and overall group performance goals. To understand how computer-mediated communication channels affect group performance, it is necessary to first evaluate what the group is trying to accomplish. We will classify tasks according to the difficulty of completion, the procedures employed to accomplish it, and the criteria used to determine when the task is complete. With some tasks, all group members perform identical activities. Secretaries in a typing pool at a state's motor vehicle department, for example, might all process new-vehicle registration requests, modify the existing data base of registered vehicles to reflect address changes, and issue forms for renewals. Such tasks are *unitary* because the secretaries have similar typing skills and perform all activities.

When members perform different—but complementary—activities, the task is called *divisible*. A divisible task involves a division of labor and a convergence of roles among the members. Software development activities are often divisible tasks. Some members of the organization may specify the interface design, others write the application code, and still others test the performance of the resulting product. Group productivity for a unitary task requires three conditions for successful performance.

First, all group members must possess the skills needed to do the task. Second, the group members must be sufficiently motivated to perform the activity. Third, the group must understand what is expected of them and have feedback regarding their performance. Successful performance is more difficult to achieve for divisible tasks than unitary tasks. In addition to the skill, motivation, and feedback requirements, individual group members must be assigned to subtasks commensurate with their experience and individual goals. Rules for coordinating the group's activities must be carefully established and conveyed to the members. Failure to follow the prescribed course of action will negatively impact the objective of completing the task in a timely manner.

Group Size

Group size can influence group productivity, but the nature and magnitude of this relationship is complex. A large software developmemt team has a greater information and skill pool to draw on when attempting to resolve problems, and consequently, has the potential to be more productive than a smaller group of developers. However, large groups need extensive organization and coordination among members, the absence of which inhibits productivity. Determining the effects of group size on productivity requires an analysis of the type of task to be performed and the self-organizing capability of the group. For some classes of tasks (called *additive* tasks), the addition of extra personnel facilitates completion of the job. Even here, however, there is some maximum point beyond which the addition of extra personnel no longer improves productivity. If 50 people tried to produce the software, difficulties in coordination might increase to the point where the group is actually less productive than a group of 10.

Tasks can also be classified as *disjunctive* or *conjunctive*. A disjunctive task is one in which group performance depends entirely on the strongest or fastest member, while a conjunctive task is one in which group performance is constrained by the efficiency and effectiveness of the weakest or slowest member. Tasks performed by a software development group may be either disjunctive or conjunctive. If the problem entails resolving a particularly sticky but basic design issue, the task is disjunctive because a solution by any number is equivalent to a solution by the entire group. If the problem is one of typing application code, the task is conjunctive because the group's performance (as measured by the speed of completing the project and number of errors encountered) will be constrained by its slowest member.

Team performance will (1) increase directly with group size when the task is disjunctive and (2) decrease with group size when the task is conjunctive.[7] When the task is disjunctive, larger groups are more likely to contain members of high ability. Since a solution offered by any member solves the problem, performance increases with group size. When the task is conjunctive, an opposite outcome is possible. Larger groups are more likely to have some members who are weak in some area. Because these weak members can reduce the overall productivity of the group, large groups should perform less well than small ones on conjunctive tasks.

Accurately defining how many individuals should comprise a large versus small group for any type of task is not well understood. One of the problems is a lack of agreement in the literature about classification of tasks.[8] This point is central to our understanding as to why organizational design and technology diffusion must be jointly optimized. Understanding how work gets done is not straightforward. As we push towards self-organizing work groups empowered to create the group structure they want, the required technological support requirements will also change.

Group Cohesiveness

Highly cohesive groups are not always more productive. Cohesiveness affects productivity in combination with other variables such as group norms and task structure. If a group is highly cohesive and has norms of high productivity, it will exert that influence on the members and will be highly productive. On the other hand, if the group is highly cohesive but has norms of low productivity, it will spend more time socializing than working. In general, cohesiveness enhances productivity norms existing within the group rather than directly affecting the amount produced.

Group cohesiveness also interacts with task structure to affect performance.[9] Figure 2-4 shows how these task and affect (socio-emotional) dimensions are related. Productivity occurs when a balance of communicative behavior takes place along dimensions of task coordination and affect (cohesiveness) remain in the "Zone of Function." When groups move outside this zone, they either "break down" because of lack of cohesiveness or they "melt down" because interaction becomes all process and no output. There is a rich literature to support this contention, which seems to have been lost to contemporary systems developers. Early work in group dynamics clearly supports the contention that cohesive groups are productive groups.[10]

This is especially being seen in workgroups in organizations that are downsizing. As "do more with less" runs headlong into "create a high-involvement culture," the zone narrows to the point it can't be found. Balance of these factors (or the attempt) relies on this cohesiveness and exaggerates its tendencies.

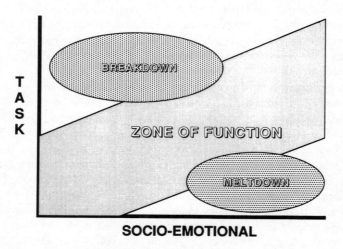

Figure 2-4. Group Interaction Factors

Communication Network Structure

A communication network is the pattern of communication opportunities within a group. Communication patterns among the members of a group are affected by the relative status of its members, the nature of the group's task, the physical distance between members, and the size of the group. A completely connected network (Comcon) allows each member to talk freely with all other members. Other networks impose restrictions on communication. In the wheel network, one individual (or computer) is at the hub and all communication must pass through that person (or machine). With a chain network, information transmitted from the person at either end must pass through other individuals (nodes) to reach the other end. Different network configurations thus affect opportunities for interaction among a group's members and can influence productivity. Examination of these opportunities for interaction is central to understanding the nature and function of cooperative work.

Social-Psychological Aspects of Computer Mediated Communication

Conversations between humans go beyond the task of giving and receiving information; they also involve the social goals of making a good impression, increasing one's status, and influencing others. The nature of a conversation is influenced in part by the person's initial attitudes toward the recipient of the information and the receiving individual's attitude toward the subject of the conversation. Each social situation contains nonverbal

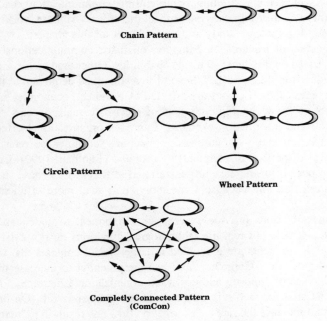

Figure 2-5. *Communication Patterns*

cues[11] that influence the initial attitudes, even before the participants are present. A casual conversation over lunch on the nature of a person's work establishes a different atmosphere than if the person were interviewing for a new job. Although the topic of the conversation is the same, the different social context is likely to result in a different conversation. Conversations are also influenced by the relative social roles and status of the participant. The interaction during the interview is likely to be more formal and constrained than what would occur over lunch. These social roles affect both the social and task goals of the conversation. On a social level, there may be a desire to strengthen an existing role or establish a new one. At the task level, the social role determines who controls conversational flows, what topics are acceptable, and how long the conversation lasts.

Computer-mediated communication differs both technically and socially from traditional communication technologies. Face-to-face and verbal communication is faster and more efficient than computer-mediated communication. Computer communications typically lack the nonverbal behaviors (smiles, head nods, eye contact, vocal cues) common in face-to-face encounters. The presence of these cues provides the listener with an efficient vehicle for letting the speaker know the subject matter is understood. The absence of these cues hinders the communicator's ability to achieve the same level of understanding.

Computer-mediated communications restrict the bandwidth of communication. For example, social status or position and power relations are not always communicated accurately with electronic communication. In addition, with asynchronous E-mail non-verbal cues are missing.[12] Later, in Chapter 3, we discuss the emotional impact that can be brought on by mediating patterns of interaction among team members. Central to this issue is that restricting, or structuring, communications that impart social status and power relationship cues can impact the process of team work. This point is amply illustrated in the case study at the conclusion of this chapter.

A great deal of research on computer mediated communications evaluates the technologies based on task and technical capabilities, rather than on the social influence processes underlying their usage.[13] Several investigations demonstrate that organizational effectiveness and efficiency are affected by technical, economic, and ergonomic characteristics of the technology. Studies of electronic mail systems show that the speed of electronic information exchange improves organizational effectiveness because tasks are completed without regard for people's schedules, secretarial assistance, or geographical dispersion of recipients (Vaske and Grantham 1990). Computer mail has been proposed to increase organizational efficiency because it discourages "off-task" interaction and because some individuals read more efficiently than they listen.

Such investigations provide a necessary component to understanding human–computer interactions, but real-life technological functions do not exist in isolation. Technological components are embodied in larger social contexts that trigger social-psychological processes. Computer mail has the potential to increase the amount of communication, across *and* up and down the organization's hierarchy. The nature of such organizational impacts, however, remains controversial. On-line computer conferences that increase the rate of information flow can result in premature decisions for reasons we will discuss later. Conversely, because computer-mediated communication channels reduce status and power differentials, and lessen the impact of other social cues, the quality of the decision can be enhanced or lessened.

Computer-mediated communication has at least two interesting characteristics from a social psychological perspective: (1) depersonalization of the communication and (2) lack of social protocol governing its use. Authors such as Sproull and Kiesler suggest three factors that affect communication via a computer:

1. Reductions in social feedback and unpredictable message style complicate efforts to coordinate communications.
2. Social influence among communicators tends to equalize because hierarchical dominance and power information is hidden.
3. Social standards are less important and communication is more impersonal because the rapid exchange of text alone, the lack of social feedback, and the absence of norms governing social interaction redirect attention to the message instead of the other person.

However, most existing software only emulates certain types of human conversations. The software available today is a little more extensive than simple electronic mail in that it can help mediate communication through meeting enhancements, bulletin boards, and conversation tracking.[14]

Researchers have identified four underlying dimensions of people's perceptions of interpersonal relations: cooperative/competitive, equal/unequal, intense/superficial, and formal-task/informal.[15] Most computer conversations tend to be cooperative, equal, intense, and task-oriented. This predetermined social style and role influences the effectiveness of computer-mediated communications by restricting the social repertoire used by people in communicating with one another.

ROLE RELATIONSHIPS AND ORGANIZATIONAL BEHAVIOR

One of the key aspects of workgroup behavior is the way in which decisions are made. More to the point, what are the decision rules that are used to make decisions affecting the entire group? Different decision rules lead to different decisions. There are differences between groups whose members are coordinating actions, being cooperative, or functioning at a collaborative level.[16] Table 2-1 relates types of decision making to decision rules and characteristics of the communication style and the level of group functioning.

Groups may decide that rewards are distributed on a input/output basis. You get out rewards directly proportional to your input. This is seen as an equity-decision type and is characterized by impersonal relationships, mostly task oriented. The group is functioning at a coordination level in this scenario.

Groups may decide to treat everyone the same and call their decision type, equality. These communications are built upon strong social network relationships among workgroup members. This is a cooperative group. Incidentally, a lot of organizational development work has been done in the past decade around the "quality

Table 2-1   Principles for Decision Making in WorkGroups

Decision Rule	Decision Type	Communication Characteristic	Level of Group Functioning
Input = Output	Equity	Impersonal	Coordination
Everyone the Same	Equality	Strong Ties	Cooperation
Neediest	Requirement	Intimacy	Collaboration

movement" to shift workers from decisions based on principles of equity to ones of equality.

Finally, you may see groups using a determination of who's the neediest to make reward distributions. They base their decisions on requirements that may shift over time. Their communications are characterized as intimate and the group functions at a collaborative level. The common literature would see these groups as 'high performing.'

The style of communication must match the group task at hand. If group norms are being decided, then communication should include a significant socio-emotional aspect. If decisions about who does what are paramount, then a more task-oriented style is appropriate. If the style of communication (e.g., in type and context) does not match performance requirements, then communication becomes dysfunctional.

The second orienting principle for the communication map is how do groups make reward decisions? In our schema, we link these decision rules and types to characteristics of the communication level of functioning. This provides a design map. We attempt, in ideal situations, to move communication from an impersonal level towards intimacy, which means an increasingly common understanding of values and respect for differences. Also, we see these groups moving from simply coordinating the activities to acting in a collaborative fashion. The structure of the communication network is the substrate upon which you can build tasks and hence organizational effectiveness.[17]

Theories of Communication

Communication is the core process of organizational functioning. Increasingly technology is mediating that core process. We believe that the heart of integrating technology diffusion and organizational change is the human communication process. The next few sections of this chapter deal with establishing a foundation of theoretical understanding of communication. While this may seem tedious and somewhat off the track of the main theme of the book, we would suggest that trying to manage organizational change without a solid theoretical base is pure folly. For example, we have witnessed repeated examples of system designers adding features to software and then exposing users to the product. When the product is rejected, they start all over without any understanding of the forces operating. This creates a confusing and time-consuming process. Maintaining your communication within a *zone of understanding* requires matching your intended communication to the recipient in several ways. Time considerations and cultural rules of exchange all require matching the impedance of sender and receiver. There is a very rich literature on each of these topics. In the interest of brevity, we will focus on a synopsis for each of these two points. Additional references are provided in the references for this chapter for the reader interested in more in-depth discussions.

Temporal Aspects[18]

Consideration of the temporal aspects of computer-mediated conversations is very important.[19] People perceive time in two fashions: linear and cyclic. The cogent dimensions of time effect are *scale, sequencing, pace, and salience*. Each of these dimensions requires explicit system-design decisions. When you design a computer-mediated conversation system, you need to consider all of these factors and how the technology will change people's perception of these dimensions. For example, how will this technology change (alter) people's perception of the pace of conversation?

LINEARITY

Communication can be seen as linear and therefore constant. It can also be seen as cyclic and signify change. There are psychological implications to these differing perceptions.

> A linear dimension contains the continuum of past/present/future, as well as the idea that phenomena contain both continuity and change. A cyclical or "spiraling" dimension focuses on recurrent events but acknowledges that—at least in Western thought—even recurrent events change somewhat from enactment to enactment.[20]

The system-design implication here is to give people anchoring information. There are also corresponding implications for organizational change. Change takes time. Is this communication intended as an action item, implying linearity; or is it meant as a planning, thinking item, implying a cyclic pattern? The same principle holds at the dyad, or workgroup level, when you are structuring communications. The practical question really is: How do we give people the proper cues to understand the temporal context of the message? Is this something that needs to be acted on now? or is it something that should be thought about and carried into action at some later time? Without information about when responses are expected, you increase the chance of misunderstanding. Communication technology that speeds up the process has the power to compound misunderstandings, which are very costly in terms of group effectiveness.

SCALE

Temporal scale refers to the duration of events and can include the interval between events. Many people propose that computer-mediated communication has the effect of speeding up processes. It is possible that these processes are speeded up (temporal scale reduced), to the point that they have become shorter than normal cognitive processes necessary for adequate planning. Many activities require a certain amount of "soak time" to process alternatives, seek advice, and reflect. There are different temporal scales for thinking and doing. These disruptions can have the deleterious effect of not allowing enough time for people to proceed through normal stages of cognitive processing. The implication, again, is to apply technology enhancement in those situations where it can match group-decision making processes.[21]

SEQUENCING

Sequencing is the pattern of specific communication activities. Turn-taking is a very good example of this. If you have ever experienced someone who would not let you talk, you can understand the frustration that can accompany the lack of proper sequencing in a conversation. This sequencing of conversations provides a way to give structure and meaning to the conversation. Sequencing is a principal aspect of how people derive meaning from conversations. Lack of knowledge of the expected, or required, sequencing can lead to confusion and prevent people from synchronizing their conversations. People report an increased dissatisfaction in conversations that are not synchronized or predictable in their pattern. The design implication is to allow people the flexibility to incorporate their expected sequencing of actions into the communication system.

PACE

Pace can be a subjective experience.[22] The pace of communication is a person's perceived experience of time within the communication. Did it seem to go fast or slow? Matching paces is another important design aspect of communication systems. Gibson has defined pace as a perception of events seen as changing in contrast to a relatively stable background.[23] In his terms, pace is the experienced perception of the difference between the speed of current events compared to an experience of background events; pace is contextual. What is a fast pace for one group may be seen as relatively slow in another. For example, when on-line bulletin boards are made available to people in a corporation where written correspondence has been the norm, the change would probably be viewed as rapid. However, the same event in a workgroup used to local-area-network connections and departmental fileservers would perceive the pace of interactive communication as actually slowing down. Often, people report feeling anxiety when the pace of events seems to outstrip their ability to digest what is going on. For example, in our experience, the pace of organizational change cycles takes anywhere from 18 to 24 months to effect significant shifts in values and behavior, whereas groups can adjust in a few weeks.

Disruptions in expected pace result in delays in reestablishing rhythms of business. This is especially critical when you are dealing across organizational boundaries where pace of communication is vastly different. This is an experience most Americans have in dealing with Japanese businessmen. The American pace is much faster than the Japanese and causes difficulty for both parties. For example, in one of our conversations with Japanese colleagues, we noticed that they were slow to respond to E-mail requests for information. Sometimes, a response took weeks. This was at variance with our expectations of almost instantaneous responses from American colleagues. Upon investigation we discovered that the Japanese group decision-making process takes time so that all members can agree on the proper response. Responses come from the group, not from individual members. Consequently, we adjusted our expectations of response time and suffered less anxiety in these cross-cultural communications.

SALIENCE

"Temporal salience refers to the degree to which an individual's thoughts, feelings, and actions are past-, present-, or future-oriented."[24] People at different organizational levels have different temporal orientations. Communications across these boundaries must include such difference in temporal salience if they are to be effective. Computer-mediated communication tends to be present-oriented, whereas middle management is past-oriented and top executives are future-focused. Again, it is a matter of matching. Lack of temporal salience may explain why computer communication systems are not as widely used in executive offices as they are on the floor. Matching salience contributes to the future of relationships; vastly different time orientations impede development of long-lasting relationships. The practical question is: "What time perspective are these people using?"

In summary, temporal aspects of communications are important as system-design considerations. System characteristics must meet user's expectations in terms of their normal communication pattern. For example, in the incident we cited of cross-cultural communication, our expectations for rapid communications were not met because the system allows asynchronous exchanges. This resulted in anxiety until we understood the expected temporal characteristics of communication within the Japanese culture. There are corresponding, temporal, design constraints on organizational change strategies. People take time to adjust to new ways of working. There is a natural pace to it.

Rules of Exchange

The next important aspect of communication theory is understanding what the rules of exchange are. Meeker describes a set of expected norms of communication, which, when violated, create disruptions and impede work flow.[25] There are three major expectations for exchange in a communication between two or more parties: rationality, reciprocity, and equity. When people engage in communication behavior, they bring to that exchange a set of expectations about *how* the communication will take place. If these norms are ignored, a breakdown in communication occurs. Therefore, it is important to clarify what these expectations are in order to design a system that can support them.

Rationality is of several types: Decisions may be based on traditional, emotional, calculative rationality (means/ends evaluation) or on generative rationality (an evaluation of means without regard to ends).[26] Principles of group decision making, different types of rationality may be operative in any given circumstance (e.g., input equals output, everyone the same, or neediest). You need to know what principle is operating to design a system to support it.

Reciprocity is the most important aspect of social exchange rules for system design. It means simply, the return action, or communicative behavior, expected. There is an implicit quid pro quo in communication exchanges. People expect something to happen as a result of their behavior. Having a question go unanswered is a very visible violation of the principle of reciprocity. When you ask a question you expect a reciprocal action or response. The reciprocal action includes expectation for temporal qualities, rationality, and perhaps equity. If a logical statement is followed by an overly emotional response out of keeping with expectations, communication (exchanges) becomes somewhat dysfunctional.

Equity, as referred to by Meeker, is only one factor. We believe her analysis must be extended to incorporate the decision types of equality and requirements already described in Table 2-1. In Meeker's formulation, equity is ascribed to a social role, not necessarily to the person occupying that role. Ascribing rules of exchange to roles makes them impersonal in the sense that the relationship between roles exists without consideration of characteristics of the person in the role.

More research is needed to fully explicate the "equitable" basis for decision making. For now, we believe it sufficient to explore the basis for group decision making, and the linkage of that principle to the method of communication. In other words, what is the purpose and how is it correlated (or supported) by the use of specific technologies.

The Paradox and Pragmatics of Communication

Another important aspect of communication is its multilevel effectiveness. We often hear people say, "They're talking the talk, but they're not walking the walk." That is a way of seeing the paradoxical impact of communication in organizations. Often the spoken word and the deed are not consistent. Paradox creates tension, disbelief, and mistrust. All of these conditions are the antithesis of an environment in which teamwork can be enhanced. The paradox comes from communication being a larger, richer process than spoken words.

Consider the injunction, "Do Not Read This Sign." That is a paradoxical communication. How can you not read the sign? You have already read the sign. What emotional state does this paradox generate? The existence of paradox, "not only can invade interaction and affect our behavior and our sanity, but it also challenges our belief in the consistency, and therefore the ultimate soundness, of our universe."[27]

Paradoxes can be logical and pragmatic. Pragmatic paradoxes are those involving the influence of behavior and are of interest to communication-systems designers. When people are placed in paradoxical situations, where they have no power of choice, adverse psychological effects result. The practical implication is that you should pay attention to paradoxical communications in the organizational change process. The "Do as we say, not as we do" injunction is inherently flawed. Executives demanding that secretaries use word processors, but refusing to answer their own E-mail set up a paradox with easily anticipated results. When words (or any communication) and deeds are not consistent, communication falters and effectiveness falls off.

Current Perspectives

There are two major perspectives currently being used in the development of communication tools to enhance group effectiveness through application of computer technology.[28] They are speech-act theory as depicted by Terry Winograd and "diplans" promoted by Anatol Holt. Both approaches have failed to yield significant and consistent results in workgroups, However, they represent some of the first attempts to define the problem and understand what work must be done before developing a technological aid to workgroup functioning. At this time, they are primarily important from a historical perspective. The case study in this chapter is a detailed analysis of the failure of one of these approaches.

A commonly used perspective on cooperative work is based on the linguistic theories of J. Austin and J. Searle. The core of this approach is that language itself is action in the context of human behavior. Although this perspective may not give sufficient attention to the socio-emotive dimension of symbolic interaction, it does emphasize the point that human interaction (and possible human–computer interaction) is, to a large extent, symbolic in nature.[29] This theoretical approach holds that language is the primary dimension of human cooperative activity. The essential feature of the software is the use of conversational templates, based on the theory of speech acts, also known as speech pragmatics. This approach deals with "language as an activity, not as the transmission of information or the expression of thought." A speech act is evaluated not so much in terms of its semantics (meaning) as by its felicity (appropriateness to context).[30]

Another major theoretical approach to the design of workgroup cooperation technology has been developed by Anatol Holt. Holt labels the approach "coordination mechanics" and traces its development to the examination of Petri nets in computer science. Petri nets are a means of symbolizing the flow of information among elements in a computer program. They are a design tool based on the formal mathematics of information theory. For example, individuals could be viewed as points where information comes together in groups. Within these points (technically called nodes), information is subject to modification and interpretation. A diagram of these points and communication links would be referred to as a Petri net diagram of the group.

Holt's approach seeks to isolate a pattern of coordination activities in an organization. These activities can then be expressed in a graphical language called "diplans," which specifies bodies, operations, involvement and aspects. These technical terms can be seen as analogous to people, interpretation, communication links, and languages in a human group. Diplans appears to bear a close resemblance to object-oriented programming, which sees "objects" or "people" taking on characteristics that describe the rules they use to manipulate language or "communication." From the viewpoint of organizational theory, "coordination mechanics" looks like a formalized version of Frederick Taylor's scientific management. The activities of a workgroup are broken down into a set of elements (people), and actions then take on information and become a constrained network of communication.

Creation of Shared Realities

Communication is a *process* of constructing social reality. This fact is what makes the study of communication important to organizational development. Most organizational interventions begin with manipulating the communication process. For this reason, organizational interventions need to be designed with knowledge of what the anticipated outcomes of communication process will be—on the individual, workgroup, and organization.

The most current perspective on communication behavior is developing rapidly to supplement the structuralist approach described above. It is interesting to note that this development of communication theory corresponds to a similar evolution of organizational theory, which shifted from structural to human relations and finally to a systemic perspective.[31] Communication allows people to create a shared vision of the workgroup, its purpose, and the methods it will use to complete the tasks at hand.

Social Construction of Realities: Phenomenology[32]

Subjective interpretation of experience also gives rise to felt states of person/object relatedness. Recent research indicates that this phenomenological process can generate emotional states correlated with behavior. For example, if I "hate" my computer I am less likely to use it. This theoretical perspective assumes that social order emerges from the agreements that exist between actors engaged in joint activity, and upheld in a series of negotiations that crystallize in mutual expectations. Furthermore, social agreement is needed to produce a realization of the significance of the ritual, symbols, and myths found in the workplace. The meaning people take from interpersonal interaction at work has both a utilitarian (task-oriented) and emotional component. My previous work has indicated the importance of the social-emotional component of worklife. By social-emotional, we mean those emotive states generated through interpersonal interaction such as liking, happiness, guilt, and anxiety. Primary emotional states of fear, anger, depression, and satisfaction are mediated by patterns of social interaction and therefore can be affected by the nature of the medium in which interpersonal communication takes place.

Phenomenology is also linked conceptually to the emergent perspective of semiotics. Semiotics holds that objects do not exist in separation from the "experience" of the object. A triad of objects (events), their signs (representations), and interpretants (objects/persons) comes together to yield the subjective experience of social life. Analysis of these relationships can take a syntactic (sign-sign), semantic (sign-object), or pragmatic (sign-interpretant) form. In other words, this theory of linguistics can be used to sensitize the organizational-development specialist to what to look for in high-tech environments. Semiotics points out the necessity to take a systemic view of the work environment and include the things that are happening (events), such as a directive to perform a task; how coordination directions are communicated (representations), such as face-to-face or written communication; and, finally, the person involved. When we use these theoretical tools to analyze workgroup activity, we quickly see that people do take meaning from their work activities. That is, workplace actions become important to them, motivate them towards particular behavior patterns, and form a basis for a sense of self-worth and esteem. In the context of CSCW, technology that mediates a process of human interaction can become an object in itself and therefore influence the process of meaning-taking in the work environment. The phenomenon of work can be a subject of case study in itself. That is, different forms of communication can impart different interpretations—quite apart from the content. For example, a summons to the boss's office is seen quite differently if it arrives via telephone instead of as a written message. As "groupware" becomes more prevalent in the office, people will have more communicative options to use. It will quite literally become, "not what you said, but how you said it."

Theoretically, the phenomenological approach should be seen as a complementary perspective to existing theories of workgroup behavior, because it provides a specific framework for understanding variations in interpretive behavior. However, the more practical question still remains unanswered: Why is this important for a CSCW software designer to understand? Or, why should an organizational development specialist working in the office environment be concerned? We assume that any self-esteem-enhancing meaning taken from work activities correlates positively to a subjective evaluation of the work environment. Further, this evaluative belief is linked to the formation of attitude structures which, in turn, are correlated with higher usage rates of new communication technologies. That is, a person's evaluation of the work environment plays an important part in the formation of attitudes towards work, tools, and their workmates. These attitudes are also linked very closely to the actual behavior that occurs in this environment. Therefore, if we can better understand the social-interaction process that yields these subjective states, we can inform a design strategy to augment multiperson work processes. We should be able to reduce barriers to use of new tools, support the negotiation of meaning in the work environment, and provide a basis for intervention to improve the quality of worklife.

Summary

All these hypotheses about group communication behavior are difficult to reduce to something a manager can use on the job. Table 2-2 is an attempt to summarize this material at a high conceptual level. This conceptual map of human communication is intended as a design guide for software developers building groupware products. These products when introduced into an organization will effect changes in the way people work. Then, these guidelines can be used as a basis to measure change in organizational process. Again, we would like to reiterate that one of the most significant problems in using technology to mediate human communication is that the design and implementation processes proceed without any conscious connection between technology and organizational change. At the same time, the development/implementation cycle is not grounded in any theory of human behavior. A central purpose of this chapter is to provide you with that basis of action.

In Table 2-2, the vertical dimension is an enumeration of the components of the various theories we have discussed. The horizontal categories are aspects of group behavior that we believe are directly impacted by communication patterns and qualities. The marks in the boxes signify which categories of group behavior are most highly

Table 2-2   Computer System Design Factors

Factor	Productivity	Level of Function	Meaning	Continuance	Reliability	Clarity	Trust	Context
Size	S	P						
Task	P							P
Network Structure		S			S			
Time								
Linearity	P			S				
Cyclic					S			P
Scale		P						S
Sequence	P					S		
Pace	P				S			
Salience				P			S	
Rationality	P		S					
Reciprocity				P		S		
Equity	S					P		
Equality		P	S	S				
Need			S				P	
Paradox			P	S				

KEY: P=primary effect; S=secondary effect

impacted by a particular aspect of communication. Both primary and secondary effects are noted. For example, the size of the group is seen as primarily impacting the level of functioning (see Figure 2-4) and, secondarily, productivity.

Another way to use this table is to reverse-engineer a group intervention. Let's say that as a manager you were concerned with making sure that your workgroup was stable and that its interaction persisted over time, given the long-term task they were engaged in. How, then, would you design a communication system to support that group, given what you now know about communication theory? When you examine Table 2-2 under the continuance column, you find that primary effects are given for salience and reciprocity; secondary effects for linearity, equity, and paradox.

Therefore, you would make sure your communication system provided for a high degree of reciprocal communication (i.e., easy response to messages), and high salience (i.e., taking future orientation and emotional states into account). Finally, you would also provide a step-by-step outline of stages of group development correlated with task-accomplishment needs, making it explicit that decisions were based on equality (see Table 2-1) and that pragmatic paradoxes were excluded from communication and behavior patterns. Conversely, if the group dynamic were assessed to be headed toward dissolution of the group, we would focus on these issues as diagnostics.

CASE STUDY

This case study is intended to demonstrate the application of communication theory to computer enhancement of group functioning. It is taken from practical experience and has been reported previously; albeit not as a practical guide to group communication. As you read through the case, we suggest you use Table 2-2 as a guide to see if you can spot areas where the design of the software was flawed and how that flaw comes from a lack of thoughtful application of communication theory.

Computer-Supported Cooperative Work: The Phenomenological Approach

This case case study examines the pattern of social dynamic associated with small-group work activities. As noted earlier, the concepts of "groupware" and "computer supported cooperative work (CSCW)" have recently gained interest among researchers.[33] From a communication-theory perspective, CSCW can be seen as a natural, evolutionary extension of existing technologies (e.g., Rogers, 1986; and Rice et al., 1984). While it is to some degree simply the latest buzzword, it does serve to highlight a critical point often obscured by other terms: namely, the fact that office work is inherently cooperative, involving both reciprocal and serial interdependencies among often diverse individuals and groups. The one worker/one product model simply does not apply to most of what goes on outside of the manufacturing sector. Models derived solely from human-factors engineering perspectives have also tended to neglect this vital perspective.

Case-Study Context

This case study began as an investigation of the process of implementing CSCW technology in a workgroup. This implementation involved one software product designed to increase group effectiveness: The Coordinator I^{TM}. While the case study being recounted here began as an examination of a process of introducing "groupware" tools in the office, we approached it from a well-articulated theory of group behavior. Our understanding of the prevailing approaches (e.g., speech-act theory and coordination mechanics) fell short in their power to explain the relationships between value structures, attitudes, and ultimately interpersonal behaviors. Specifically, we sought an orientation that could:

- Account for dynamic re-structuring of interpersonal systems
- Explain how implicit rules of behavior are made explicit in terms of informal relationships, authority lines, and lateral communication patterns
- Account for sub-optimizing behavior such as "exception to policy" actions
- Increase our understanding of adaptive learning and feedback loops of communication

The theoretical approach best suited to these issues is symbolic interaction. This perspective overcomes the existing theoretical inadequacies published in the groupware literature by incorporating explanations for dynamic negotiation processes into an explanation of behavior. Symbolic interaction and phenomenology are related to one another in the sense that they both come from a paradigm of explaining human behavior that has been called social definition. Symbolic interaction holds that human interaction is mediated by the use of symbols, by interpretation, and by ascertaining the meanings of one another's actions. Phenomenology is a social-definitionist approach that "seeks to examine the data of experience as they appear in consciousness with the theoretic tools of philosophic science."[34] Therefore, the approach we choose for this case study was a combination of theoretical orientations, with an emphasis on discovering *how people attributed meaning to the experience of using the software to communicate with one another.*

Methodology

Examination of patterns of interaction should be central to understanding just what cooperative work really is. People use words as symbols to mediate their interactions. The important point is that the language (symbols) used can take several different forms (i.e., substantive, annotative, and procedural). Examination of these symbolic interactions should precede the development of a computer-based technology to support cooperative work. The social dynamics of small-group interaction are very complex in nature. Cognitive, attitudinal, and behavioral factors all operate simultaneously. It can also be shown that there is an association between the pattern of interaction or communication and the generation of affective states. Because of this symbolic complexity and the lack of cogent empirical studies in computer-supported cooperative work, we decided to employ a triangulated research methodology that could capture several dimensions of the workgroup interaction.

A pre/post within-group comparison methodology was used to evaluate changes in the subject's cognition, attitude, and behavior patterns. It was felt that ultimate behavioral effects might not become evident as quickly as changes in cognitive evaluation or shifts in the affective component of attitudes. Qualitative data were collected by using participant observers and personal interviews. Three separate instruments were administered to all case study participants: a semantic differential scale, a social network analysis questionnaire, and a communication-technology usage matrix. The same instruments were used in pre- and post-tests. Instruments were coded to maintain anonymity and tabulated by a researcher who was not a member of the case study.[35] Changes in subjects' cognition were assessed, using a series of semantic differential scales. This technique allows the measurement of changes in peoples' evaluation, potency, and activity valuations towards selected target items (e.g., computers, work team, collaborative work, action orientation, new language, and workgroup effectiveness). Changes in participants' attitudes towards members of the workgroup, and their intragroup communication patterns were measured using a network-analysis questionnaire (developed by R. A. Schmeideck) called the Personal Sphere Model. This instrument has been employed elsewhere to assess the relationship between social-network structure, form of communication, and affect.[36]

Participant observers recorded their data in narrative format on a regular basis and were debriefed by a non-case-study researcher. The ethnographic interviews were conducted over a period of several months, beginning before the case study and continued after the case study was terminated.

Subjects

The subjects of the case study were 15 technical professionals employed in a large high-tech industry on the West Coast. The subjects ranged in education level from two years of college to Ph.D. The majority had extensive training in computer science and programming. The group was characterized by less than ten years of job experience, on average. All subjects volunteered to participate in the case study. Four members of the groups were located approximately 30 miles from the remainder and communicated quite frequently via electronic mail and telephone with the others.

No member of the group had any previous experience with "computer-supported cooperative work" either as a subject of case study or with any commercial products. The group was newly formed by members from several other functional groups within the larger organization. Therefore, each member brought to the group different background experiences and histories.

The Software

The basic case study design was to measure a number of subjects' attributes, interject a software based group communication medium and after six months re-measure the same attributes. The particular software chosen, The Coordinator I, imposes a structure on the communication among group members. The design of the Coordinator is based on the theory that language is the primary dimension of human cooperative activity. The software's essential feature is the use of conversational templates, based on the theory of speech acts, also known as speech pragmatics. This approach deals with language as an activity, not as the transmission of information or the expression of thought. A speech act is evaluated not so much in terms of its semantics (meaning) as by its felicity (appropriateness to context).

By combining electronic mail, calendaring, and word processing and providing a framework for conversations, the software makers claim to improve group productivity by making communication within a workgroup more focused and orderly. The basic unit of work is a conversation, not a message. Since messages within a conversation are explicitly identified by type, one may retrieve them either by conversation or by type: for example, "commitments we have made" or "responses due me today." Conversations are of two basic types: For Action or Possibilities. Conversations For Action have a structure that leads towards closure of some kind: either by fulfilling a request, declining to fulfill a request, accepting an offer, declining an offer, or cancelling an offer.

Conversations for possibility, or free-form messages within a conversation for action, do not necessarily lead to behavioral closure and do not have as much formal structure. Messages and responses are linked in the software so that one can always retrieve the context of any given message. The dates of commitments and promises in one's conversations are automatically included in the calendaring function. The intent of the software is to provide an environment that fits the structure of everyday communication so well that the user need no longer be aware of the software or its interface. The software would thus be "transparent" and permit the user to focus on the content of the communication.

Findings

We found that the preexisting pattern of communication in the group was varied and included all existing forms of communication (i.e., telephone, electronic mail, and face-to-face). Little written communication existed in support of the organizational structure. Subjects' attitudes towards computers, work, and technology in general were normally distributed on the semantic scales. Clinical indicators of communication as measured by the Personal Sphere Model were not notable.

The basic, objective finding of this case study was that members of the group did not find that the CSCW tool facilitated their interaction as a workgroup. Only one significant cognitive shift was found in the semantic differential data: a move toward reporting "collaborative work" more boring during the trial period.

Other trials of The Coordinator I have been reported that cite anecdotal data indicating user acceptance. Our experience was that the implementation and support requirements for cooperative work systems are more difficult than anticipated by developers and novice end-users. The test group was not convinced that software offered functionality that was worth the effort involved in learning to use the product. An improved interface, more flexible terminology, and better implementation support are needed for a successful installation.

However, the data taken from the Personal Sphere Model of interaction revealed an interesting pattern of communication. The patterns of communication revealed by the questionnaire are seen as precursors to a decline in the quality of the socio-emotional functioning of the group. The geographic structure of the group allowed us to differentiate a core group from a peripheral subset of the group. Within this structure, we found:

1. An increase in number of connections between periphery and core clique members.
2. A decrease in the density (i.e., the ratio of actual to possible connections among

group members taken as an indicator of group cohesion) of the social network connections of the periphery group.

3. An overall decrease in the reported use of electronic mail to "coordinate work group activities," with no associated increase in other methods of coordination.
4. A decrease in the amount of affective communication in the group using electronic communications.

The participant observers recorded their subjective experiences about how these documented changes in group communication were experienced. The ethnographic interviews served to provide more detailed information about the subjective nature of the group process revealed by the test instruments. The basic finding was that use of the software prompted expression of emotional or affective states in almost all subjects. In most cases, these expressions were not solicited but occurred freely. The most cogent observation was simply the stoppage of use by a majority of subjects. In this sense their actions spoke louder than their words. When questioned, they stated that the format to their interaction pattern encouraged by the software was "unnatural," "uncomfortable," and "made no sense" to them.

Subjects reported feeling overly restricted in "how they can talk to one another" in the speech-act paradigm. Although most admitted not understanding what the underlying language paradigm was, they felt that an intellectual understanding would not allay their felt emotional states. During the ethnographic interviews, it was revealed that a large part of the communication occurring during the trial period was designed to formulate new rules of group behavior. The group in actuality did not exist as such: no shared meanings were present at the onset of interaction. What was happening was the formation of a group, in the social sense of shared identity, patterns of communication, and interaction expectations.

Subjects openly expressed the need and desire for a communications medium that would augment their search for common understanding. Open-ended, free-flowing, unstructured, almost serendipitous conversations were the norm for the subjects. In this case, the group was in the process of forming its own identity. In such a situation, structured communication appears to inhibit a natural social process.

Their fourth finding was that there was a decrease in affective communication using the software tool. However, the qualitative data indicates almost an explosion of affect. How are these findings reconciled? This apparent contradiction gets to the heart of the experienced phenomenon of work. When one mode of communication inhibits the natural negotiation of meaning (i.e., affective states "How do you feel about that?"), another mode will be used. It appears that the Coordinator I inhibited this normal part of group interaction and it found another outlet, in acting out behavior.

Discussion

As software becomes more and more a key element in mediating communication among people, its impact needs to be addressed from research, design, and clinical perspectives. The fact that people take meaning from work, and that this process is mediated by software technology, warrants efforts to more clearly understand the dynamics of computer-augmented personal interaction. The phenomenology of computer-supported cooperative work is that the intersubjective meaning of work includes a significant emotional component. Experienced interaction mediated by technology can attenuate, or amplify, meaning. Technology that does not purposefully encourage the negotiation of meaning through interaction is reacted to with negative emotional states. The phenomenological conclusion is that the software interfered with the transparency of the assumption of everyday communication and therefore was reacted to in a negative way. These negative feelings lead to the development of attitude structures correlated with decreased use of the computer-mediated communication channel.

Cicourel[37] discusses how people take different meaning from symbolic structures in part based on their "mastery of the language." Cicourel calls this process "generative semantics" and signifies that meaning is generated from use of symbols. We believe that this points towards development of a primary concern for the intermediation of computer systems between object and sign, as expressed in the semiotic literature. That is, the interpretive process varies with individuals. Different people can take different meaning from a shared experience or communication. Sending a message saying that a person has missed a deadline can be seen variously as intrusive or as a helpful reminder.

Cultural norms in the use of language also provide some basis for extracting meaning. The meaning that people take from these interactions with computers is not necessarily "hardwired." That is, not everyone will take the same meaning from the interaction, partially dependent upon their cultural and perhaps even professional background. A software designer's major task, then, becomes one of clearly identifying the symbols in a way that allows users to develop a common understanding they can take from the situation. In the case of The Coordinator I, these interpretations were constrained by the stereotyped message templates in the software, which led to a feeling of dissatisfaction with the interactions.

The development of cultures of productivity[38] emphasizes the point that high productivity, which we assume to be a goal of cooperative work settings, can only be fostered when its features are legible, symbolically coherent, and open-ended. Different cultures or subcultures vary with the extent they expect these features to be commonly understood—for example, the difference between high-context cultures where much is implicitly understood and low-context, where things need to be made very explicit. Computer-mediated communication is very low context—which may, at a minimum, make high-context communication uncomfortable and, most likely, impossible (Hall, 1984).

We conclude, therefore, that The Coordinator I failed to be incorporated into a normal workflow pattern because it, and its underlying paradigm of work, failed to acknowledge the experienced phenomenon of work. The assumption of the underlying speech act paradigm that all communication can be highly structured (low context) violates the phenomenology of work, which embeds a process of symbolically negotiating the agreement of meaning among workgroup members.

Pask's (1980) conversation theory emphasizes this by making a distinction between communication and conversation. Communication is a process of transmission of information between, and among, group members. Conversation is distinct in that it implies a process of concept-sharing and development of agreement of the interpretation of events. In this sense, the Coordinator I supports a process of communication, but does not necessarily support the process of conversation or the negotiation of interpreting meaning among group members. These facts of social life, which are informed by a phenomenology of workgroups, need to be explicitly incorporated in the design of CSCW software if it is to be used effectively by workgroup members.

Final Analysis

If you now refer back to Table 2-2, which relates communication characteristics to group functioning, you can see that the results of this trial were very predictable from theory. Finding 1 reported an increase in the scale of communication with a resultant increase in level of function, perhaps moving the group to the level of information processing. On balance, however, Finding 2 reports a decrease in network-structure density and a consequent decrease in level of function. Findings 1 and 2 seem to balance each other out in terms of overall impact on the group.

Finding 3 shows a decrease in pace of communication because the interface made it difficult for free-flowing communication and the expected decrease in productivity was noticed (at least subjectively). The key finding appears to be the fourth finding, in which a decrease in communication salience is found and which can be seen from post hoc analysis to have contributed significantly to the discontinuance in the use of the communications system.

This case study concludes our discussion of communication. Remember that communication is the foundation for managing organizational change. For this reason, we have spent considerable time discussing it in detail. We are now ready to move onward to the next step of our process using the Enneagram. This chapter has corresponded to Point 1 (Communication); we now move to Point 2 (Design). The concept that connects these two processes is that design cannot proceed without good communication between designer and user.

NOTES

1. While it may be argued that interventions could improve the quality of worklife without affecting business performance, this does not appear to be the trend in organizational development (H. G. Katz, T. A. Kochan, and M. R. Weber (1985), "Assessing the Effects of Industrial Relations Systems and Efforts to Improve the Quality of Working Life on Organizational Effectiveness," *Academy of Management Journal,* vol. 28(3), pp. 509–526.)
2. Their work is reported in Johansen et al. (1991) *Leading Business Teams,* Addison Wesley. The point is that at certain stages of team formation, different communications technologies are most appropriate. I will return to this topic later in Chapter 4.
3. We often think that faster is better. Technology can also make slower better. A colleague of mine reports that he likes to communicate with electronic mail when he is dealing with people from other cultures. E-mail gives him time to consider his response, check with coworkers, and generally slow down the communication process to allow time for clear thought.
4. Chapter 5 is devoted to linking specific technologies to organizational structure.
5. This section has been adapted from Vaske and Grantham (1990), Chapter 2, and is reprinted with permission of the publishers, Ablex Publishing Corporation.
6. The first technical conference on the topic was held in late 1986 in Austin, Texas (Krasner, 1986).
7. Steiner (1972, 1974).
8. Tasks can also be characterized by dimensions of uncertainty and/or complexity. In Chapter

6, on Organizational Structure, we expand this discussion to include equivocality. The interested reader should refer to McGrath (1984) for an expanded discussion.

9. Nixon (1977).

10. Berkowitz (1954), Libo (1953), and especially Stein (1976).

11. For example, "flaming" behavior in E-mail communication sets a tone of interaction before people meet face to face.

12. See Sproull and Kiesler (1991) for an expanded discussion of this point.

13. See, for example, Rob Kling's discussion of "technological utopianism."

14. E-mail is the most common form of computer-mediated communication. Peter and Trudy Johnson-Lenz, principals of Awakening Technologies, who coined the term "groupware," are using a computer system to mediate the human spiritual growth process. Personal communication, December 1992.

15. Murray and Bevan (1985).

16. Admittedly, the term cooperation is somewhat emotionally-laden. Cooperation in the CSCW sense does not imply that there is no competition among cooperating work units. Often the terms coordination, cooperation, and collaboration are used interchangeably. Such use blurs the distinction between different levels of human harmony.

17. See earlier work by Grantham (1982) for extensive discussion of the relationship between social-network structure and intimacy.

18. Additional references are Gersick (in press), Kiesler et al. (1984); readers interested in the psychological analysis of time and work should consult McGrath (1984).

19. See Hesse, Werner, and Altman (1988).

20. Op. cit., p. 4.

21. This theoretical point made by Hesse et al. (1988) appears to be supported by field experiments reported by Johansen et al. (1991).

22. Pace can also be seen as an objective property of events, such as bits per second in a modem. We emphasize the subjective nature here in order to remain focused on the social aspects of communication.

23. Gibson, J. J. (1975).

24. Hesse et al., op. cit., p. 11.

25. See Meeker (1971).

26. Today's scholars build upon Weber's work by distinguishing between calculative (traditional Weberian) and generative rationality. *Calculative* rationality is found in production environments where the rules for acceptable behavior and the methods for accomplishing tasks are based on efficiency goals. Such environments tend to be relatively stable, promote standardized operating techniques, and have established procedures for implementing change.

   Generative rationality is characteristic of a product-development group, where the goal is to create or invent technologies. There is a rational, systematic process operating, but the results are often unpredictable.

27. See Watzlawick, Bavelas, and Jackson (1967), p. 187.

28. There are other examples of groupware such as Lotus Notes[TM], Awakening Technologies, Inc., and many more every day. We have selected these two approaches because there is some documentation and research available that provides a basis for software design that we can examine. Most other approaches are, in our opinion, ad hoc designs based on designer intuition, without an understandable and accessible basis in human-communication theory.

29. See Carasik and Grantham, 1988.

30. For additional details see Winograd (1986) and Winograd and Flores (1989).

31. See Vaske and Grantham (1990), Chapter 3, for a fuller discussion.

32. Phenomenology, and the symbolic interactionist approach, have been used variously to delve deeper into the intersubjective meaning of everyday events. This approach yields richer understanding than that obtained through experimental or survey-based research. It begins to get to the development of belief structures that social psychologists take as antecedent variables to the attitude/behavior relationship. Technically, both phenomenology and symbolic interaction are sociological approaches subsumed under the category of the "social definition paradigm" (Ritzer, 1975).

33. The term "office automation," with its associated images of the assembly line and robot workers, was perhaps one of the most unfortunate vocabulary choices. It should be noted, however, that it was successful in getting many managers' attention precisely because of those associations and the implication that applying such industrial models to the office could raise productivity and lower costs (Curley and Pyburn, 1982). The spirit of Frederick Taylor has never been far from the hearts of white-collar management.

34. Ritzer, 1975.

35. Copies of study instruments are available from the authors.

36. It is used as a clinical assessment tool to show the relationship between location in social structure and therapeutic interventions. The goal here was to see if provision of a new communication method facilitated a change in subjects' social networks (Grantham, 1982).

37. See Cicourel (1975).

38. See Akin and Hopelain.

REFERENCES

Akin, G. and D. Hopelain (1986) "Finding the Culture of Productivity," *Organizational Dynamics*, pp. 19–32.

Attewell, P. and Rule, J. (1984) "Computing and Organizations: We Know and Don't Know." *Communications of the ACM*, pp. 1184–1192.

Auramaki, Esa, Erkki Lehtinen, and K. Lyytinen (1988) "A Speech-Act Based Office Modeling Approach," *Transactions on Office Systems*, Vol 6(2): pp. 126–153.

Austin, J. (1962) *How to Do Things with Words*. Cambridge, MA: Harvard University Press.

Bales, Robert F. (1958) "Task Roles and Social Roles in Problem Solving Groups," in Maccoby, E. E., Newcomb, M., and Hartley, E. L. (eds.), *Readings in Social Psychology* (3rd ed.), Rinehardt and Winston: New York, pp. 437–47.

Bateson, Gregory (1979) *Mind and Nature: A Necessary Unity*. New York: Dutton.

Bavelas, Alex (1951) "Communication Patterns in Task-Oriented Groups," in Lerner, D. and Lasswell, H. (eds.), *The Policy Sciences*, Stanford University Press.

Berkowitz, L. (1954) "Group Standards, Cohesiveness, and Productivity," *Human Relations*, November, pp. 509–19.

Blumer, H. (1962) "Society as Symbolic Interaction," in Rose, A. (ed.), *Human Behavior and Social Processes*, New York: Houghton–Mifflin.

Brown, J. S. and Newman, S. (1985) "Issues in Cognitive and Ergonomics: From Our House to Bauhaus," *Human-Interaction*, 1:351–391.

Cartwright, D. and Zander, A. (eds.) (1968) *Group Dynamics: Research and Theory*. New York: Harper & Row.

Carasik, R. and Grantham, C. (1988) "A Case Case Study of Computer Supported Cooperative Work in a Dispersed Organization," in *Proceedings of SIGCHI 1988*, New York: Association of Computing Machinery.

Cicourel, A. (1975) *Cognitive Sociology*. New York: Penguin.

Culnan, Mary J. and M. Lynne Markus (1987) "Information Technologies," in *Handbook of*

Organizational Communication: An Interdisciplinary Perspective, Jablin, F. M., Roberts, K. H., Putnam, L. L. and Porter, L. W. (eds), Newbury Park, CA: Sage Publications.

Curley, K. F. and Pyburn, P. J. (1982) "Intellectual Technologies: The Key to Improving White Collar Productivity," *Sloan Management Review.* 24(1):31–39.

Fisek, M. Hamit and Richard Ofshe (1970) "The Process of Status Evolution," *Sociometry,* 33(3), pp. 327–46.

Gersick, Connie (1989) "Marking Time: Predictable Transitions in Task Groups," *Academy of Mgmt Jrnl,* 32(2), June 1, pp. 274–309.

Gersick, C. J. (In press) "Time and Transitions in Work Teams," *Academy of Management Journal.*

Gibson, J. J. (1975) "Events Are Perceivable, But Time Is Not," in J. R. Fraser and N. Lawrence (eds.), *The Study of Time II. Proceedings of the Second Conference of the International Society for the Study of Time,* pp. 295–301, New York: Verlag.

Grantham, C. E. (1982) *Social Networks and Marital Interaction.* 21st Century: Palo Alto, CA: 21st Century.

Grantham, C. E. and J. J. Vaske (1985) "Predicting the Usage of an Advanced Communications Technology," *Behavior and Information Technology,* 4(4): pp. 327–336.

Hesse, B., C. Werner, and I. Altman (1988) "Temporal Aspects of Computer-Mediated Communication," *Computers in Human Communication,* (4): pp. 1–19.

Hiltz, S. R. and Turoff, M. (1978) *The Network Nation: Human Communication Via Computer.* Reading, MA: Addison–Wesley.

Holt, Anatol (1988) "Diplans: A New Language for the Case Study and Implementation of Coordination," *Transactions on Office Systems,* Vol 6(2): pp. 109–126.

Holt, Anatol (1985) "Coordination Technology and Petri Nets," in *Advances in Petri Nets, Lecture Notes in Computer Science, No. 222.,* G. Rozenberg (ed.), Springer–Verlag: Berlin.

Husserl, G. (1969) *Ideals.* London: Collier–MacMillan Ltd.

Jefferson, G. (1972) "Side Sequences," in Sudnow, D. (ed.), *Studies in Social Interaction,* New York: Free Press.

Johansen, R. (1988) *Groupware.* New York: Free Press.

Johansen, R., D. Sibbett, S. Benson, A. Martin, R. Mittman, and P. Saffo (1991) *Leading Business Teams.* New York: Addison–Wesley.

Katz, H. G., T. A. Kochan, and M. R. Weber (1985) "Assessing the Effects of Industrial Relations Systems and Efforts to Improve the Quality of Working Life on Organizational Effectiveness," *Academy of Management Journal,* Vol 28(3): pp. 509–526.

Kemper, T. D. (1978) "Toward a Sociology of Emotions: Some Problems and Some Solutions," *The American Sociologist,* Vol 13: pp. 30–41.

Kemper, T. D. (1987). "How Many Emotions Are There? Wedding the Social and Autonomic Components," *American Journal of Sociology,* Vol 93(2): pp. 263–289.

Kiesler, S., Seigel, J., and McGuire, T. W. (1984) "Social Psychological Aspects of Computer-Mediated Communication, *American Psychologist,* 39: pp. 1123–1134.

Kling, Rob (1991) "Cooperation, Coordination and Control in Computer-Supported Work," *Communications of the ACM,* Vol 34(12): pp. 83–85.

Krasner, Herb (1987) "CSCW 86 Conference Summary Repot," *ACM SIGCHI Bulletin,* 19(1): pp. 51–53.

Libo, L. (1953) *Measuring Group Cohesiveness.* Ann Arbor, MI: University of Michigan Press, Institute for Social Research.

Markus, M. Lynne (1987) "Toward a Critical Mass Theory of Interactive Media," *Communication Research,* 14(5): pp. 491–511.

McGrath, J. E. (1984) *Groups: Interaction and Performance.* Englewood Cliffs, NJ: Prentice–Hall.

Michener, H. A., DeLamater, J. D., and Schwartz, S. H. (1986) *Social Psychology*. San Diego: Harcourt Brace Jovanovich, Publishers.

Nixon, H. L. II (1977) " 'Cohesiveness' and team success: A theoretical reformulation," *Review of Sport and Leisure,* 2:36–57.

Nwankwo, R. L. (1973) "Communication as Symbolic Interaction: A Synthesis," *The Journal of Communication,* Vol 23: pp. 195–215.

Meeker, B. (1971) "Decisions and Exchange," *American Sociological Review,* 36: pp. 485–495.

Mick, D. G. (1986) "Consumer Research and Semiotics: Exploring the Morphology of Signs, Symbols, and Significance," *Journal of Consumer Research,* Vol 13: pp. 196–213.

Murray D. and N. Bevan (1985) "The Social Psychology of Computer Conversations," in *IFIP Conference on Human-Computer Interaction,* pp. 268–273, London: Elsevier Science.

Pask, G. (1980) "The Limits of Togetherness," in *Proceedings of INFORMATION PROCESSING 80,* S. H. Lavington (ed.), North-Holland Publishing.

Rice, R. E. (1984) *The New Media: Communication, Research and Technology*. Beverly Hills, CA: Sage.

Ritzer, G. (1975) *Sociology: A Multiple Paradigm Science*. Boston: Allyn and Bacon.

Rogers, E. M. (1986) *Communication Technology*. New York: Free Press.

Scheff, T. (1986) "Micro-Linguistics and Social Structure: A Theory of Social Action," *Sociological Theory,* 4: pp. 71–83.

Schmeideck, R. A. (1978) *The Personal Sphere Model*. New York: Grune and Stratton.

Schutz, G. (1964) *Collected Papers Vol. I*. The Hague: Martinus Nijhoff.

Schutz, G. (1970) *Collected Papers Vol. III*. The Hague: Martinus Nijhoff.

Searle, J. (1969) *Speech Acts*. Cambridge: Cambridge University Press.

Shott, S. (1979) "Emotion and Social Life: A Symbolic Interactionist Analysis," *American Journal of Sociology,* Vol. 84(6): pp. 1317–1334.

Sproull, Lee and Sara Kiesler (1991) *Connections: New Ways of Working in the Networked Organization*. Boston: MIT Press.

Stein, A. (1976) "Conflict and Cohesion: A Review of the Literature," *Journal of Conflict Resolution,* March, pp. 143–72.

Steiner, I. D. (1972) *Group Process and Productivity*. New York: Academic Press.

Steiner, I. D. (1974) *Task-Performing Groups*. Morristown, NJ: General Learning Press.

Vaske, J. J. and Grantham, C. E. (1990) *Socializing the Human Computer Environment*. Norwood, NJ: Ablex.

Watzlawick, P., J. Bavelas, and D. Jackson (1967) *Pragmatics of Human Communication*. New York: Norton and Co.

Westrum, R. (1984) *The Effect of Electronic Communications Technologies on the Large Corporation: Basic Theoretical Framework*. Minneapolis, MN: Honeywell, Corporate Information Management.

Winograd, T. (1984) "Computer Software for Working with Language," *Scientific American,* 251: pp. 130–145.

Winograd, T. (1986) "A Language Perspective on the Design of Cooperative Work," in Krasner, H. (ed), *Proceedings of CSCW 86,* pp. 203–220.

Winograd, T. and F. Flores (1989) *Understanding Computers and Cognition: A New Foundation for Design*. Norwood, NJ: Ablex.

3

Designing the Organization

This chapter moves from an analysis of interpersonal communication mediated by technology to an analysis of the relatively persistent patterns of interactions called organizational structure. Once we have an understanding of group communication, we can then move to thinking about the best interplay of technology to change the organization.

Central to this chapter is our belief that it is the responsibility of the designer to be conscious of the precept that *a way of doing things is as important as the result*. People who design technology and organizations must behave in a socially responsible way and seek to serve a purpose higher than themselves.

Where We Are

Step 2 of the Enneagram is "set up tools" (see Figure 1-3). The basic tool of organizational intervention and technology development is a design process. This chapter gives the theoretical background and details of the design process we use in organizations undergoing change because of technology diffusion. Looking forward (in our planning process) we see Step 8 of the Enneagram, "finishing touches." This means that we need to look ahead to finishing the intervention process, as we begin the design process. How will we know, when we are through, that we have been effective. This is the key question to keep in mind as you go through this chapter. For this reason, we have moved around the Enneagram to Step 2, where we decide on what tools (interventions) to use. We base these decisions upon understanding our

50

purpose (Chapter 1) and developing adequate communication within the organization (Chapter 2).

There are four major sections in this chapter: (1) a theory of design, (2) descriptions of the process of design, (3) design application to organizational change, and (4) a concluding case study demonstrating the use of design as an organizational-change tool. The process of design builds off the general Enneagram model and explicates a thinking and doing process in steps that can be used in the workplace.

The third section builds on our organizational diagnosis model developed from the sociotechnical literature. The model has six elements that characterize a healthy organization. Through a vector analysis, we spell out the linkage between communication processes and relative health in each area. The case study includes information on symptoms of dysfunction and the etiology of these dysfunctions.

THEORY OF DESIGN

"The future of software design is philosophy." This headline appeared in a nationally syndicated column on Innovation by Michael Schrage in November of 1991.[1] This small article probably went unnoticed by many, but it clearly focused on the dominant technology-design issue for the 1990s—and perhaps beyond. Design of technology systems, and hence working organizational structures, proceeds from a set of philosophical assumptions. Sometimes these assumptions are explicit; sometimes not. Schrage's point is that not only should they be made more explicit but also examined. We second that point. The philosophy underlying much of this book comes from the moral philosophy of John Bennett,[2] itself a distillation of several schools of thought. For these reasons, we would like to begin this chapter by making explicit our underlying philosophical assumptions about human behavior. Our philosophical design guidelines follow:

1. People strive to develop in a positive fashion towards greater self-actualization.
2. The meaning of work is derived from the phenomenon of interaction with others and the environment.
3. Symbiotic evolution of people and social groups is facilitated by open communication.
4. Purposeful communication provides a material benefit to human action.
5. A person or group has meaning only within the identity of a larger social context.
6. Development of technology tends to increase the scope and rate of human interaction.
7. Clear, concise conversations, based on mutual nonjudgmental respect, provide a clear pathway for people to transcend narrow self-serving behavior.
8. The creative aspect of people arises from the act of serving beyond self.

Design as Opposed to Engineering

Before we go much further it probably is a good idea to stop and draw a distinction between *design* and *engineering*. They are not mutually exclusive concepts or activities. However, we believe that the central issue facing organizational designers is how to deal with the conceptual shift in decision making from the perspective of engineering to that of design.

One of the best ways to understand a distinction is by analogy. Our analogy is that of *architects* and *builders*. That is, we believe that *designing* is to *engineering* as *architecting* is to *building*. Each of these processes of creation is correlated with a social role, world outlook, and value set. In other words, design and architecture move concepts to an actualizing stage.[3]

Figure 3-1 outlines some of the differences we see in these approaches. The importance here is to make a distinction. As Gregory Bateson once said, "The only difference is a difference."[4] Without distinction, we can't comprehend context or meaning. To bring meaning to this discussion of participatory design, we begin with this distinction.

The point to this figure is that a paradigmatic shift in how *we think* about design is occurring. Similar shifts in thinking appear to be occurring in numerous disciplines. This represents a general direction of change in cognitive mindset from a mostly linear pattern to a more systemic mindset we feel is well described by the Enneagram differences in patterns of thinking and doing. These patterns are not mutually exclusive, but complementary. Both designing and engineering perspectives have merit—when applied in the proper context.

The point is that, although the roles of software architect and software engineer may be linked and overlap, where you start the process of creating software can yield a vast difference.[5] Drawing on our analogy, beginning construction of a house by a builder yields a vastly different outcome than one that begins with an architect. No value judgment is intended—it just works that way. Well, why? Should a different design perspective really make a difference in end results?

A builder usually begins by looking at what constrains the process: cost, time, and material availability. On the other hand, an architect usually begins with looking at the potential. True, both of these perspectives need to be eventually reconciled, but the process is different. Beginning with constraints means that you then move toward opening up—a divergent thinking process. The other way around leads to moving

(Old Paradigm) ENGINEERING	(New Paradigm) DESIGN
Builder	Architect
Implementation	Creation
Logical	Intuitive
Actual	Potential
Manager	Leader
Analytical	Integrative
Clarity	Ambiguity
Efficiency	Elegance
Solid	Fluid
Substance	Style
Data	Information
Plans	Heuristics
Objectives	Values

Thanks to John Perry Barlow for these insights

Figure 3-1. *Paradigms of Thought*

toward the center—a thinking process of convergence. The point is that where you start changes the types of questions you ask your customer.

We certainly know that attitudes and behaviors are linked together. Your attitude toward your job, the task at hand, and towards a customer impacts your behavior—and consequently your business performance. Your attitudes towards a technology, its possible use, and your ultimate goal are related to your behavior in developing or creating the product. But more to the point, these attitudes are based upon a relatively stable set of personal *values*. The shift from engineering to design is driving the change in paradigms of software development.

Therefore, the contrast between roles (e.g., designer and engineer) is most critically evidenced in the difference in value sets held by these groups of people. The shift in values has been towards the inclusion of technology users in the design and development process. This value is crystallized around the principle of building technology in the service of the user. Systems are never goals in themselves. The purpose of the system is to serve users and control the business process embedded in a group of larger systems. As a corollary, software is increasingly designed and built by *groups* of people for use by *groups* of people. The dynamics of group interaction clearly affect the process, as well as the acceptance of the product.

History of Technology Design

Doubtless, the history of technology design can be traced back as far as the creation of fire by humans; the details of the process are lost in antiquity. However, for the purposes of this chapter, we will limit our comments and analysis to the period of the Industrial Revolution to the present; that is, from circa 1750 to now.

Technological development of steam power, transportation, clock mechanisms, and architecture began with a goal of economic gain. The criterion for gain was based on goals of *efficiency, speed,* and *cost.* These design forces came directly from the intended application-value of the technology.

Technology was created for purposes of profit and control of the means of production—not from an aesthetic motivation. Brute force and ignorance were often the energy behind development. Bigger bridges, deeper mines, faster ships were the way success was measured.[6] The underlying philosophical bent seemingly was the control of nature by man. Concerns of despoiling the environment or impact upon the general human condition were remote from the minds of most people engaged in creating and using these developing technologies.

About 50 years into this process, a social revolt of sorts began to challenge these values. Child-labor laws were passed in England; workers were guaranteed some degree of comfort in terms of sanitation and work conditions. This pattern continued relatively intact through the end of World War II. Actually, the period of 1910–1945 can be viewed as one last technological push to ultimately conquer the forces of nature and divide the spoils of natural resources among a few. Toffler echoed this point in describing how the search for wealth based on economic power in the first half of the twentieth century occurred in correlation with an expansion of military might based on a technological infrastructure.[7]

An interesting sidenote here is that some preeminent Japanese social scientists see a corresponding change in Japanese politics and thought that led to World War II, and the consequent recovery.[8] When the values of Japanese society changed from trade/exploitation to wealth-building, the entire way in which technology was viewed changed. Again, value shifts led to attitude shifts and behavioral changes.

The pace of change increased, and *at an increasing rate.* The United States developed international telecommunications networks, created nuclear power and the rudiments of present-day computer technology by 1949.[9] It is interesting to remember that the very beginnings of a new design paradigm were born at this time. The Tavistock Institute was working in the coalfields of Southwestern England using something termed socio-technical design both to gain productive efficiency and to improve the quality of work life.

Design was still something that engineers did. Scientists in white lab coats created wonders and were greatly admired (Edison, Alexander Bell, Einstein, Fermi). Their legacy passed to the engineers who took concepts and made them usable. Telephones, automobiles, washing machines flowed into the marketplace. Whole economies shifted and the world balance of power became the issue of who controlled technological production. Technology design was based upon technology capability. What could be done reigned supreme. Bigger was better—more horsepower, faster, faster, more, more, more . . .

During the late 1960s, a fundamental shift happened. People began to see the finite nature of the natural resources of the globe. Not everyone wanted to admit it—but this point became clearer every year. The Club of Rome issued a report on the *Limits to Growth,* Rachael Carson wrote *Silent Spring,* and—finally—we experienced the "oil crisis." Industrialized countries went into a panic. One could argue whether or not this was the watershed point for a change in perspective towards design of technology—but it seems to us that we have at least a good working hypothesis.

What was the shift? Apparently, we went from a mechanistic, controlling paradigm to a more holistic, symbiotic approach to the use of technology. In the early 1970s academics began to talk openly of a paradigm shift in thinking, across a wide range of activities. Technology design was only one of these. In 1979, a landmark paper was published at Stanford by P. Schwartz and J. Olgivy, detailing a shift in cognition. There was an increasing awareness that the design of technology systems and human work organizations could not be logically separated from one another. Organizational design began to emerge as a distinct practice, allied with but separate from, management science in practice. Power in organizations began to move down and out.

Where did this leave software development? The change can be tracked with the movement of software development from the mainframe environment to smaller, decentralized approaches. As with the Industrial Revolution, software development went through a corresponding change in the way it was done. We moved from the 1950s picture of user talking to programmer and the mystery of coding in machine language, through the 1960s when we got second generation languages and made the distinction between operating and application levels. The 1970s saw the introduction of new specialties (decomposition of roles) and we got systems analysts and later, systems engineers. The process of design became formalized with many steps:

delineate, the "waterfall method," code walkthroughs, and—finally—integration testing.

All very logical, linear in form, and fundamentally bureaucratic. If bureaucratic models of economic activity led to increased efficiency and decreased variance, then why not apply it to the building of software? The simple answer is that these models don't work very well for software development. While they are excellent at hashing out the syntax of it all, they are ineffective at dealing with different semantic views. As software development projects became ever larger and more complex, a production mode of operation began to fail. Work structure modeled on the assembly-line model was not working. People began to think of concurrent engineering, database modeling, and other ways of viewing the process as a system.

So, in the late 1970s, we find computer technology rapidly moving into the hands of end-users (God Forbid!!!). PCs, networking, and—finally—workstations. We see the first examples of software that allow a moderately motivated person to begin to communicate with a computer, e.g., Lotus 1-2-3™, Framework II™, and dBASE II™. People don't have to go to the central MIS group to get a computer to help them. A revolution is brewing—but still is constrained by the forces of an embedded bureaucracy.

This puts us in the present. End-user computing, information resource managers, and fourth generation languages abound. Finally, after festering in the human consciousness for 30-odd years, comes *participatory design* built upon the seminal ideas of those folks back in the English coal mines.

Current Perspective: Design as Minding

Recently, a train of thought has developed within the field of product design that parallels the socio-technical perspective in organizational design. This approach has been called product semantics.[10] A quote from Klaus Krippendorff defines the perspective.

> Product semantics is developing notions of sense, meanings, cognitive models, types, signs, perceptions and motivation as tools that facilitate communication among designers, that help pose user-enabling research questions. I contend that design is more than the subjective component of engineering, the artistic aspect of marketing, and the unspeakable part of management. Design can develop a coherent discourse of its own.[11]

Krippendorf goes on to outline five characteristics of the design process as a minding process. Design becomes a creative, conscious process of "creating meaningful interfaces in the social practice of living."[12] The minding-as-designing metaphor assumes the following:

1. Different people have different cognitive models of the same thing—including the workplace that has emerged during their lives. This follows closely from the school of cognitive anthropology.

2. This perspective provides people with the capability to construct their own realities of the workplace. It (the product of design) can be manipulated by users.
3. It is based upon user-centered research, which seeks to understand the shared meaning people take from function, experience, and purpose.
4. Design is a recursive process. It feeds upon itself.[13]
5. It embodies an idea of social organizations. That is, the concept of product semantics implies that things take on meaning from embeddedness in social context.

These distinguishing characteristics of the contemporary design perspective fit quite well with our own assumptions and suggest that they can be applied to the process of organizational design as well as to more conventional product design. The reason is that Krippendorf's perspective is, at its base, interactive, social, and experiential. Those three qualities lie at the heart of any human organization's function.

Six Principles for Organizational Technology Design

Theory differentiates design as a intellectual process from engineering. Many disciplines of design (e.g., architecture, graphics) have developed "Principles of Design" that guide the activities of people working in the field. Creativity in design becomes the utilization of these principles in new and innovative ways. Principles are not stand-alone elements. They are part of a systemic relationship—and must be considered as a *system*. Emphasis on interrelatedness is essential and defines the elegance of the design.

We have developed six principles of design to guide our activities in helping people create technologies to serve the purposes of organizations. In large part, these principles are borrowed from the field of architecture and modified by our own experience (Pye, 1979). The underlying philosophy, of course, is to design technologies to support the healthy functioning of an organization over time. Alternative principles could be employed; but, in our opinion, these alternative methods would sacrifice functioning, a sense of connectedness, and, the ultimate purpose of organizing to do work. These six design requirements follow:

1. The requirements must embody the essential principle of arrangement. Design must connect elements of your social world.

Technology systems must open your social world—not restrict it. The analogy here is an open-systems approach in both networking and operating systems for computer platforms. A technology must, in this sense, become a conduit for communication among people within the work group. A technology that restricts, inhibits, or disconnects people from each other would be in violation of this principle. This principle does not provide access but merely provides the avenue for access.

This is the freeway of the information infrastructure of the organization. Current developments in promotion of the National Research and Education Network (NREN) are a fine example of an attempt to put this design principle in place for the United States.

2. *Parts of the environment must relate in time and space, which reflects your requirements of use.*
It is necessary for the system to preserve a history of its operation and provide an avenue to project itself into the future. This relates parts of the enterprise in time. The most common manifestations of this principle would be business simulation applications which are based upon historical data. Often systems are designed that do not permit use of historical data for analysis. Such design violates this principle.

Connections in space mean a system that operates across large networks—on a global scale. Small systems which cannot connect to other entities would violate this principle. Connections in space also imply a uniformity across several parts of the enterprise process. Therefore, well-designed systems connect parts of the business enterprise smoothly. For example, having disparate electronic mail systems to support engineering, marketing, and accounting would violate this principle at the enterprise level of analysis.

Lastly, all these relationships in time and space must reflect your requirements for use—that is, not technology or functionality for its own sake. This is a key point for developers of technology to hold. Technological elegance does not always translate into good design, if it fails to meet the end users' requirements for use (as defined by them).

3. *Components must be designed in ways that work against the strong tendency towards entropy.*
All systems tend toward entropy.[14] Components of the technology system must be constructed to guard against this tendency. For example, systems that encourage the cloning of information and automatic dispatch will overload the communication structure with uselessly replicated information.

An additional element could be a method to seek out relevant information and present it in an easily understandable form. In other words, we are seeking systems designs that promote the "essentialization" of information flowing in the system.

4. *Open access must be provided.*
Perhaps this is the most obvious of systems design principles today. The proliferation of networks is making the idea of "interoperability" a key concern of designers in the 1990s.[15] Questions about who has access to what become designer concerns. With use of this principle, inherent social values become embedded into system design. At least, designers should try to make these social decisions conscious ones.

Just as handicapped access is mandated in public building, we suggest that access to information networks (both public and private) be an essential design principle. The Apple platform opened access to many people for the use of personal computers.[16] The spread of Metropolitan Area Networks (MANs) and Electronic Data Interchange (EDI) are making this access principle a critical feature of all system designs.

5. *Cost of use must be acceptable.*
People won't use systems they can't afford. Overpriced systems fail in the market—no matter how well they function. The Apple LISA, and—more recently— the NEXT platforms are examples of failure to incorporate this principle of design.

However, the issue is more complicated than simple price points. True business value is as much a phenomenon of perception as it is a fact. People often pay premiums for real-estate locations that imbue them with status or for designer labels. We suggest that the same psychology operates with technology and must be considered in the design of the systems. The cost of a system has an added social-psychology component based upon how effective they are found to be in actual use.

6. *Technology systems must be aesthetically pleasing.*

Aesthetics is the study of art and beauty. Beauty is often defined as the "quality of being pleasing in form."[17] It is difficult to say in words what an aesthetically pleasing system design is. This is the most subjective design principle. Simplicity, elegance, and grace are words that come to mind. One way out of this mental trap is to look at good aesthetic designs as ones that create in the user a desire for use. You are drawn to it and find it pleasurable in use.

Elegant designs are often the signature of the designer. You see the design and you know who designed it. Apple platforms carried this distinction during the 1980s and have lost it as their systems move closer to other PC designs. The essence of design is uniqueness with purpose. That is our definition of systems aesthetics.

These six principles of design are not isolated from our perspective on what a healthy organization looks like. Quite the opposite. These principles, taken largely from the field of architecture, can easily be related to our perspective of organizational design. There is a mapping of these principles to a sociotechnical approach to organizational design. We will elaborate on this relationship in the following sections on organizational design and the case study.

PROCESS OF DESIGN

Workplace Design

Designing the workplace is an activity that requires the integration of several design perspectives: ergonomics, graphics, interior arts, technology, and organizational form. Existing bodies of literature exist for ergonomics, graphic design, and interiors. This section focuses on the latter two factors. The overall thrust of this book is to integrate designing technology platforms and organizations—the marriage of two otherwise unlinked practices.

But because of technology, workplaces have always been the result of information architecture. Work is being separated in time and space with the advent of the distributed organization. For the purpose of this chapter on design, assume that information environments are the basic unit of organizational design.[18] These environments are coming into increasing use as a design tool.

Designing the workplace means, in essence, putting data into context so that it can be used as a basic ingredient of the productive process. There is a fundamental shift in the quality of information in today's economy.[19] The basic laws of economics hae been upset—no longer does scarcity operate as a central principle of determining value. Information can be made ubiquitous instantaneously. As a result, fixing value becomes complicated. It is within this context that workplaces, information environments, must be designed.

Information is different from data. Data becomes information when it is placed in a social context. Information technologies are co-evolving with human organizational forms. Entirely new forms of human networks are growing around us, spurred on by the increasing pervasiveness of accessible information. For example, these information environments are sometimes called "distributed business enterprises." But the real trend is to reverse the separation of home and workplace that began with the industrial revolution. Designing information environments for work today is really engaging in *community reconstruction*.

The workplace is no longer a distinct element from other human habitations. The workplace, school, home, and community center are moving closer together. Now, when we embark on a workplace design process, it becomes a much larger enterprise. We must consider the social factor in the design process. These new values—the new paradigm—become a driving force. In order to include these subtle social factors in the design process, we recommend using the participatory design process.[20]

Participatory Design

The purpose of this section is to enlarge a discussion of the participatory design process in organizational design. Elsewhere, we have a new arena of investigation called "software sociology."[21] Its essence is that if software—or any communications product—is being designed, developed, built, and used by *groups* of people, then we need to apply some of our knowledge of interpersonal dynamics to the design of these products. Hence, software sociology. The issue of participatory design is merely an extension of this approach, based on design methodology.

We are limiting the scope of this discussion to the technology development process. Specifically, we will focus on software development, because we feel that it is the core technology for information environments. Although we believe we can extend this process into other technology-development areas, that will have to be left for another time. In our view, software is a communcation medium, in the best McLuhanian sense. It is the vehicle by which people communicate with machines, machines with machines, and—finally—machines with people.[22]

So, what are the semantics and syntax of the participatory design process? At this time, they are not clearly defined. Interest in the topic has been growing for a few years and has taken its clearest expression in a conference held in the spring of 1990. The Participatory Design Conference '90 was sponsored by Computer Professionals for Social Responsibility and brought together about 120 people from the international community who were interested in the topic. The center of discussion was the Scandinavian experience in work redesign.

More recently, a distinct professional organization has been formed to promote the development of software design as a distinct practice. The purpose of the organization is:

> The Association for Software Design (ASD) is an educational nonprofit organization whose purpose is to create, support and further the profession and community of software design. Although the ASD will start in the California Bay Area, it is expected that, it will grow into a national organization and include foreign members as well. In pursuit of this mission, the ASD will undertake the following activities. . . .[23]

That is, this perspective on design is more than an academic exercise. It is firmly rooted in an action-research tradition and is aimed at the practical application of design theory.

Designing and using advanced software platforms seem to consist of three basic stages as depicted in Figure 3-2. The first stage is a translation of people's needs into functional specifications that can be taken by software developers (through coding) and made into machine-language instructions. The second stage is a reverse translation of machine appearance and capability into a human understanding for practical use. This two-stage process introduces numerous opportunities for mis-understanding and errors. It is because of this translation complexity that participatory design holds so much power. Power to reduce errors, increase quality of product, and reduce barriers to use of the software. The boundary between each stage of the process is one of communication and interpretation. We have seen in Chapter 2 just how complex this process can be. We have also expounded on the principle that communication needs to be interactive and—to some extent—structured. Participatory design is an interactive structure supporting this design process.

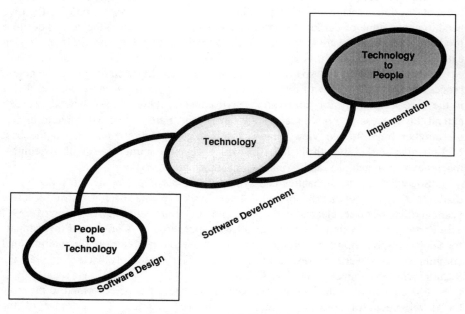

Figure 3-2. *Software Technology Development Process*

The Process of Design

The participatory process can take several forms. The most often cited is the use of focus groups, a rather naive approach. Many more techniques exist to involve users in the design process itself—not as observers or bystanders but as full participants, equal with designers and developers. Ideally, users begin working with technology creators at the conceptual stage of development. Usually, they form into teams of seven to fifteen people and the team itself goes through a "teambuilding process" to clarify goals and vision. As much attention is paid to team development as product development, and a by-product of the *design team* process is that communication patterns among members are clarified and strengthened. The users on the design team become advocates for the use of the technology and assist in the reverse translation of product capabilities into the workplace.

Figure 3-3 is a diagram of the staged participatory process. Each point in the loop actually contains another series of loops so that the process can iterate around any issue. The value of the process is that it is complete. That is, no critical factors are left out of the design process if the pattern is followed. For example, you cannot jump from design to action, or full-scale implementation, without prototyping and planning.

The participatory process should extend beyond more traditional concerns for interface appearance and clarity of instruction manuals. Software is as much form as substance. As with architecture, there is a certain aesthetic to software. Elegance and simplicity are guiding design principles when users are involved in the process. As capability grows, so does the complexity of the software. This places a design premium on constructing a good, extensible foundation. If you have to go back and rewrite core modules in order to add a field to a database, you don't have elegance.

Users can inform this process by recounting how they actually could and would use the product. Live testing helps considerably. Part of the process is to bring a genuine business problem to the design group. This insures that the design is grounded in practicality. You can't design skyscrapers in the absence of consideration for gravity,

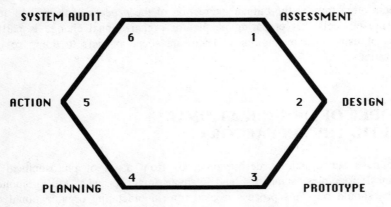

Figure 3-3. Grantham and Nichols Design Process

nor can you design good software in the absence of practical utility. Because users are the experts in this domain, the participatory process is gaining credence among advanced system developers.

Later chapters will expand on the use of this design process. This process is an extension of the Enneagram model, the overall architecture of this book. The six steps in the process represent the internal points of the Enneagram, specifying the *doing* part of the model. It is linear in construction; but embedded within a larger more systemic model (i.e., the Enneagram).

The design process needs to be followed in order (1-2-3-4-5-6-1). As it is iterating, it is repeated as many times as necessary to achieve the desired results with increasingly finer-tuned design and increased granularity. The key to success in using this design team model is not leaving any steps out. As we have said, people often want to jump from point 2 (Design) to point 5 (Action) without going through the necessary intermediate steps. This leads to disaster and failure of design. On the other hand, some people, groups, and companies never get past step 1.

The heart of the participatory process is that each step is an interactive process jointly involving the designers and end-users. It is far more intrusive than bringing in end-user groups and showing them the product as it exists and asking for input. Participatory design means just that: users of technology have roles as equal partners in the design process. Myriad techniques to facilitate group interaction can be used in the process, depending upon group characteristics, history of interaction, and time constraints.

Participatory design is necessary in its application to *organizational design*. The idea of consciously designing a work organization is taken as radical in some circles of managerial thought. However, recent experiments in Scandinavia have shown that organizational design can be practiced as a discipline, with positive results. In fact, given the economic drivers of business enterprises we speak about elsewhere, organizational design is a necessary component of contemporary management practice.

Pelle Ehn has stated that "democratization of the workplace is mandatory for a successful enterprise." Further, he states, "technology changes the way we work. We must understand and appreciate the politics of this in design. What designers often miss is the human interaction of the *process of work*." In addition, Kari Thorsen feels that preparing people for organizational change is part of the process of using new technologies. There are social barriers to doing so in most organizations.[24]

A MODEL OF ORGANIZATIONAL HEALTH: THE SIX FACTORS

As we have stated before, design proceeds from a set of philosophical tenets, guidelines, principles, standards, and even an image of what the components of elegance should be. This process is also true in practicing organizational design. Previously, we have outlined our particular perspective in the philosophy and principles of design. Now, we turn to a more explicit model of what the ideal, healthy, or successful organization would look like.

Organizations process information to manage uncertainty and equivocality.[25] The way that they manage the flow of information can indicate the relative health of large, formal, complex organizations. We are proposing that an organizational-design model based on information flows can be used as a diagnostic tool—as well as a design template for the organizational development practitioner.

Bennett sees a multiterm system composed of six elements as one that describes a concrete "event." That is, something that has come into existence and is complete. Therefore, a six-term system becomes the basis for describing a work organization—because it does exist and is complete. In systems-theory terms, the organization has a boundary, requisite variety, and has its constituent parts connected to one another.

There are many models of healthy organizations. The sociotechnical approach of Passmore,[26] the diagnostic approach of Kotter,[27] the cybernetics model of Beer,[28] and the comparative approach of Morgan[29] are some of the most popular used today in the practice of organizational design. We do not attempt to argue the validity of their or our model of organizations. We are much more concerned with the idea of reliability in the use of the model for comparative analysis. Our model is an application of Bennett's work to our own information flows, extended into the process aspects of organizational interaction.

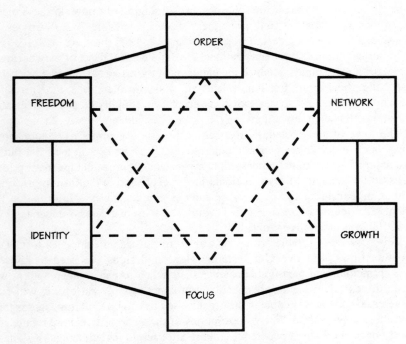

Figure 3-4. *Elements of Organizational Health*

More traditional ways of analyzing organizations have included dimensions of structural complexity, formality, size, technology, effectiveness, etc.[30] Our model is one of *process,* where others have been focused on *structure.* We believe that these are merely different levels of description. We hope that the relationship of more traditional ways of analyzing organizations to our unique approach would become the center of an applied research program in the future.

The requirements for sufficiency of organizational description include the process of interaction, systems that support these interactions, and finally the material structure that emerges from the interactions. Bennett's work provides the basis of this model by relying on structural aspects. Our additions of information flow and associated socioemotional aspects, along with the model, provide us with an organizational design framework that has proven itself useful in everyday practice. Figure 3-4 is a diagram identifying these elements of organizational health. This figure is meant to indicate the interconnectedness of the six elements. The dark lines forming the outer border signify that all elements must be viewed as a complete whole. The dotted lines inside the figure form two triangles that are the two subsets of the entire process. Freedom, network, and focus unite to build potential for action. Identity, order, and growth are the manifestations of that potential. Thus, the elements can be examined as unique items, in sets of three, or as a whole. Each of these structural elements has an analog in information-system flow, outlined in Table 3-1. Therefore, each of these structural elements is characterized as a pattern of information flow. We can, by definition, diagnose the relative functioning of an organizational element by examining the associated information-flow characteristic. This principle becomes the basis for the creation of our unique diagnostic (and design) paradigm. But how do these elements relate to our previously stated principles of design? Table 3-2 illustrates these relationships.

In our experience, the Organizational Health Vector (OHV) of networking is an analog of design principle of connecting elements of the organization. Identity becomes the aesthetic dimension; freedom relates to cost considerations; order relates to organization in time and space; growth is access; and finally, focus is related to an organization's tendency toward entropy.

The logic of these relationships stems from the organizational design process. Our principles of design are general guidelines that must be kept in the forefront when intervening in organizational processes. Our particular approach maps these principles to six essential elements of organizational health expressed in the form of information flow in an organization. In this way, we can examine a pattern of information flows, trace that to a principle of organizational health, and—in conclusion—understand which general design principle is involved.[31]

This may seem a rather complex way to relate design principles to OHV and information flows. But this is a systemic view of design. We need to know how concept, principle, and measurable characteristic relate to one another. Often, we are called in to help diagnose an organizational problem and several people will explain the issue in several ways. People in the organization have a difficult time understanding how all these apparently different descriptions of the same problem are related. What is usually occurring is that people are talking at different logical levels.

For example, a senior manager may express an issue in terms of a design

Table 3-1   Dimensions of Organizational Analysis

Network	Measure of Interaction Pattern Density and Reciprocity
Identity	Measure of Uniqueness Boundary Permeability
Freedom	Rate of Innovation Measure of Creative Ability Measure of Cooperative Challenge
Order	Measure of Sequencing of Operational Steps Steps done for the Right Reason
Growth	A Measure of Organizational Scale coupled with Rates of Change
Focus	Efficiency of Operation Output Variance REduction

Table 3-2   Organizational Health Elements and Design Principles

Organizational Health Vector	Design Principle
Network	Connect Elements
Identity	Aesthetics
Freedom	Cost
Order	Time/Space
Growth	Access
Focus	Entropy

principle: "Parts of my organization don't seem to be connected." A middle-level manager expresses the feeling: "We don't know who the hell we are anymore." And the line worker says: "Upper management makes me very anxious about our future." All of these are indicators of one central problem: imbalance in the networking OHV. Our conceptual map allows us to relate these various expressions to an underlying concept of organizational health so that we can begin the intervention design process.

The next section of this chapter lays out the process of moving from isolating an OHV to development of an intervention strategy.

Diagnosing the Organization

Every organization is characterized by three basic vectors of description, as follows:

1. Definition is the boundary condition of the system: Who are we?
2. Distinction is the uniqueness dimension: How are we different?
3. Direction is the evolving characteristic: Where are we going?

Entropy is continuously defeated as we strive to answer and reanswer these questions. The elements of the Bennett model of organizational health can be mapped to these three dimensions and begin to yield a framework for asking questions, performing assessments, and offering prescriptions for return to balance in the organization.

Figure 3-5 is our concept of how these elements of Bennett's model align with the critical questions. The social-psychological dynamic of organizational imbalance is that individual striving toward healthy, personal functional goals is frustrated by organizational goals.[32] These organizational goals are manifestations of the desires and imagination of the leaders of the organization. The desires, concerns, and fears of leaders are expressed in the rituals and symbols of the corporation, which implicitly control behavior by prescribing what is right and what is wrongful behavior. Our design for intervention should be aimed at opening up channels of power and removing the obstacles that impede harmonious interaction of people in the organization.

We believe that when a particular issue becomes the dominant concern of organizational members, this is a sign of imbalance in that particular area of functioning. When questions surface, they are indications that something (or some elements) is out of balance and needs to be corrected. Further, these questions are

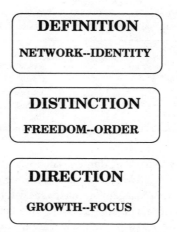

Figure 3-5. *Structural Elements of Organizational Health*

indicative of fundamental attitudes towards interaction and what kinds of behaviors are seen as harmful within the organization. These attitudes and behaviors are then linked to specific patterns of interaction, which yield emotional states.[33] These emotional states and imbalances can be corrected through a set of prescribed interventions aimed at the *process* of interaction within an organization. We call our diagnostic framework an *ecology of interaction*.

Relationship of Values, Emotions, and Intervention Strategies

Figure 3-6 is a diagram of the relationships between personal values; patterns of interaction, status, and power; and the consequent emotional states generated in people. We see this as a diagram of the social psychology of organizational health. Our reasoning is that value sets will shape how we interact with fellow workers and that this pattern of interaction establishes status and power relationships among people. Status is that dimension of social relations that expresses the relative amount of prestige you have within the workgroup. Power is the ability to control and shape others' behavior. Status and power can be viewed as being in excess ("I've got more than I deserve") or deficit ("I don't have as much as I deserve"). The cause, or agency, of the amount you have can be seen as being determined by others or self. Thus, you may believe that you have more power than you deserve and that power has been given to you by others; your profile would be Power-Others-Excess. Further, these power/status relationships yield emotional states. The active intervention that organizational developers employ is therefore aimed at bringing these emotional states into harmony throughout the organization. It is our belief that you cannot deal with social-psychological systems without focusing on the shifting values held by employees, managers, and executives. In other words, organizational development begins and ends with personal development and value change.

Organizational Health

Table 3-3 is an overview of how we see organizational health vectors expressed in terms of values, harmful things, status/power, emotions, and finally, interventions. This is the model we use to decide what is unbalanced in the organization and where to begin the intervention. For example, the OHV of Order expresses a valuing of efficiency in an organization. When this is out of balance, questions regarding the use of external standards for evaluation are seen as harmful. People perceive that their status is in deficit and that this deficit is caused by themselves. This perception results

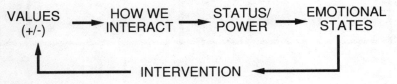

Figure 3-6. *Social Psychology of Organizational Health*

Table 3-3 Organizational Health Vectors Diagnostic Framework

	Values	Harmful Things	Status/Power	Emotions	Intervention
Network	Realization of Unity	Honesty	Status Other Deficit	Anxiety Outward	Town Meetings
Identity	Understand Purpose	Potential	Status Self Excess	Alienation Fear	Ethics Spirit
Freedom	Creation	Risk Taking	Power Self Excess	Hostility Outward	Theatre & Planning
Order	Efficiency	External Standards	Power Self Deficit	Hostility Inward	Quality Control
Growth	Customer Needs	Looking Outside	Status Others Deficit	Confusion Imagination	Customer Satisfaction Systems
Focus	Status Quo	Change	Power Others Excess	Diffuse Anxiety Denial	Work Flow Analysis

© 1992 Grantham & Nichols

in emotions of inward-directed hostility and we have found Quality Control workshops an effective initial intervention.

In the following pages, we will describe each of these dimensions in detail and relate the elements of our social-psychological model to each of them. Table 3-3 presents a synopsis of our organizational intervention approach, which is a prescriptive approach to diagnosing a dysfunctional organization. The negative emotional states expressed are, in our opinion, manifestations of imbalances in underlying organizational functional parameters.

INTERACTION VECTORS

Definition–Network

This is the expression of life and activity of the organization. It is the pattern of interaction among organizational elements and with their environment. This is a process of determining and realizing the *context* of the organization—both internal (part to part) and external (whole to whole). When this process is out of balance, there is a continuous expression of activity—which is not directed toward purposeful action.

Key Questions Dominant in Discussions
- How can we communicate better?
- What's going on around here?
- How can we get feedback?
- How can we tell management what's going on?

Existence of these questions indicates to us that the *valued* attitudes are:

1. Realization of unity
2. Being more connected externally
3. Being more related internally

Almost paradoxically, Open Communication and Honesty are seen as *harmful*. The shutdown of honest, open communication actually creates the situation where indicator questions arise and people strive toward value-based attitudes. Control of communication behavior gives rise to attitude shifts. This situation is characterized by the following interaction pattern.

Interaction Pattern
Status determined from external Other, usually in *Deficit* mode. People preceive that their status is determined by somebody else, without relation to their intrinsic worth. Most people believe that they are not being given status commensurate with what they perceive they deserve. This pattern results in specific emotional states.

Emotional States
Anxiety focused on outside forces. Passive–aggressive behavior. Anger. You may see a lot of useless behavior (rearranging the deck chairs) in acute cases, such as constant

reorganization. Paradoxical and unclear communication also occurs. When this situation exists, we recommend the following intervention.

Intervention Strategies
Produce open forums for two-way, honest communication. Town meetings with the presence of executives also work quite well. Programs that promote the relatedness of internal elements can be helpful; "the everyone is a salesperson" approach.

Definition–Identity

This is the development of the *relationship* between the individual and the organization. The aesthetic appeal of the organization is a central design concern. Distinction with purpose. People viewed as unique and contributing to the overall mission and purpose of the organization. A constant defining of activities is the negative pattern. Potential is not valued and not discussed.

Key Questions Dominant in Discussions
- Who are we?
- Why do we do what we do?
- What qualities define us?
- Where are our boundaries?

Existence of these questions indicates to us that the valued attitudes are:

1. Understanding our purpose
2. Linkage to larger universe
3. Spirit and will

Questioning why we exist, being seen *only* as a part, and talk about potential are seen as *harmful*. Again, the paradox of controlling behaviors shifts attitudes toward what really needs to be dealt with in the organization. Personal meaning exists within a context—in this case personal meaning is missing. This situation is characterized by the following interaction pattern.

Interaction Pattern
Status excess is defined by self-referent. People feel that they have *status* in excess of what they actually deserve. This pattern results in specific emotional states.

Emotional States
Paranoia and constant audit/monitoring behavior. *Fear* and *guilt* are primary emotions. May be accompanied with alienation from work and self. We recommend the following intervention.

Intervention Strategies
Most successful strategy centers around showing possibilities for individuals and the organization. A lot of work required centers around *purpose* definition, with *status*

equalized. Workshops on values and ethical behavior are also found to be effective in opening up linkages to bigger things. Emphasis on Spirit.

Distinction–Freedom

The continuous improvement of the potential of the organization by freeing up the creative energy of its members. Internal generation of increased capability. When the vector is out of balance, paralysis results and denial of creative ability. People cannot be themselves. Self-actualization is seen as prohibited. From a design perspective, cost is the primary concern.

Key Questions Dominant in Discussions:
- How do we renew our products?
- How can we create things?
- How do we move to higher levels of functioning?

Existence of these questions indicate to us that the *valued* attitudes are:

1. Creation and renewal
2. Building of capabilities

The conflict between these personal values and organizational values produce a situation where being receptive to positive input, doing business a different way, and experimentation are seen as *harmful* behaviors. This situation is characterized by the following interaction pattern.

Interaction Pattern
Power from Internal Referent in *excess*. People believe that they have too much power and the cause of this is their own fault: "I really don't deserve this much power."

Emotional States
Negative emotion is denial. Outward Hostility and anger towards competition and customers. Shame results. Extreme cases result in powerlessness and serious self-esteem issues. We recommend the following intervention.

Intervention Strategies
Affirmation activities that demonstrate goodness, potential, and inner creative capabilities not restricted by the environment. Actions that release and acknowledge emotional states are positive. Creative exercises such as brainstorming and planning to follow through are critical. Theater as a metaphor is very effective in Freedom-deficit cases.

Distinction–Order

This is the process that eliminates variance from operations. Sequencing of events is important. Further, making these sequences visible to all members can assist in coordinating activities across functional boundaries. When this process becomes unbalanced, subjective items become objective, and circular reasoning results. Time and space relationships are the dominant design factor.

Key Questions Dominant in Discussions

- What is the right sequence of events?
- What do we mean by quality?
- How can we track and forecast input/output correlations?
- How do we achieve consistency in product and service?

Existence of these questions indicate to us that the *valued* attitudes are:

1. Do it right the first time
2. Smoothness in operation
3. Efficiency

External Imposed Standards and Randomness in Process are viewed as *harmful* behaviors. This situation is characterized by the following interaction pattern.

Interaction Pattern

Power with Internal Referent usually in *Deficit* mode. Things are "out of control." A preoccupation with internal processes—digestive and neurological things. A lot of blaming behavior and "only ifs."

Emotional States

Inner-directed Hostility, anger at others. "It's all their fault." Schizophrenic behavior. Some depressive states. Guilt. We recommend the following intervention.

Intervention Strategies

Put standards in place. They need to be consensual in nature and worked from the outside to the inside. Variance monitoring and control systems need to be structured in a positive sense *for improvement*—not blaming. Emphasis on developing systems for Quality Control that can lead to new ideas and services.

Direction–Growth

The organization is expanding in both time and space. New markets are identified and expectations of customers are met. When this vector moves away from balance, a state of imagination exists. People construct their own realities not based on objective, outside information. Things are OK, and denial of reality. This vector is linked to the design principle of Access.

Key Questions Dominant in Discussions

- What can we become?
- How do we grow?

- How big do we want to be?
- What market share do we need/want?

Existence of these questions indicate to us that the *valued* attitudes are:

1. Meeting externally defined needs
2. Knowing what customer expectations are
3. Comparison to industry quality standards

Looking Outside, External Comparisons, and Believing Customers are seen as *harmful*. This situation is characterized by the following interaction pattern.

Interaction Pattern
The clinical interaction pattern is characterized by inward focus with emphasis on *Status* based on control by Others, usually in terms of *Deficit*. In other words, your status is viewed as insufficient and controlled by others.

Emotional States
Negative Thinking state is *Confusion* and *Imagination*. Depressive feelings and behavior with some delusional tendencies. We recommend the following intervention.

Intervention Strategies
Primary strategy is to open up communication to get Outside view. Customer satisfaction systems put in place and have reward systems tied to these *objective* measures. Reality testing is a secondary intervention. Basically, getting to "What does the customer think and feel about us" as a pathway to improvement.

Direction–Focus

Removal of unnecessary activities and material from the processes of the organization are represented by this vector. Eliminating these impurities and concentrating the process is a prime concern. When this factor becomes unbalanced, activity for continuous improvement is removed from the system. Entropy results.

Key Questions Dominant in Discussions:
- How can we do it better?
- Where can we save on time, energy, and organization?
- How can we simplify our internal processes?
- How can we balance allocation of resources?

Existence of these questions indicate to us that the *valued* attitudes are:

1. Status quo
2. Internally-defined efficiency
3. Cutting costs.

Effects Towards Change, Questioning of Ego Force, or Quick Actions are viewed as *harmful*. Sometimes this situation results in "paralysis by analysis" and results in the following pattern.

Interaction Pattern

Power issues are predominant topics. Rule by dictate from above. Power goes to person, not position. A lot of codependent activity. Other and Excess orientation. Efficiency is stressed to the excess.

Emotional States

Diffuse anxiety and emotional paralysis—denial of feelings. Very ego-centered with self-worship reinforced by subservient feelings. The "con" is being practiced. Very addictive. This is a very difficult cycle to break because the god of "efficiency" is a deep cultural value (especially in the United States). We suggest the following intervention.

Intervention Strategies

Workflow analysis can help the objective and visualize the real business process. Cross-functional impact groups dealing with focus for link to a larger whole. Reinforcement for building capability—investment in people. Slow down the "ready–fire–aim" syndrome.

How to Use These Guidelines

Obviously, we can't pretend to make you an expert in the application of this organizational-design template by reading this chapter—even repeated readings. We offer our process outline to you in hopes that it will spark some deeper understanding of the complexity of organizational interventions. They need to consider the values, interaction patterns, social relations, and emotions that accompany situations where OHV factors are out of balance. Later in Chapters 5 and 6, we elucidate another process map for actual interventions. These maps should be combined when designing both the form and function of the intervention.

CASE STUDY: DIAGNOSIS OF SYSTEM IMBALANCE

The final part of this chapter is a case study, which illustrates how this Organizational Diagnosis framework can be applied in a work setting. The case study involved a requested intervention in an organization undergoing a significant leadership change and an expanding market.

The presenting complaint was not actually a complaint, but a request for assistance. The past leader had been very autocratic in style. However, recent additions to the professional staff of the organization were beginning to create a situation where status relationships were shifting and old power structures were being upset. The purpose of the assessment was to provide the temporary leader with data to develop an organizational intervention in preparation for new leadership.

The intervention was structured around an exercise called the "Spider Diagram" (see Figure 3-7). This is a visual metaphor of the core concerns of people within the organization. Respondents are asked to write down their concerns on the Spider Diagram. These are collected and data is derived. These written documents are supplemented with personal interviews to verify findings.

Report on the "Spider Diagrams" from Staff and Professionals

The purpose of the "Spider Diagram" exercise was to identify areas of concern among staff and professionals about current functioning in a way that would lead to plans for management action so that we could enhance our service to our customers (employers).

We received 21 completed forms from a variety of staff, professionals, and administrators.[34] Although we can not generalize from this data, it appears to be fairly

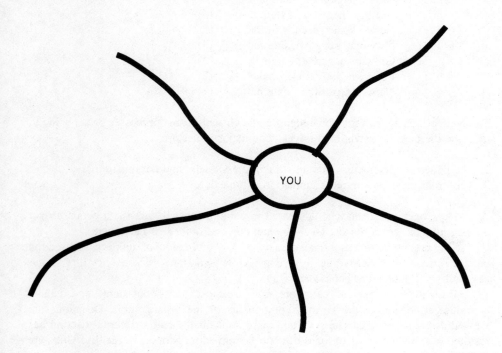

Instructions: Please write down your primary concerns as an employee of this organization. Place each concern in a separte area of the diagram. If you need more areas, add more legs to the Spider.

Figure 3-7. Spider Diagram

consistent internally and therefore can be assumed to reliably reflect the "state of the organization."

The model that Bennett developed, which closely resembles a modern complex social organization, is called a *hexad* because it contains six terms or elements. The hexad represents a coalescence of *time* and *space* dimensions of different processes that occur when an organism is evolving. According to Bennett, this structural model formed the essential basis for the dynamic nature of organisms. We have adapted this model in my work with organizational-change efforts as a symbol of organizational robustness. The model has proven to be an excellent diagnostic tool that parallels work done by sociotechnical systems practitioners. Figure 3-4 is a diagram of the six terms and their relationship in triads and as a whole system.

Table 3-1 is an abbreviated explanation of the elements of the hexad structure.[35] The content analysis of the spider diagrams categorized comments as either negative (indicative of concern) or positive (things we do right), with reference to internal (within) or external locus (outside) of the issue.

Results indicate areas of concern in priority order:

Order, negative, internal	(10)
Identity, negative, external	(6)
Network, negative, external	(5)
Network, negative, internal	(4)
Growth, negative, external	(3)
Focus, negative, external	(2)
Network, positive, external	(1)

The Network categories may be collapsed and Growth/Focus processes be set aside to examine the core organizational issues. The major issues are:

1. The pattern of interaction among staff, professionals, and administrators
2. The orderliness of internal administrative procedures

A tertiary concern that may be addressed in conjunction wih these is a concern over the *negative image within the larger community and among its customers*.

The predominant emotional climate is a combination of anxiety focused on outside forces—with passive-aggressive behaviors—and inner-directed hostility, anger at others, and depressive behavior.

Basically, it appears that there is a lack of clear, consistent, and valued communication among the various components of the organization. Decisions are viewed as being made capriciously and in an unplanned fashion. Internal friction has resulted from recent shifts of locus of control from administrators to faculty. Units are not well connected to one another nor viewed as being related in a value adding change. The negative process underway is one of continuous accidental expression of useless activity.

The existing administrative processes are not seen as ones that are sequenced to minimize variance in output, produce quality and in service of the entire organization. Activity for activity's sake without a careful examination of the underlying need for administrative procedures. The negative process underway is solipsism—the theory that one's self (own administrative procedures) is the only existing reality.

Recommendation: Organizational Intervention with Use of External Resource

1. Produce open forums for two-way, honest communication. Town meetings with presence of executives can work quite well to initiate the communication process. Programs which promote the relatedness of internal elements can also be helpful. Draw a picture of how everyone is connected in the process of developing and delivering quality educational programs.
2. Put standards in place. They need to be developed in an interactive fashion working from the outside (students) to the inside. Variance monitoring and control systems need to be structured in a positive sense for improvement—not blaming.

Results of the Intervention

Three specific behavioral actions resulted from this diagnosis. First, the interim leadership immediately began having monthly open-forum meetings and used these as a way of introducing the mission, concerns, and interests of each functional group to the others. New leadership began with a series of briefings to cross-functional levels of the organization, soliciting input for improvements in organizational functioning.

The second result was commissioning a more extensive analysis, which included job descriptions and an attitude survey of staff and professionals. Client groups, both current and former, were also interviewed to determine levels of customer satisfaction and problem areas to be addressed.

This in-depth analysis resulted in development of a strategic marketing plan intended to drive structural reorganization decisions. The intervention is still in process at this writing, but a higher degree of morale is reported—along with increased responsiveness to customers.

NOTES

1. *San Francisco Examiner*, p. E-14, Nov. 10, 1991.
2. *The Dramatic Universe*, Claymont Communications, 2d ed, 1987.
3. "Builder" would be a more accurate description of what activities are actually completed by whom. However, "builder" and "engineer" have socially-laden roles assigned to them. Therefore, we hope to have readers move beyond that artificial distinction and look to the actual tasks performed.
4. Bateson, *Mind and Nature* (1979).
5. Thanks to Mitch Kapor for pointing out this subtle political point.
6. Forty (1986).
7. Toffler (1990), *Power Shift*.
8. Professor Shumpei Kumon, Los Angeles, April 1991, "Japan and the United States: Creativity and Constructive Coemulation During the Great Transformation," paper presented at the Multimedia Roundtable in which Kumon makes the distinction of a shift in behavior from "Trade/Exploitation" and the "Wealth Game," to a behavior of "Persuasion/induce-

ment" and a "Wisdom Game," which he dates as occurring during the post WWII time period. See Boulding (1968) and Galbraith (1973).

9. Emery and Trist (1965).

10. See, for example, *Design Management Journal* 5 (2), Spring 1989, containing the proceedings from the Product Semantics 89 conference, University of Arts, Helsinki, Finland, 1989.

11. K. Krippendorf, "Imaging, Computing and Designing Minds," *Design Management Journal,* Winter 1991, pp. 29–36.

12. p. 35, op. cit.

13. See Bateson (1979), *Steps to an Ecology of Mind,* Chandler: New York.

14. This is the Second Law of Thermodynamics operating in organizational systems. They tend towards disordered activity with no purpose. We often see this in action, when people have meetings just to have meetings—with no business result. It takes considerable energy to prevent this from happening.

15. Why hasn't "interoperability" occurred: Esther Dyson has put it quite succinctly. She feels that the problem inhibiting true networking is that all the disparate systems keep improving individually, and not enough time is allowed to stabilize platforms for connectivity. *BYTE,* 16(11), pp. 117–120.

16. Perhaps this is no longer an accurate term. What about *public* computers instead? Computer platforms could be public in the sense that everyone could use them—not just the technologically sophisticated.

17. *Webster's New World Dictionary,* 1987.

18. Bob Jacobson of the University of Washington is developing the idea of information environments from an extension of the "virtual reality" technologies. See *BYTE,* June 1992 for additional information.

19. Toffler, op. cit.

20. The subtle point is that participatory design is essentially a political process which proceeds from a set of assumptions about human nature. Pelle Ehn, the best-known Scandinavian practitioner of participatory design states: "Participatory design concerns questions of democracy, power and control at the workplace. In this sense, it is a deeply controversial issue from a management point of view."

21. Vaske and Grantham (1990).

22. The interesting question is, "Is software design different from other forms of product design?" When this question was put to Tony Wasserman of UNISYS, he responded: "It's another domain. Intelligence products have the peculiar capacity to change their very natures by reprogramming the software. We have no idea what people are going to do with its capability. Designers have to deliver systems that are not just technologically open, but sociologically open. The design job is to see what people do and then learn how to enhance systems to better support what they're doing."

23. Taken from the original charter.

24. Comments from a panel discussion at the Participatory Design Conference 1990 in Seattle, Washington.

25. Deft and Lengel (1986) p. 107.

26. William Passmore (1988), *Designing Effective Organizations,* J. Wiley: New York.

27. John Kotter (1978), *Organizational Dynamics,* Addison-Wesley: New York.

28. Stafford Beer (1985), *Diagnosing the System for Organizations,* J. Wiley: New York.

29. Gareth Morgan (1986), *Images of Organizations,* Sage: Beverly Hills, CA.

30. See Vaske and Grantham, chapter 3, for a review of this literature.

31. Chapter 5 sets out the details of these information flows. For now, just use them as analogs of organizational functioning.

32. This thought runs through most of the organizational-development literature. It has been most eloquently expressed by Chris Argyris in his seminal article, "The Individual and the Organization," *Administrative Science Quarterly,* vol 2(1), June 1957, pp. 1–24.
33. The assumption that a pattern of interaction among people yields an emotional state comes from Kemper (1978). Perceived differentials in status and power among social actors generate a corresponding emotional state.
34. This was a 46 percent response rate. We interpreted this rate to be reflective of some passive-aggressive behavior.
35. We consistently use this structure to analyze organizations. Cross-references may be found in Chapters 5 and 6.

REFERENCES

Bateson, G. (1979) *Mind and Nature: A Necessary Unity.* New York, NY: Dutton.

Beer, Stafford (1985) *Diagnosing the System for Organizations,* New York: John Wiley.

Bennett, John (1987) *The Dramatic Universe.* 2nd ed. Charles Town WV: Claymont Communications.

Boulding, Kenneth (1968) *Beyond Economics: Essays on Society, Religion and Ethics,* Ann Arbor: University of Michigan Press.

BYTE. (1991). 16 (11), October.

Emery, F. and E. Trist. (1965) "The Causal Texture of Organizations" *Human Relations.* 18:21–32.

Daft, R. L. and Lengel, R. H. (1986) "Organizational information requiremnts, media richness and structural design." *Management Science.* 32(5): 554–571.

DeForest, A. (1990) "Wasserman." *International Design.* March/April, pp. 68–71.

Forty, A. (1986) *Objects of Desire,* New York, NY: Pantheon.

Galbraith, John K. (1973) *The Anatomy of Power,* Boston: Houghton-Mifflin.

Kemper, Theodore (1978), *A Social Interactional Theory of Emotions.* New York: Wiley-Interscience.

Kotter, J. P. (1978) *Organizational Dynamics: Diagnosis and Intervention,* New York: Addison-Wesley.

Krippendorf, K. (1991) "Imaging, Computing and Designing Minds." *Design Management Journal.* Winter, pp. 29–36.

Kumon, Shumpei. (1982) "Some Principles Governing the Thought and Behavior of Japanists (Contextualists)," *Journal of Japanese Studies.* 8(1):5–28.

Kumon, Shumpei. (1991) "Japan and the United States: Creativity and Constructive Coemulation During the Great Transformation." Paper presented at the Multimedia Roundtable in Los Angeles, April 1991.

Morgan, G. (1986) *Images of Organizations.* Beverly Hills: Sage Publications.

Pye, D. (1978) *The Nature of Aesthetics of Design,* New York, NY: Van Nostrand Reinhold

Schwartz, P. and J. Olgivy. (1979) *The Emergent Paradigm: Changing Patterns of Thought and Belief.* Analytic Report no. 7. Values and Lifestyles Program. Menlo Park, CA: SRI.

Toffler, A. (1990) *Power Shift,* New York: Bantam.

Vaske, J. and C. Grantham. (1990) *Socializing the Human-Computer Environment.* Norwood, NJ: Ablex.

Weisbord, M. (1978) *Organizational Diagnosis: A Workbook of Theory and Practice,* New York: John Wiley.

4

Customer Service and Quality

One of the major forces driving a technology change in modern organizations is customer demand for better, quicker, and higher-quality service. Service is an interaction between organizational structure and customers. Gaining an understanding of this external influence is a key concept in this chapter, as it moves the reader from an internal design process to a look at the demands of the environment. Also, this chapter builds on practical experience in helping clients to design and use advanced communication technologies to improve customer service.

Customer satisfaction is built on quality programs within a company. Quality programs are designed to improve the communication process between customers and the enterprise.[1] As shown by the segments of the figure, Strategic Customer Service™ and Quality are two sides to the same coin. Healthy companies and healthy people go together. The point here is that both customer satisfaction and quality rest on *standards*. Standards are the acceptable rules of business operation that specify the criteria used.

Profits are a result of the relationship between revenue and cost. Our approach is to work first on the revenue side of the equation. Although we do not ignore the importance of internal efficiencies, it is our belief that increased revenues result from increased customer satisfaction. Furthermore, customer satisfaction is a balance between expectation and the actual experience of dealing with your company. Elements of customer satisfaction come from the six senses and are a judgment process arising from the *customer's* values.

80

Quality varies externally by customer; not internally by your process. Quality is not a program and it can't be mandated or budgeted. It is determined by your customer.

Another core concept of this chapter is expanding the readers' thinking to the notion of Strategic Customer Service. That is, serving your customers' customer. It's not only whom you sell to, but what is done with your product or service. For example, in the health-care industry, service is not only providing physicians with computing technology, but also how that technology is used to improve patient care.

The current trend in American business is "downsizing" or "rightsizing" [2]—in essence, businesses are laying off employees as fast as they can, in order to improve bottom-line performance. At the same time, workloads remain the same or increase. This creates a productivity gap (see Figure 4-1). Managers are faced with the question: How do we improve performance with fewer human resources? The answer doesn't lie in continuing to do business as usual. This point is often missed. To be successful in this environment, enterprises need to discover how to fundamentally reengineer their business.

Peter Drucker has stated, "The single greatest challenge facing managers in the developed countries of the world is to raise the productivity of knowledge and service workers."[3] This chapter deals with our vision of how to accomplish this required increase in productivity. We believe, as did Drucker, that this process must be driven

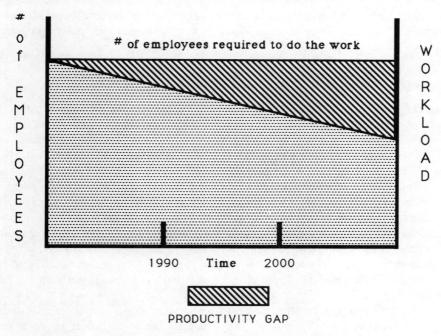

Figure 4-1. *Downsizing and Productivity*

by the establishment of external standards. These external standards are the cornerstone of the Quality Improvement movement in American business.

Drucker goes on to identify five key elements in improving productivity:

1. Define the task.
2. Concentrate on the task.
3. Define performance.
4. Establish partnerships with employees.
5. Build continuous learning into the organization.

The four stages of our Strategic Customer Service process incorporate these five vital ideas. As you will see, productivity cannot be defined in narrow terms of units of production over time. Service and information workers (managers among them) don't always operate that way. Ask yourself, "How do we define productivity of software engineers or movie producers?" Is it how fast they work? Is it how long the program or movie was? Productivity for these emerging central occupations is more difficult to define, and rests largely in the minds of the consumer of the product. You are productive when you meet your customer's expectations. Anything else is wasted effort.

We have developed this Strategic Customer Service process over years of working with clients who ask us, "What comes after quality?" This question in itself is rather cynical. Most managers assume that quality is a management fad that will fade, and a new concept will appear in the business schools. Then another horde of consultants will descend upon CEOs with the answer of the decade. In our opinion, the cynicism is well founded. Quality, Management-By-Objective (MBO), and Zero-Based Budgeting are all parts of a larger issue. A more systemic view of organizational change is required. That systemic view, as espoused in this book, includes quality programs, but goes far beyond them.

Plan of the Chapter

This chapter is laid out similarly to those preceding. An overall view of Strategic Customer Service is presented, followed by detailed discussion of each of the steps in the process. The chapter concludes with another case study in which the process was successfully applied in a business setting. Let's begin by stepping back and find where this fits into the general Enneagram model.

This chapter represents Point 3 on the Enneagram (see Figure 1-1). This is a special point because it shows where new energy is put into the business process. The first energy input was concerned with *purpose,* or the *why* of the business. This point concerns itself with energy from outside the business—input from customers. In a sense, this is the *what* question. We know why we are organized to work; now we need to determine what we do. This chapter focuses—from the perspective of the *customer*—on what we are doing. In following chapters we will deal with the *how* question.

The four stages of the Strategic Customer Service process are Strategic Customer Service, Business Process Analysis,[TM] Partnerships, and Continuous Improvement. Figure 4-2 diagrams these stages.

Each step in the process can be related to the overall Enneagram, the process cycle of action and work on various elements of organizational health. In terms of the Enneagram, energy is injected into the system at each stage of Strategic Customer Service. For example, Stage 1 (customer service definition) works on putting energy into defining purpose and vision; Stage 2 (business process analysis) puts energy into the customer-satisfaction process, and Stage 3 (partnerships) works on internal capability. Each of these stages is completed sequentially.

In the previous chapter, we outlined our six-step process for moving through any organizational intervention (see Figure 3-3). Strategic Customer Service stages correspond to various points in that overall process. Stage 1 looks at assessment and design; Stage 2, design and prototypes; Stage 3, prototypes and planning; and Stage 4, linking planning and action. Notice how each stage overlaps with the previous one so that continuity is designed into the intervention process itself.

Strategic Customer Service intervenes in the organizational process at the specific elements of organizational health that we also outlined in the last chapter (see Figure 3-4). Stage 1 joins Network and Freedom; Stage 2, Focus and Identity; Stage 3, Network and Growth; and Stage 4, Order and Growth. Therefore, our intervention strategy (Strategic Customer Service) is directly tied to our theory of organizational functioning, to our process map, and ultimately to the Enneagram as a planning and action-guiding cognitive tool.

Each stage is designed to work on a specific business need. Defining Customer Service works on focus. Getting a workteam to isolate what they should be working on is the necessary first step to process improvement. This stage corresponds to Drucker's first step of "defining the task." The next stage is business process analysis. Here, we concentrate on efficiency of operation. This stage is the heart of business

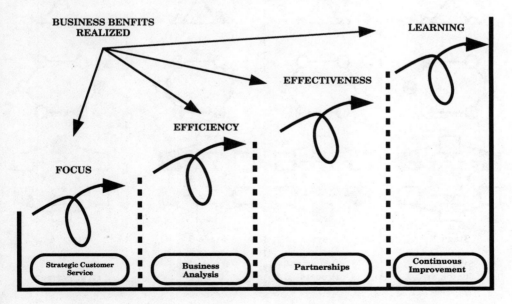

Figure 4-2. *Quality-Focused Customer Service Phases of Organizational Change*

reengineering. It is treated in summary here. Treatment of the specific techniques is expanded in the next chapter, as a bridge between what we do and how we do it.

The third stage is building partnerships with internal and external stakeholders and examines business effectiveness—"doing the right thing." This stage gets to Drucker's partnership idea, along with use of customer feedback developed in Stage 1 to define performance criteria. The final stage of the process looks at developing a learning unit through a continuous improvement segment.

Each stage of Strategic Customer Service points to a different phase of organizational change associated with development of a quality-focused customer-service organization. The diagrams of Figure 4-3 symbolize increasing capability through each transformation within the stages. The underlying dimension is that we move people from a view outward (Stages 1 and 3) to alternating views inward (Stages 2 and 4). Managers find themselves going through the process of looking at customers, then tracing the implications of what they find back toward themselves, and repeating this process repeatedly.

There is a design linkage between Strategic Customer Service (SCS), the Enneagram, and organizational health factors. In other words, within each stage of SCS, you are working on specific topics related to your location in the overall systemic change process.

Stage 1 represents an energy input from the overall business environment, or Point 9 on the Enneagram. This stage also corresponds to Steps 1 and 2 in our design

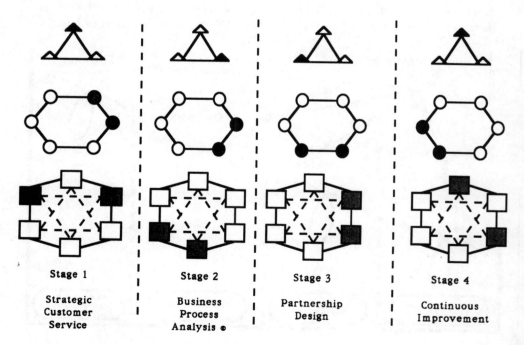

Stage 1	Stage 2	Stage 3	Stage 4
Strategic Customer Service	Business Process Analysis ©	Partnership Design	Continuous Improvement

Figure 4-3. Strategic Customer Service

process—assessment and design. Lastly, this stage deals with issues of freedom and networking in terms of organizational health.

Stage 2, Business Process Analysis, is another energy input from specific customers—or, rather, the implication of their wants, needs, and desires for how you organize to produce the required product or service. This l[ ]ks to Steps 2 (design) and 3 (prototype) of the process cycle. Stage 2 of SCS looks at issues of focus and identity of organizations.

Stage 3 represents energy coming into the system from individuals within the organization—an internal input. Building partnerships harnesses the creative forces within the group. Steps 3 (prototyping) and 4 (planning) are represented. Lastly, partnering concerns itself with issues of freedom and growth of the organization.

Stage 4 both ends and begins the cycle. Energy is now flowing back into the system as a result of the previous stages. This stage deals with Steps 4 (planning) and 5 (operations) of the process cycle. It is also linked to issues of growth and ordering of organizational processes.

The first three chapters of this book have really built a foundation for facilitating organizational change. Now we begin the process of working on the organization by use of our methodology, Strategic Customer Service. However, the process itself is a systemic intervention and is inextricably connected to all our methods of viewing process and structure within organizations.

Learning Objectives

This chapter will give readers knowledge and guided practice in:

- Understanding the relation between customer satisfaction and business performance, as well as how they can improve each other
- Building high-performance, quality-service-oriented workgroups
- Establishing a *Customer Satisfaction Measurement System* for enhancing quality in the core business process.

WHAT IS STRATEGIC CUSTOMER SERVICE?

Strategic Customer Service is putting your business into the service of your customer. The three most critical questions facing business in the 1990s are:

1. How to increase customer satisfaction
2. How to enhance quality of your product and services
3. How to take time out of business operations

This isn't an easy task, but it *is* the right challenge. The key to addressing the challenge is to deal with these three issues in an integrated fashion. The Federal Government has instituted the Baldrige Award to encourage investment in the customer satisfaction area, and popular writers such as Tom Peters continue to emphasize the importance of customer service, quality, and time.[4] This chapter targets the intersection of the three key business questions above for the 1990s. A good measure of how effective your customer-service efforts and quality programs are is in the time between customer request or complaint and an implemented organizational response. The shorter this time loop, the more effective you are.

Automation can certainly help in this process. Speeding up communication among organization elements can improve response time. However, you must also remove the redundancies and excesses. The greatest improvement in operational efficiency comes from stopping unnecessary activities.[5] You not only have to do things right, but do the right things. Therefore, we believe that *Strategic Customer Service is the only sustainable competitive advantage in service industries.* As computer products move toward commodity production, advantage can be gained by focusing on service, quality, and usability. Quality reflects the attitude a company has about its customers. Quality is expressed in tangible form in a product. However, quality is harder to define in a service industry. It is found, or not found, by customers where your organization meets them and is determined by the nature of the relationship between you, your customers, and *their* customer.

It is much more difficult to develop an effective business structure to deliver customer service than it is to organize to manufacture a product. The introduction and promotion of the Baldrige Award process is indicative of this problem. To date, no service-based industry has successfully competed for this award. This chapter continues with a discussion of the social psychology of customer satisfaction. It combines our insight and experience in the service industry to help clients gain a new competitive advantage by understanding how quality can be brought to the customer service organization.

STAGE 1: STRATEGIC CUSTOMER SERVICE

The first step in the development of a Strategic Customer Service plan is realizing that customer satisfaction is a psychological state resulting from the interaction of your business with that customer. That is, satisfaction—or lack of it—develops based on how customers view the interaction they have with your business.[6] Attitudes come from values and are shaped by many things. There are several steps within this stage of the process. The desired output is a determination of just what items, actions, and appearances keep your customers satisfied.

Step 1: Elements of Customer Satisfaction[7]

What's important to your customer? When you ask people this question, they usually spit out a listing of several things that refer to the product you sell. Well, this is part of the answer, but not the total picture of what makes customers satisfied with your business. Customer satisfaction is based on value, expectations, product attributes, and customer experience of the transaction process. Let's look at each of these in turn.

Different customers have different values, or—more appropriately—beliefs about the world around them. These beliefs affect the creation of attitudes customers bring to their experience with your business. They have beliefs about what is right or wrong and good or bad. These beliefs shape their attitudes and need to be considered. We define an attitude to be "a relatively enduring organization of beliefs around an object or situation predisposing one to respond in some preferential manner."[8] Customers bring this predisposition to their interaction with your business. You need to understand what these predispositions are to develop a business process that increases their satisfaction with you.

A key part of this predisposition is customer expectations. Experiences, rumor, and much else come into play to form an expectation. Customers expect transactions to take place in certain ways, to be treated in a specific fashion, and to receive something of value. When these expectations are met or exceeded, customers are satisfied with the transaction and product. When expectations are not met, satisfaction declines. Any good salesperson can attest to this. A key part of the sales process is to first determine what expectations are and then position the product to meet those expectations. But what about a service? Often, customers have a difficult time expressing their expectations—especially if the service is something new.

Given the customer's belief systems and expectations, you can position your service (or product) appropriately. But what attributes of the product do you emphasize and what others do you minimize? The most cogent are price and quality. But these are not the only ones. Price is relevant to expectations and is most important in markets where commodities are exchanged. For example, personal computers are rapidly becoming commodity items. Customers look at price foremost, and manufacturers compete on this basis.

Product quality is a complex issue. Defining quality goes beyond the traditional "fit and finish" viewpoint.[9] It extends into an area we call utility. Utility means just how effective the product or service is when it gets used.[10] You can certainly use a shovel to move leaves, but it is not as effective a means as, for example, using a rake. This utility measure becomes another element in determining customer expectations and satisfaction. Thus, when you are trying to determine what makes customers satisfied, you need to look beyond simple cost and quality to the utility of the product for its intended purpose.

The final component of customer satisfaction is the most elusive—service. Simply defined, service to the user means the ease of doing business. The harder it is to do business, the lower the degree of service. If you have to travel to specific locations to buy a product, that travel raises a barrier to doing business and decreases the perceived quality of service. We call this the transaction mechanics of business. What does the customer have to do to conduct business with us? That is the *key* question. Your work redesign efforts should be targeted toward making this process as easy for the customer as possible.

The old saw, "Never let customers stand in line with cash in their hands" comes to mind. Ordering, shipping, and invoicing systems are key targets for improving quality of service. Customer-service functions have become more of a core business process in recent years. Customer-service systems are error-correction systems for the other parts of the business. We suggest that if core business operations are designed with ease of transaction in mind, the need for the customer-service organization becomes minimized, unless they really are structured as sales forces.

Look at the pattern of doing business with your operation. Focus on the transaction pattern and on how a *relationship* is built with your customer. *Good business is built on good relationships*.

Step 2: Assessing (Cold, Hard Facts)

In the words of Joe Friday, "The facts, ma'am, just the facts." Assessing the degree of customer satisfaction is often a task managers don't like to engage in. Hearing that your customers are not happy is something to be avoided in most business organizations. What happens is that these organizations wait until orders fall off and blame the competition. That leads to the death spiral we have seen in the steel and auto industries in the United States. It may not be pleasant to deal with customer dissatisfaction, but it is essential to staying in business—and to prospering.

Businesses need a system in place that reliably measures customer satisfaction and produces an assessment of how your customers view your business. A system that is based on internal measures ("this is what I think the customers want") is inadequate.

SEGMENTS

	A	B	C
Price Imposition	5	3	3
Service	1	5	3
Quality	2	2	2
Utility	4	1	5

Rate on a scale of 1-5; 5=Most important

Figure 4-4. *Elements of Customer Satisfaction by Market Segment*

There are several ways to accomplish a reliable measure. Right now, we would like to look at the elements of such assessment systems and leave the mechanics of operations to a later time.

Figure 4-4 is a matrix of elements that suggests the questions to ask during the assessment. Four basic variables are shown: price, service, quality, and utility. These perceptions of your customers also vary by segment of market or product line. The key to assessment is making correct distinctions across market segments. We have no magic solution of this issue other than to say it is an iterative process that is ongoing and self-reflective. The point is that different segments have different priorities within the categories of price, service, quality, and utility. Within each category you need to ask specific questions to create an overall map of the customer-satisfaction drivers you are dealing with.

Often, this process of customer-satisfaction assessment is automated and a database created so that trends in changes can be objectively tracked. Of course, this process in itself can become onerous. We suggest that a customer-satisfaction process be built into another ongoing process—such as customer service or marketing.

Step 3: Design (Fabric for Basic Infrastructure)

Designing a system to assess and analyze customer satisfaction is a serious business operation. It is not a nice-to-have, easy-to-cut part of your business. The Baldrige Award, for example, grants a full 30 percent of its points to an assessment of the customer-satisfaction system in place in candidate organizations. The overarching point of the design, however, is not that it is in place, but how it is linked to other parts of the business. To simply conduct market research and generate a group of reports is not enough.

The system design must link output of assessment to input of product development and strategic planning. This necessarily implies that there must be some overall organizations plan to use the information coming into the organization, with the goal of improving system performance. The first part of this plan is system *integrity*. If managers don't believe the validity of the data produced, they won't use it in a serious fashion.

Data architectures must be consistent with what exists elsewhere in the organization. For example, you would want to be able to correlate changes in level of customer satisfaction with employee attitudes and revenue figures. This type of information-architecture integration allows for simulation and "what if?" kinds of analysis throughout the company.

Finally, we believe that these customer-satisfaction assessment systems can ultimately provide managers with Computer-Assisted Decision Making™ (CADM) platforms. Elsewhere, we discuss our theories of information flows in organizations as indices of health.[11] Customer satisfaction data should form a core of this database.

Step 4: Where You Are (How to Start)

The way to get started in this process is to first perform a self-examination. Using such guides as Figure 4-4, you can have the management team rate your own business.

We have found it particularly useful to break groups into different functions, such as operations and marketing, and compare the results of the self-rating process. This comparison usually leads to realization of the complexity of customer satisfaction, when you see that even groups within the same business have differing perceptions of the state of the business.

Also, you need to have a clear statement of company mission and purpose. If the purpose of the company is to serve only selected segments of the market, then customer satisfaction in other segments may not be totally relevant. However, with this context, you need to ascertain where the entire Strategic Customer Satisfaction process fits within your strategic-planning process. So, you must first define the business context, then the company's direction, before an assessment of specific segments against elements of customer satisfaction makes any sense.

One of the most revealing points in assessing where you are is the idea of competitive benchmarking. That is, during your process of self-rating, also rate your competitors along the same criteria. More often than not, you can spot some glimmer of your competitor's strategy in that process. Once this is done, you can verify your perceptions against your customers' by using field surveys, focus groups, and interviews.[12]

Step 5: Your Business Issues (What to Work On)

This assessment process yields a great deal of information. At this point, managers often become confused and paralyzed. We suggest that summaries of the information be reviewed by key stakeholders so that the following issues can be examined:

- Clarity of purpose
  What business do our customers think we are in?
  How does this compare with our own view?

- Your key issues
  What areas do we need to work on, in our customer's opinion?
  Where are we at a relative competitive disadvantage?
  Where do we have an advantage?
  What trends seem to be emerging?

This kind of analysis can be quite sobering to most managers. Almost by definition, this assessment process leads to realization of a need to change. For example, this kind of process has led both IBM and General Motors toward radical restructuring. They both came to realize that they were not providing what customers expected, wanted, or needed. Not only was that in terms of price, but also in terms of utility and service. So, if you know where your customers are and what your business is capable of, what do you do next? Simply, you have to plan for change. That is the topic of this book, but it should be made much more concrete before any action takes place.[13]

We suggest that you ask some key questions at this point of the process that point you in the right direction. Look at the following:

- Resistance and roadblocks
  What entrenched political interests can impede change?
  How can these either be co-opted or neutralized?
  How can this resistant energy be channeled in a more productive direction?

- Principles of action
  What principles will guide us in developing priorities for action?
  What beliefs and values lie behind these principles?

- Tactical Focus Points
  What is our plan for moving forward?
  Who has responsibility?
  What are the standards of accountability?

All of this is a lot of work, and it's only the first stage of a process. Is it worth it? Well, the answer to that lies in the question, "How serious are you about improving business performance?" Perhaps there are other issues that seem more pressing or more important. This business reengineering based on customer satisfaction is not easy, cheap, or fun. It simply is a requirement of continuing to be in business in an ever-increasingly competitive global environment. At this point, you have the basic information you need to move forward. The external environment has told you a lot and helped you focus on key issues to be addressed. Now we turn inward and see what business operations need to be changed to be more effective.

STAGE 2: BUSINESS PROCESS ANALYSIS

Chapter 5 is about Business Process Analysis (BPA) in a general sense. In this chapter, we would like to discuss the business-engineering process of BPA in the limited arena of determinating customer satisfaction. That is, how do you engineer a process of assessing customer satisfaction? BPA (as a methodology) produces five steps.[14] They are:

1. Prototype (What would the assessment system look like?) *(input)*
2. Roadmap (Where are we going with this?) *(transform)*
3. Blueprinting (the management model) *(transform)*
4. Value-adding stream (Where does this fit into the business?) *(output)*
5. Start in the middle (What's out there?) *(link to next cycle)*

Step 1: Prototype

The basic task in this step is to build a picture of what the system would look like as a separate business process. This picture needs to be built on the input required, or available, from customers. As we outlined above, the expectation of the customer is a key element of satisfaction. There are three basic techniques for determining attitudes and expectations: in-depth interviews, focus groups, and surveys. Whichever method you choose to use needs to be designed by an expert in the field. The field of market research is highly developed. Because each market or business is different, consultation with people knowledgeable in the field will pay off in the long run. During this step of system design you need to determine (at a minimum):

- Survey design (questions, format, degree of qualification)
- Customer sampling frame (how many people and by what segments)
- Personnel training (your personnel or subcontracted support for data collection)
- Computerized support (database structure compatible with yours)

All of this goes to construct a Business Intelligence System. A Business Intelligence System is a computerized database of customer attitude data. This data can be linked and correlated with customer behavior patterns (i.e., purchases, refunds, complaints, and suggestions) and is integrated with other cogent business-performance data, such as profit and loss records. The reason for computerization of this function is to increase your business's ability to rapidly isolate and spot changes in customer attitudes. Attitude changes usually precede changes in behavior that directly impact performance. The quicker you can spot these, the more time you have to respond.

The final part of the input process of the assessment system is the synthesis of this information with external environment-trends information—for example, gross economic indicators and competitor performance measures. All of this allows managers to ask questions of the data that they might have not thought of before the system was put together. The input side of your customer-satisfaction assessment system contains data on customer attitudes, behaviors, general economic trends, and competitor performance.

Step 2: Roadmap

Step 2 begins the transformation process of the data. This step answers the question about where this business intelligence fits into the overall business operation. At the highest level, information gathered needs to flow into and inform several strategic processes of the business. Product planning, production, and operations are the three areas that can most effectively be impacted by customer-satisfaction information. The design implication is that this data needs to be consistent and reliable across these functions. The requirement for uniformity of customer data implies a centralized information database.[15]

At the tactical level, this kind of information can quickly identify specific customers who need special attention or production processes that are out of control. Tactical information needs to be limited and focused. There is a tendency to overwhelm people with data—but give them little business intelligence. For example, people working one market or product line do not necessarily need customer satisfaction information for all product lines. Some sort of filtering mechanism needs to be installed between the centralized data base and front line operations. The best way to devise these filters is to place frontline managers and systems designers together.

A business-intelligence roadmap provides the manager with an idea of what lies ahead by forecasting and by trend analysis. It should also give them signposts along the way. Key indicators of change are good signposts such as leading indicators of change. Leading indicators can only be developed with an historical analysis of past events. What cannot be placed on the roadmap are events that are radical departures from past events. Entry of a new competitor in a market or significant sociopolitical events are common examples. However, a roadmap of customer satisfaction with an overlay of the desired direction can be a useful guide.

Step 3: Blueprint (The Management Model)

Now that we have a data-collection process in place and a roadmap of what we are looking for in the data, what step is next? The final part to a transformation is action. If management does not have a plan for action, the data and roadmap sit on a shelf and are dusted off each year at the beginning of the so-called planning cycle.[16] While we cannot give you an explicit set of instructions to implement business changes based on customer input, we can offer some advice on using general approaches to the situation.

A blueprint is a specific set of instructions for assembly. The blueprint for a business process built on customer information is more like an architectural drawing with some areas shaded in. The design model with six stages explored in the previous chapter is the best model we have found for constructing a business-process blueprint. We would like to add that this process can occur in parallel in several parts of the organization. Critical to the process is identifying the information flow cross-connections between functions.

Instead of a static functional blueprint, you really need a wiring diagram or a map of the information pipes in the organization. We have found that people who manage paper-pulp plants and oil refineries are very good at constructing these blueprints. The reason is that they manage a *systemic* process and subconsciously understand the subtleties of conflicting influences and interdependencies. You need a visual metaphor of the organization that is sensitive to—and can display—these interdependencies.

In addition, your business-operation blueprint needs to contain some instructions for assembly. Our suggestion is that you always start on the outside and work your way into the business. Don't design the survey questionnaire first. Figure out what is happening in your business environment, *then* proceed to implementation. There is a frightening tendency in American business to jump right into action without thinking. Many executives have found that the stream wasn't as deep as they hoped and that there are rocks right under the surface.

Step 4: The Value-adding Stream (Are you in the river or part of it?)

By now, most business leaders are familiar with the idea of a value-adding stream. The value-adding stream is a picture of the different steps in your process that may be influenced with customer information. Where do you feed this new data into your system for maximum impact? A good analogy to a dynamic business process is a river.

There are constrictions that impede flow, there are tributaries that drain off energy, and there may be dams that totally stop any flow.

If you look at your business in this way, your customers can probably tell you where things are not flowing smoothly. For example, if it takes longer to order material than customers want, you probably would want to take a closer look at invoicing and shipping procedures.

In a process, we like to use symbols of boulders in the stream to be avoided, whirlpools that can cause action to circle around and go nowhere, or eddies that are quiet pools off to the side of the main flows. All of these may have positive uses. A beaver knows quite well how to use a boulder as an anchor to a dam. In a similar fashion, a crafty manager may find that a person (or department) that impedes information flow can be leveraged into an anchor for slowing a process down until it is complete. Financial analysts are very good at impeding the planning process in this way—so that all options are examined before commitment to action is made.

The quiet eddies may be product-development efforts or skunkworks. Whirlpools are to be avoided if throughput is a concern, but can be very helpful if you are attempting to time a market entry or holding action while events unfold. Using the metaphor of a value-adding stream in this sense provides a new mental image of how a business operates. If the stream exists in service of the fish, what implications are there for building the stream to promote continued health of the fish? Do you make it wide? Narrow? Make it deep or shallow? Provide sheltered places?

Step 5: Starting in the Middle

The last part of integrating the Strategic Customer Service approach to performance improvement is to link this BPA effort to other similar business reengineering processes. The quality movement is the most widely known of these other efforts. All of the quality-improvement programs key off of customer input to manufacturing practice. Many of these approaches may be in place in your business and any other approach must add value to what's already there. Let's begin with a brief review of some principal approaches to quality.

W. Edwards Deming, Joseph Juran, and Phil Crosby are the three most prominent names, the quality gurus.[17] The central message of all these management consultants is commitment to the process. In some sense, they are saying it doesn't matter which approach you choose, but stick with it and don't deviate. This is good advice to any organization-change effort. It is very tempting to change direction every year or so when things start to get sticky. But follow-through is what works.

In our opinion, the similarities in approach among the gurus are more striking than the differences. All take a systemic approach to removing variances in production, stress the importance of customer input, and use a suite of quantitative process tools to reveal sources of error in the process. We don't see much difference between these tenets of quality and what we propose in this book. There is, however, one difference that is significant.

We stress the use of these techniques on the design and analysis of information flows. The current quality programs work very effectively (if applied consistently and over time) in a manufacturing environment. Our message is intended more for the service sector of business, where information is the product that moves between producer and consumer. The quality of information is a judgment call made by the user of the information. Further, we believe information's effectiveness is only in use. It must be used to have value. Therefore, in a service environment, looking at your customer's customer is the *only effective* way of gaining competitive advantage.

We believe our approach complements the current spate of quality programs when it is applied to the information-flow–intensive parts of a business operation. Again, customer satisfaction comes *after* information has been used. One quality dictum is, "Do it right the first time!" We believe that Strategic Customer Service and BPA can help you design it right, before you do it the first time. This is an important distinction. BPA is a Stage in a process that promotes planning for zero defect BEFORE you act.

We are often asked, "What comes after Quality?" We believe that the next wave of innovation in management practice will be anticipatory planning and structural design. Simulation of business process in an information environment is the next wave if you will. We offer one model of that process here. Undoubtedly, others will follow. The basic approach is to anticipate, not react.

STAGE 3: PARTNERSHIPS

The next stage in the Strategic Customer Satisfaction process is the building of partnerships. So far, we have developed a process to assess customers' satisfaction and analyzed internal business processes in light of that information. Now it is time to turn outward again and begin the formation of ongoing relationships with our customers. We call that relationship state a partnership.[18] These relationships are built upon strong communications linkages. We have expounded on communication in a previous chapter. This chapter is devoted to the "how" of building a partnership aimed at improving the quality of the relationship in a business context.

The primary question is, "Who do we need to be partners with?" The answer to this question should come from the previous two stages of the process: your customers, and the people immediately upstream and downstream from you in the value-adding stream of your business. Those are the two key groups.

Skill Sets Required for Forming Partnerships

Several social skills are needed to form an effective partnership. One of the first is to add some structure to the interactions. This insures that both parties are always clear on the nature of the conversation, how the interaction will take place, and what is expected. Each interaction should begin with both parties explicitly agreeing on the answer to four basic questions:

1. Why are we here?
2. What do we expect to accomplish?
3. How are we going to do that?
4. What do we need to be successful?

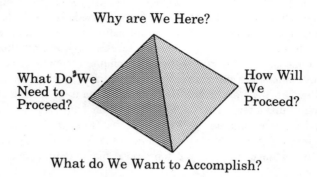

Why are We Here?

What Do We Need to Proceed?

How Will We Proceed?

What do We Want to Accomplish?

Figure 4-5. *Structured Meetings*

Figure 4-5 is a diagram of a meeting pyramid. The pyramid represents a three-dimensional system that has as its pinnacle the purpose of the meeting, supported by the other questions. It represents the four key questions above for meeting with partners. The "Why" question is crucial to make sure everyone has the same purpose in mind before beginning a discussion. The "What do we want to accomplish?" question helps set expectations of outcomes for the interaction. The "How" is really about setting an agenda for the process. What you need to proceed sounds rather simplistic, but really isn't. You will need to have the necessary data handy, a place to have a meeting, and—more importantly—a state of mind to govern the process.

If these questions are not answered to both parties' satisfaction, then the interaction should be terminated until agreement can be reached. Think about how many times you have had a meeting with a group and walked away wondering why you needed to meet with these people. Getting clear on *what* and *how* can move the partnering process forward very quickly.

The second skill-set is using assigned roles for each interaction. Trading off roles allows each party to experience the other's position in a neutral setting. The interaction itself takes place around an issue in which both parties have a vested interest. However, the *process* of interacting is a metastructure. It is in this metastructure that people can directly experience another's position. For example, if each person takes a turn at organizing the meeting, they both can share the experience of organizing as separate from the discussion itself. This sharing gives everyone a common experience base and tends to build trust over time.

There are three basic roles that must be fulfilled to balance all factors in an interaction: leader, facilitator, and recorder. Group Decision Support Systems have come into use lately to support the role of recorder through technology. Again, this is an example of technology beginning to be used by people practicing the art of organizational development. We do not recommend that one person try to perform two roles. Our experience is that this is ineffective for groups of more than five people. In Chapter 2, we discussed the need for balance in task and socioemotional factors in social interactions (see Figure 2-4). The leader takes responsibility for the task dimension and the facilitator has responsibility for the socioemotional factors in the meeting.[19] The recorder role is the one most often overlooked. The job of this person is to create explicit records of the meeting that can be fed back to partners for clarification and a quality-assurance mechanism. It prevents the "Well, I thought you said . . ." syndrome.

Before we proceed to the mechanics of establishing a business partnership, you may want to ask yourself three questions to focus your awareness.

- What are the characteristics of a healthy partnership?
- What causes a partnership to become unhealthy or dysfunctional?
- What is unique about a business partnership?

As with other stages of the SCS process, there are several distinct, ordered steps to forming partnerships. Each of four steps is worked through by both parties. In other words, the process of moving through these steps is the foundation to forming the partnership relation. It is the first issue you partner around.

Step 1: External Influences

This is a joint examination of what external forces are impinging upon both parties to make forming a partnership an important and beneficial issue. We suggest that a series of questions be posed so that everyone can reach agreement on the answers:

- What is the boundary between us and the external business environment?
- Who are your most significant suppliers?
- What is required from you to be a successful partner with your supplier?
- Who are the ultimate end-users of our joint business activity?
- What are the regulatory forces we have to concern ourselves with?
- What are the competitive forces in the environment?

Answering these questions usually creates awareness of the critical nature of partnering. For example, we have found in some industries that forming partnerships with regulators is often the key element in improving business performance. Moving from an adversarial stance to a partnering posture is a fundamental shift in business approach. These questions are designed to bring that kind of awareness to the interaction.

Step 2: Internal Influences

Again, the focus shifts to the internal state of your business. What is going on internally that impedes forming true partnerships? Are there differences in values or attitudes that get in the way? Where do these differences come from? What can be done to overcome these? These are the kinds of questions that should guide your discussions. It is usually very revealing to potential partners that they are using the same type of restraining actions that prevent a different relationship from emerging.

For example, a manufacturer says to a parts supplier, "Our accounting people say you don't invoice us on time." The supplier says, "Our shipping people say you don't return packing slips immediately after receipt of goods." So, the internal restraint to partnering is the existence of an us vs. them attitude. Now, however, there is a specific issue to resolve. It is not so much forcing a partnership to emerge as it is simply removing the barriers.

Two of the most successful techniques for forming internal partnerships are cross-functional teams and teams of teams. Cross-functional teams are *not* task forces, which are by definition task-oriented. This orientation ignores a fundamental aspect of human interaction, as we discussed in Chapter 2. Also, task forces usually break down. Teams are *not* just groups of people; teams are people working to be collaborative. That means you spend as much time working on relationships as you do trying to "get the job done." One of the great success stories of the Japanese is that they spend a great deal of time on building relationships and teams. Once cross-functional teams are formed, the time required to get something done decreases dramatically. The partnership process is front-end loaded.

Teams of teams are the next level of aggregation. Your team and our team get together to work on a mutual issue. This situation is politically difficult. In business, as in government, power is assigned to identifiable groups of people. When you start to break down these boundaries, you begin to dissolve old power structures. Leaders, and loyal lieutenants, have a natural tendency to try to preserve the status quo. Teams of teams come together to collaborate for sustainability. Perhaps the most technically correct concept here is a *confederation*. The emergence of the European Common Market and the Confederation of Independent States are two excellent contemporary examples of teams of teams.

The reason this is an as yet relatively rare event in business is that the psychological model is one of collaboration, not competition. That is the bottom line to partnering: moving from a competitive to a collaborative model. Witness Apple Computer and Novell.

Step 3: Permeable Boundaries

When you form partnerships with people, it is sometimes difficult for an outside observer to distinguish between the partners. The boundaries become permeable. That means the information glides through the boundary.[20] This opening of boundaries brings up the issue of internal system integrity. For example, how do we maintain our integrity if customers have access to their account records?

The question to be addressed in the partnership discussion is, How far inside you and how far inside them are we or can we be? If only two parties are involved, there may be no need for a distinction between partners. However, life is more complex than that. As in social life, in business you become known largely from the company that you keep. Your identity as a business entity is defined by the web of relationships that you have with suppliers and customers. Thus, with any individual partner your respective boundaries could be so permeable as to appear nonexistent. However, when viewed at a higher level, a system of boundaries with varying degrees of permeability emerges.

There is a very good biological metaphor for organizational permeable boundaries: the blood/brain barrier. This is the boundary between the cardiovascular and neurological systems in mammals.[21] Chemicals and fluids pass through this boundary in a controlled fashion. Certain molecules are too big to pass through and are blocked.

The same is true in reverse. Chemicals can be released that open or close down the degree of permeability. The boundary exists, therefore, in a relative degree for different objects. The analogy holds for organizational boundaries. Boundaries may be sensitive to the size of transactions or, perhaps, limited in their frequency. The point is that the degree of permeability is a topic for negotiation between partners.

Step 4: Five Phase Process—Your Customer's Customer

Once you have jointly examined external, internal, and boundary issues and gained some proficiency in purposeful interactions, a new question comes forward. What should the structure of partnership negotiations look like? We suggest a five-part process. But, by way of prologue, certain capabilities are needed *before* those discussions start. In our experience, the following state of mind is required to accomplish successful partnering:

• There is concentration on something larger than both parties. Mutual sustainability is a good place to begin. The whole purpose of a business partnership is to help insure continuity of interaction—the partnership is in service of something larger than any one part.
• The arena of action is clearly identified. What field are we playing on and what are the rules of the game? These issues need to be clarified and made explicit.

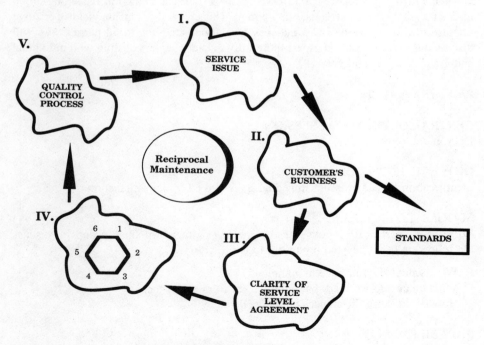

Figure 4-6. Partnership Design Process

- Reciprocal maintenance is required. There will be give-and-take in all good partnerships, although at no point will a strict quid pro quo exist. Over time, however, the rule of exchange is governed by need.[22]
- All three parts of partnerships need to be valued: you, your customer, and your customer's customer.

Figure 4-6 shows the relationship of the five parts of the partnering process as we use them. The partnership design process is highly structured at first, but begins to loosen up as people become more experienced. It is, above all, iterative and dynamic. One discussion covering key issues in each of the parts is not sufficient to establishing and maintaining a partnership.

Each of these steps is designed as a separate event. We usually devote a two-day management-development session to each of these steps. That may seem like an inordinate amount of time to spend on addressing just a single issue within a larger process. We have found that the time spent together working on service-quality issues and building partnerships with customers takes more than just moving through a task-oriented agenda. We design each session using some of the thinking frameworks you are experiencing in this book. Each session is then tailored around the issue identified, but in a way that builds capability along the basic dimensions of organizational functioning.[23]

Each of these steps builds upon the previous one. For this reason, the capabilities required increase as you move through the process. The central questions posed at each step are actually questions that must be answered by the group in order for it to become a high-performance team.[24] We consistently use a method of managing group interaction that creates differences in opinion. This creation of tension yields a creative impulse to rise above the issue and seek a solution satisfying to all parties. We will discuss this creative-tension aspect more fully in later chapters dealing with individual and group-learning abilities.

Phase 1: Key Issues

CENTRAL QUESTION OF SESSION:
Do you want to be here?

OUTCOME EXPECTED:
Identification of salient issues impeding increased customer satisfaction.

SUGGESTED PROCESS:
Mixed (i.e., parties from both sides of growing partnership) small groups to discuss the following questions and report out to entire group:

- What values do you have in common?
- What values do we hold that are different from each other?
- How could those differences be reconciled?

CAPABILITY REQUIRED:
Open, honest communication; social interaction skill sets.

Phase 2: What Does Your Customer Expect?

CENTRAL QUESTION OF SESSION:
What level of trust is there between us and our customers?

OUTCOME EXPECTED:
Who has responsibility to clarify commitments?

SUGGESTED PROCESS:
Mixed (i.e., parties from both sides of growing partnership) small groups to discuss relevant questions and report out to entire group.

CAPABILITY REQUIRED:
Reliable data on current customer satisfaction

Phase 3: Standards for Measuring Success of Final Ideal Outcome

CENTRAL QUESTION OF SESSION:
What are we going to do?

OUTCOME EXPECTED:
• Clarity of service-level agreement
• What are we going to do and how are *we* going to do it?
• Explicit targets and objectives—the warranty

SUGGESTED PROCESS:
Mixed (i.e., parties from both sides of growing partnership) small groups to discuss relevant questions and report out to entire group.

CAPABILITY REQUIRED:
Ability to simulate service-provision process so that contingencies can be examined.

Phase 4: The Process Within the Process

CENTRAL QUESTION OF SESSION:
How are we going to do it?

OUTCOME EXPECTED:
Mastery of a design process.[25]

SUGGESTED PROCESS:
Mixed (i.e., parties from both sides of the growing partnership) small groups to discuss relevant questions and report out to entire group.

CAPABILITY REQUIRED:
Maximum purposeful interaction. Emergence of leaders, facilitators, and recorder roles in a stable fashion.

Phase 5: Quality Control

CENTRAL QUESTION OF SESSION:
How will you know when you are there?

OUTCOME EXPECTED:
Plan for comparing expected to actual results. Process designed to incorporate these known variances into the next iteration of Strategic Customer Service planning.

SUGGESTED PROCESS:
Large-group discussion led and facilitated by members of the group with external coaching.

CAPABILITY REQUIRED:
Ability to design group process.
　　As we said, this is an overall design. Details are worked out dependent upon the unique situation, time allowed, and beginning level of capability of group members. This plan is a roadmap, not the final step-by-step process.

STAGE 4: CONTINUOUS IMPROVEMENT (ALWAYS GETTING BETTER)

The last stage of the Strategic Customer Service program is the creation of a continuous improvement process within your business. But first, let's review what this is all about. By *strategic,* we mean positioning you ahead of your customers in their market and also positioning your customers ahead of their competitors. We maintain that you must be in the service of your customer. All management consultants strive to leave their clients with more capability than they found them with—at least, the consultants who are successful over a long period of time. The same is true of Strategic Customer Service as a process. Therefore, the final stage is to build the customer's ability to keep improving after you are gone. But this is more than lip service. Expending resources in the name of building capability must be more than simple activity—it must be action-oriented.

Action versus Activity

Action and activity are different. We have all heard about activity traps—"we don't have time to do that." But personal responsibility for action is the job we all have in an organization. It is important to know the difference between action and mere activity in order to be decisive in allocating our time. Knowledge of this difference, and the process for causing each, sets doers apart from wishers.

Here, we offer Nichols' First Law of Action: To increase the speed and breadth of action, reduce the set of instructions and elevate the language and objectives. For example:

- The Lord's Prayer has 56 words.
- Lincoln's Gettysburg Address has 268 words.
- The Declaration of Independence has 1,322 words.
- U.S. Federal Regulations governing the sale of cabbage has 26,911 words.[26]

When organizations reach awareness that they are in trouble, they often turn to "a manager who can get things done," someone who will "kick ass and take names"—in short, someone who will move forward with a lot of activity. However, even before this awareness, management's usual routine is to find those who are not doing things correctly and make some rules governing how they do their job. But the proper response is in the other direction—not activity, but action. Promote the use of fewer rules and operate from a basis of principle. Take the progression in the list above, and note that the Lord's Prayer expresses principles for action, while the cabbage regulations are activity-control devices.

Step 1: Strategic Positioning (How Do We Fit In over Time?)

So far, we have been dealing with the immediate business environment—in a sense, the knowable present. However, to move forward and build continuously, you must act against a larger, longer-range view fraught with increasing uncertainty. Strategic positioning may mean abandoning a market or making a significant shift in business direction, such as redefining your core business. A number of factors need to be examined in order to do so.

Many techniques may be employed to do this—ranging from consulting with experts to creating a strategic-planning department. In truth, the best method employs the largest number of alternatives so that your process has enough variety to encompass all possible turns of events.[27] As a minimum, we suggest that you examine the following four areas to determine the most appropriate positioning strategy:

- Geopolitical trends
- Related or connected industries
- How to create mutual advantage with customers
- What's the world going to be like in 100 years?

We recommend that you do this both internally and externally to create some difference in opinion. We have found that most managers are very good at this, even when they believe that they can't think in a strategic manner. Admittedly, this process is more intuitive than what has preceded and is found as a welcome break to the tedium of analyzing a wealth of hard data.

Step 2. Marketing Trends (In What Direction Are Things Going?)

Where do we want to be? is naturally followed by looking at what forces are current. A ship captain can plot his desired final destination on a chart, but before plotting the exact course he will examine the currents, winds, and weather patterns as they exist. The major marketing trends we see impacting businesses are conglomeration, pricing, positioning, packaging or distribution, and shifts toward more qualitative judgments of customers.

Conglomeration

The 1980s and early 1990s have witnessed a great deal of this phenomenon. Mergers and acquisitions have been the rule of the day. These impacts are still being felt as they result in a drive toward increased scales of economy. Partnerships are not forged—companies just swallow each other up. We believe that is contraindicative of the underlying strategic trend, which is toward the creation of smaller semi-autonomous business units connected together electronically. This is seen in the emergence of the digital workplace, where boundaries between enterprises are spanned by communications technologies. Things get bigger until the weight of internal coordination topples them over because they are slow to respond to increasingly rapid changes in the environment. IBM was the first to move with the underlying current when it shocked its investors and employees by announcing in late 1991 that it would break itself apart in order to survive.

This trend affects your business in that you will need to follow suit to keep up with changing customer expectations. Disaggregation moves business closer to customers and speeds up response time between business partners.

Pricing

Product pricing, as well as service pricing, is moving rapidly toward commodity pricing. Increased global communication creates a situation where consumers can shop internationally for the best buy and become more sensitive to small differences in pricing. This is especially true in the information-intensive industries, where costs of production and delivery are not distance-sensitive.

A subsidiary trend is toward increased visibility of true cost, as opposed to advertised price. Maintenance, replacement, and training for use are all hidden in the price but visible as a cost. Customers, we believe, will continue to become more sensitive to cost, not price. Competitive advantage can be had by aiming at adding value by decreasing cost to customer.

Positioning

The heart of this issue is what we referred to earlier as utility. Traditionally, marketing managers looked at positioning vis-à-vis their competition. We suggest that this is an ineffective business strategy for the 1990s and beyond. The interdependence of most industries has reached a point where this strategy ultimately leads to decreased market share for all parties involved.

Your position in the market has to be defined by how effective your product or service is when it is placed in the customer's hands. That is, how effectively it meets the needs of your customers to meet the needs of their customer. The core business process of your enterprise needs to be helping your customers be successful in their endeavor. Making positioning a partnership exercise is the effective strategy.

Packaging and Distribution

More than fancy soap packages or cleverly designed reusable containers, this trend gets to a major restructuring of distribution channels in America and the world. People used to go to the product; now, products must be brought to them. How many people go to the local drugstore to buy a daily paper? Very few—and increasingly the news comes to the user through the ubiquitous television network. Even hard goods—such as automobiles and groceries—are delivered to the consumer.

Obviously, information services can be distributed electronically as the telecommunication web spreads around the globe. What are the implications of this trend for providing service to your customers? The most obvious is the significant increase in no-cost customer-service operations that act as trainers, troubleshooters, salespeople, and relationship builders.

Quantitative versus Qualitative Evaluations

In the short run, this is probably the most difficult to get at. During the recession of late 1991, President Bush lamented that he couldn't understand why everyone's attitude was so pessimistic when all the quantitative indicators were above levels experienced ten years earlier in a similar economic environment.[28]

Attitudes—and, especially, opinions—come from values and expectations that are not amenable to factual analysis. Reality is as it is perceived. This is why it is extremely important to stay in close, continuing contact with customers. Their evaluation of quality, service, and effectiveness cannot necessarily be measured with the same yardstick time after time.

We believe that the move from quantitative reasoning bases to more-qualitative ones is a reflection of an underlying trend in America and the world economy. More is not necessarily better, and the accumulation of quantity is not germane in the emerging environment. Values are changing. The events in Europe are a harbinger of similar restructuring in several areas, including the world economy as it has existed since the 1930s.

Step 3: Values in the American Workplace

- American values
- Participatory design
- The source of creativity
- Employee capability building
- Teamwork and individuality

Step 4: Our Role Shift (We Move Outward)

Students leave the university; children grow up and forge out on their own. A similar process must occur with the use of management-development consultants.[29] There are several structural elements that can be put in place to wean your organization from dependence upon external sources of stimulation, allowing you to respond to customer opinions. These resources are internal consultants, champions, and customer advisory councils.

Internal Consultant Development

Train the trainers. Early in the Strategic Customer Service process we like to identify personnel who can be effective as internal change-agents. These internal consultants then receive additional process-consultation training so that they can become the agents of change to continue the process.

Champion

These are natural leaders who can carry the banner forward. Usually, these champions are the executives who initially brought the process to the business. Again, some special attention is required for them to quickly become masters of continuous learning. This begins with a very intense examination of personal strengths, weaknesses, desires, and frailties. We have never witnessed a successful change-agent who did not, in the process, experience fundamental changes in views, values, and attitudes.

Customer-Advisory Council

Another effective means to establish a continuing link between you and your customers is to set up an organizational structure. A customer-advisory council is one structure we have found helpful. The computer business is familiar with this idea in the form of user groups. These groups are composed of people who have purchased products from the manufacturer and, under their own auspices, come together on a regular basis to exchange information. These forums then serve the additional purpose of being a single location where businesses can solicit input from customers on product development, new needs in the market, and—in general—the experiences customers have in dealing with the company.

Step 5: Organizational Redesign (Sociotechnical System Redesign)

The ultimate step in this process is the redesign of the business enterprise to become more reflective of true marketplace demands. The entire purpose of this book is to provide the reader with a detailed roadmap of how to conduct a sociotechnical organizational redesign. The next two chapters are concerned with the tactical actions that managers can take to begin this redesign process. Chapter 5 looks at our Business Process analysis as a reengineering methodology of organizational *processes*. Chapter 6 then moves on to look at *structural* changes built on new technology platforms.

This chapter should have given you the insight that this redesign process must encompass three key factors:

- It must be end-to-end and carry through the entire value-adding stream.
- It must be customer-driven.

• It must include changes in value systems to produce a continuous improvement culture.

Successful large-scale interventions also need to include a revitalized board of directors. This corporate body is ultimately charged with maintaining the integrity of the business enterprise. It is the executive control function and cannot be excluded from the redesign process. Most failed large-scale change attempts can be traced either to a lack of support from the board level, leading to passive compliance with changes in vision, or outright board intervention to halt a process.

INTEGRATING THE SCIENCE OF TECHNOLOGY WITH THE ART OF MANAGEMENT

Background

Introducing technologies into large, complex organizations creates a change in the communicating process among people; a change in the routinized work-support systems; and, finally, a change in the persistent patterns of worker interaction, especially in information-intensive industries. The driving technology of such change is software—software that controls and shapes communication among workers; software that paints a picture of organizational functioning; and, lastly, software that molds how information is presented to worker and customer alike.

Our work with business managers consistently points to a lack of constructive ways of thinking about technology introduction and guidelines for managing that process as the major limiting factor in the effective use of computers and telecommunications. We have found that there is a correlation between the introduction of specific technology platforms and major organizational change issues.

Work organizations can be seen as being composed of different levels of aggregation. Figure 4-7 shows our view of these levels of organization. Work activity truly starts at the level of the individual worker. Individuals come together to form teams, which call for coordinated action and a pattern of workflow. Note that all groups of workers are not necessarily *teams*. The failure to recognize this basic distinction is often the first task we face in helping managers develop more effective organizations.

"Teams of teams" can be seen as the next level of complexity in this framework. These workgroups are cross-functional and begin to move work conduct across different task groups, such as marketing, engineering, or operations. Groups then combine into enterprise-level entities that we call businesses. Finally, we see increasing awareness that businesses are linked in whole economies functioning interdependently. However, a realization of cross-industry impact is often difficult to see except at the CEO and board level.

Technologies enter the workplace at all these levels. However, we believe a progression of technology diffusion can be seen evolving from the interface between individual and team to linkages across business units and the economy in general. Figure 4-7 also displays these core communication technologies on the right side (inside the arches). Technology bridging these boundaries entered the American workplace in the last few years and now is being diffused at the rate of several thousand LANs a month, with the implication that individual workers are being electronically connected into workteams at a maddening rate through the use of local-area networks (LANs).

At the next level of organization, wide-area networks (WANs) begin to bridge the space- and time-gaps between teams. Linking buildings and floors within buildings is the current manifestation of WANs. However, technically there is no reason why a specific business could not have functional units scattered over a large geographical area by means of dedicated electronic connections. Groups are linked together as business units through the technology of Electronic Data Interchange (EDI), a protocol for information-exchange among different technology platforms, such as various computer systems (i.e., Apple and IBM, or Digital Equipment and Univac). EDI is deployed over even greater time elements and geographic distances—sometimes spanning several time zones and states or provinces.

Finally, businesses merge into economies and Trans Border Data Flow (TBDF) technologies link them. At this level of work organization, technology transcends geopolitical boundaries and we see globalization of work activity. For example, in our practice, we see software specifications being developed in the United States; transmitted electronically to Asia, where the software is written; and the software product is then transmitted electronically to the customer in Europe or North America.

It is our experience that identifiable and specific organization-development issues emerge with the introduction of technologies into the workplace. We have begun to map the pattern that connects technology introduction to change issues. Figure 4-7 is a graphic depiction of those relationships. When LANs are installed and individual

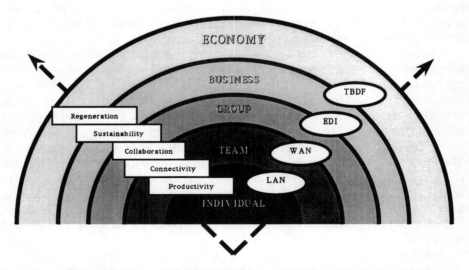

DIFFUSION OF TECHNOLOGY OVER TIME

Figure 4-7. Technology Impact in the Workplace

workers become connected to one another, management begins to focus on a concern for productivity. Concerns are voiced about cost/benefit ratios of computers and the speed of the workflow. Productivity concerns, initially phrased in terms of individuals, moves toward a concern for team productivity. Coordination of work tasks becomes the aim of management interventions.

Wide-area networks bring forth an emphasis on connectivity: How do we connect people? Who gets connected? How do we maintain security? These questions move to the foreground and shift the scope of problem deliberation to a higher level. Connectivity, in this sense, is more than just the technical dimension—it is social connectivity, as well. Organizational-design interventions begin to work on balancing the social and tasking needs of the work team. It is now that the issue of collaboration also emerges. Collaboration, in our experience, is much more than another way of saying coordination or cooperation. Collaboration means working on developing a unifying vision of the purpose of the team, its tasks, and the larger group to which it is linked.

Now, individuals and teams can begin to harness the energy of working toward a common purpose. In itself, electronic connection brings a more diverse view of work and the work environment to workers, and that diverse view leads to collaboration. As WANs evolve to Electronic Data Interchange networks, an even wider world view is made available. Collaboration among teams is subsumed by "world-view" issues about how the organization can fit in, sustain, and grow. The enterprise is now seen as part of a larger system. The organizational question becomes, "To what end are we working?" Management has the opportunity to shift its awareness to long-term growth and to questions of purpose.

As the enterprise connects itself to the global economic structure and data flows across political boundaries, it becomes possible to consider an ultimate large system and to take an end-to-end view of the whole system, while deriving sensitivity towards renewing the forces that brought the organization into being in the first place. "How can we build a learning organization?" is the question currently asked as a manifestation of the concern for generation-regeneration of individual motivation, team spirit, group loyalty, business purpose, and service to a larger society.

As we said in the beginning, the introduction of advanced information technologies into large organizations creates change in the way people interact, the processes they use to do business, and—ultimately—the structure of the organization. It is our experience that an attempt to take advantage of technology without systemic thinking and systematic planning leads to inadequacies in the development of control systems, in employee acceptance, and in strategic benefit, often resulting in a tremendous waste of financial resources. The analytic model we have presented here is our cognitive map of the relationship of specific communication technologies and the consequent organizational design issues.

We recommend creating awareness of the personal and business impacts of the change being contemplated. Where possible (not merely where necessary), incorporate users and users' customers into the design process. Demand breakthrough performance of your managers, based on the desires of your users. At the highest levels of technology, provide the intelligence arteries as well as the report capability. Demand that the technology serve not the job being done, but the stretch view of what that job should be doing. Throughout the process, develop everyone's ability to think systematically and tackle tough, emotional issues with order and skill.

CASE STUDIES

CASE 1: WHY IT DOESN'T ALWAYS WORK

Any large-scale system-redesign effort also requires a full commitment of upper management to long-term result, not short-term efficiencies. This case study began as a field experiment to test a methodology of integrating sociotechnical design, software development, and management planning for large-scale system change.

The site was a large telecommunications company that wanted to integrate current office-automation platforms into its ongoing sales-management function. The key problem was to obtain uniform design requirements and develop a reliable system-wide change strategy. Previous attempts at ad hoc development had proven ineffective, resulting in problems of communications across operating units.

Our conclusions were that a major system-development and implementation effort was required. Partial, nonsystematic efforts would not be successful. Specifically, the following six areas for action were identified:

- Increased leadership and need for automation
- Need to prioritize fiscal resources; the long-term view
- Use of advanced "networked-platform" departmental technology
- Increase in support requirements; both technical and work redesign processes
- Computer-literacy skill development *before* implementation
- Role clarification of the emerging "information manager"

All are required for success.

CASE 2: AND THEN SOMETIMES IT DOES

People must know why they have to change the way they do business in order for any organizational intervention to be successful. The reason is not always obvious—neither to workers nor to leaders. This case study involved a 200-person information-systems group that supported a major teaching hospital in the United States. When local networking technology was introduced into the hospital, the systems group began to report difficulties in intra-group communications, as well as a decrease in programmer productivity.

Our intervention consisted of a six-stage intervention labeled Strategic Customer Service. The first stage dealt with building basic communication skills. This effort formed the basis for much detailed work on the second stage of determining the level of customer satisfaction, with an emphasis on *why* customers needed information-systems support. The third stage was a detailed analysis of the unit's internal business process in response to their customers' needs. It is in this stage that major socio-technical work redesign began.

The fourth part of the intervention was building intergroup partnerships. Here we focused on proactive methods of dealing with collaboration issues within the entire system. Next, we went through a period of strategic business planning, looking at moving the group into a value-added strategic position within the system, and sought solutions to regeneration issues within the community. The final part of the intervention was a workshop on the topic of continuous learning. This final stage yielded a commitment, in terms of effort and resources, to put in place a system that would help all members of the group consistently strive to improve their functioning capability. After 24 months, the intervention remains successful by all reports and productivity has increased more than 20 percent.

NOTES

1. The most cogent explanation of Quality programs is given in David Garvin's article, "How the Baldrige Award Really Works," in the *Harvard Business Review,* Nov.–Dec. 1991. Certainly, there are many goals of most quality programs; however, we believe that improved customer input to the production process is the key ingredient.
2. One could argue the wisdom of this process where cuts are made deepest in the ranks of experienced employees without regard to performance criteria. Time will tell us which businesses went through this process in a thoughtful way and which ones simply reacted to short-term financial criteria.
3. "The New Productivity Challenge," *Harvard Business Review,* op. cit., pp. 69–79.
4. The linkage between these is often unclear. We believe that is because quality is a systemic issue, not something that can be isolated from the remainder of the business operation.
5. Peter Drucker, op. cit.
6. People take meaning from interactions based on many things. Their own backgrounds, history, and even mood. Customer satisfaction is an attitude; not a behavior.
7. Section 7 of the Baldrige Award Process deals with customer satisfaction. The most critical elements are knowledge of customer requirements and expectations, satisfaction determination, results, and comparison to others.
8. Vaske and Grantham (1990), p. 33.
9. Quality of product, or service, is the *perceived* quality. This realization that quality is a constantly shifting target is the key paradigm-shift brought about by the quality movement in the United States. It cannot be defined once and for all. Products need to change and shift with perceptions of quality.
10. Technically, you need to look at effectiveness from a perspective of necessity and sufficiency. Does the product provide the attributes necessary for the intended purpose? Is it sufficient for the intended use? And lastly, does it add some value beyond that? Can it be used for other purposes?
11. The next chapter, on Business Process analysis, explicates this point.
12. For specific guidance on research technique, refer to any market-research text. An executive overview of these techniques is given in Vaske and Grantham, op. cit, Chapter 5.
13. Managers often want to jump up and go do something to get things back on track. That leap to action without planning inevitably leads to disaster. *Stop* and *plan*.
14. BPA is a general system-analysis methodology. Its basic logic is sketching out and analyzing

the steps in a business process. The basic technique is to examine inputs, transformation, and output from any system. Applied in this context, we are concerned with input, transforms, and outputs to a customer-satisfaction assessment process.

15. We have seen cases where this data was decentralized due to organizational politics. The result was that no two officers of the company had the same basic information. Therefore, various decisions (while valid from each parochial viewpoint) often ran at cross purposes for the entire enterprise. The product-development results were disastrous.

16. Most planning systems today are cunning euphemisms for the budgeting process. Thus, actions are not planned, cash flows are merely forecast.

17. Joseph Oberle, "Quality Gurus: The Men and Their Messages," *Training,* January 1990, pp. 47–52.

18. We apply a particular meaning to partnering. The dictionary has several definitions: (1) one who joins in an activity, or (2) either of two persons dancing together. More than coordination is required—partners are collaborators. See Table 2–1.

19. Most organizational-development specialists are very good meeting facilitators. The key here is for the participants themselves to act out these roles. Partners need to be self-facilitating in order to be collaborative.

20. Our bias to is to view organizations as information processing networks. Money, goods, energy, and people may actually be the 'things' that move through the boundaries.

21. We are sure that some biologists would dismiss our analysis as overly simplistic. This may be true, but our purpose here is a demonstrate by way of analogy what a permeable boundary is.

22. See Figure 2-1 for additional explanation.

23. See Chapter 3.

24. Johansen, R., et al. "Leading Business Teams," op. cit.. The team-development model was developed by Drexler and Sibbett. The theory is that groups of people are transformed into teams when they pass through several stages of social-psychological development. Each of these stages is characterized by a central question that must be put to rest.

25. The process we used is based on the Enneagram model of action. Please refer to Chapter 1 for the discussion. The next chapter, on business process analysis, deals explicitly with this six-step model.

26. C. Nichols, personal conversation.

27. See the management cybernetics literature (e.g., Clemson 1984) for theory underlying requisite variety.

28. "Bush Puzzled by Depth of Blues," *San Francisco Chronicle,* Dec. 27, 1991, p. A-3.

29. Again, our view. Codependency can develop in any human relationship. Once your business unit has developed an ability to learn, you don't need to see the teacher every day.

REFERENCES

"Bush Puzzled by Depth of Blues." (1991) *San Francisco Chronicle,* December 27, p. A-3.

Drucker, Peter. (1991) "The New Productivity Challenge." *Harvard Business Review,* pp. 69–79.

Garvin, David. (1991). "How the Baldrige Award Really Works." *Harvard Business Review,* Nov–Dec.

Oberle, Joseph. (1990) "Quality Gurus: The Men and Their Messages," *Training,* May, pp. 47–52.

Johansen, Robert et al. (1991) *Leading Business Teams.* New York: Addison-Wesley.

Vaske, J. J. and Grantham, C. E. (1990) *Socializing the Human-Computer Environment.* Norwood, NJ: Ablex.

5

Business Process Analysis

ENGINEERING YOUR BUSINESS: INTERNAL INFLUENCES

In Chapter 3 ("Designing the Organization"), we introduced the notion that an organization's health could be assessed by examining the pattern of information flow within the organization. This chapter deals with the practical application of that idea. How do you ascertain the pattern of the information flow? We have developed a methodology to accomplish that task, to be explicated in this chapter. Chapter 4 described a system-wide intervention strategy called Strategic Customer Service. The second stage of that intervention is Business Process Analysis.

Business Process Analysis is a way to use industrial-engineering methodology to analyze workflow process. I have developed it over the past five years, in designing advanced office-automation software.[1] It has been used to develop functional specifications for workgroup computing platforms. This initial application is here extended to include a broader range of communication technologies. A key feature of this chapter is to provide managers a way to link work-role and task requirements to the socioemotional aspects of the work environment; in other words, connecting the task-oriented technology to the affective dimension of organizational functioning, found to be critical in the Chapter 2 case study.

Plan of the Chapter

This chapter returns to the theme of integration of customer satisfaction, employee attitude, and business function introduced in Chapter 2. First, we describe the model for collecting data on internal process functioning, its outputs, and its rationale. The second section of the chapter relates this information to the organizational-functioning model presented in Chapter 3. This section is followed by a discussion of the transformational nature of linking together task role and customer satisfaction as the central purpose for modifying any internal business process. The chapter concludes with the development of a six-stage intervention process designed to effect change in internal work flows.

Where We Are

This chapter represents Step 4 in the Enneagram process—"How to Work." The chapter takes you across a critical step in the process of integrating technology into your organization: the move from thinking to doing. The previous chapters have set the stage (Chapters 1 and 2) and developed keener understanding of internal (Chapter 3) and external dynamics (Chapter 4). This chapter shows the move toward action. The initial step in that "doing" process is to get a clear picture of what lies ahead.

Overall, this chapter emulates the general transform model of input, transform, and output. Figure 5-1 depicts this model. For a business process, the *input* is data collection and reduction (Business Process Analysis). The *transformational process* relates these results to the general Organizational Health model, along with customer satisfaction. The *output* of the business process is a plan for intervention: the six-stage Enneagram model that concludes the Chapter.

BUSINESS PROCESS ANALYSIS

Business Process Analysis (BPA) is an organizational-analysis methodology designed to elicit information from supervisors and a workgroup. This forms the basis of an intervention program to improve the efficiency of internal work flows. The technique becomes the basis for a higher-level organizational analysis.

BPA treats the workgroup as a system of interrelated objects. Each task performed within the group is the basic object of analysis. Interrelationships of objects are

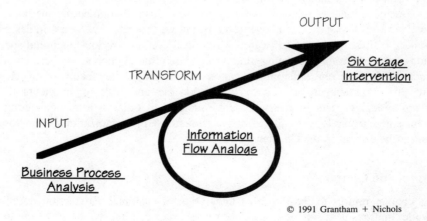

© 1991 Grantham + Nichols

Figure 5-1. *The Transform Process*

characterized as the flow of information among them. BPA is unique in that it collects data that relates performance of task to social role within the workgroup. As we described in Chapter 2, social role and communication patterns are inextricably intertwined. Therefore, any organizational intervention—including the automation of work tasks—must consider these sociological aspects of team function. These social roles are defined by BPA in terms of authority structures, work allocation procedures, and nodes of business rule expertise.

The purpose of BPA is to add value to the process of introducing workgroup computing technology to any busines process, within the context of a Strategic Customer Service intervention. The value added is the clarification and specification of the nature of the actual work that is conducted. BPA is a knowledge engineering tool that guides managers through the process of work flow analysis.

HOW IT WORKS

The basic process employed in BPA is to collect data, analyze it, and produce a series of workflow analysis reports. We will describe each step in hypothetical fashion. Four separate data capture instruments are used to collect data from the workgroup. They are:

1. Workgroup Boundary Description (Appendix 5A)
2. Work Task Outline (Appendix 5B)
3. Work Task Description (Appendix 5C)
4. Work Role Relation Matrix (Appendix 5D)

Each of these is included as an Appendix to this chapter.

BPA is designed to help you construct a graphic flowchart of the tasks performed within the work unit under study. These flowcharts allow you to "zoom in or out" on each work task object to specific actions that are being taken and isolate what data flows from tasks to task. This provides a visible, dynamic picture of the actual workflow in the organization. This flowchart, linked with BPA information, provides you with several analytical tools, such as:

1. Work process models
2. Operating procedure documentation
3. Functional role analysis

BPA organizes this information into the form that can be used as the basic-requirements document for the construction of custom-tailored systems-engineering applications. Reliable data collection and uniform formatting of workflow characteristics greatly reduce the time required to successfully implement workgroup automation procedures. BPA also provides the advantage of involving end-workers in the actual design process. The flow of work can be viewed as it exists and supervisors can perform "what-if" analyses before any decisions are made to automate specific tasks or to coordinate the tasks themselves.

The Methodology of Analysis

A set of predefined forms is used to collect data from the workers. Each form is designed to capture key descriptions of workflow. The questions asked of the workers reflect the expertise of human-factors specialists in work-flow design and have been developed after a thorough review of industrial-engineering literature. Traditionally these industrial-engineering processes have been administered by trained observers, or through interviews. We have found that BPA is more successfully employed when its application becomes the central goal of a design-team seminar. This procedure blends the data-collection process with a structured organizational-intervention process.

Design Teams

Design teams are common in corporations that develop products or analyze business processes.[2] A team of individuals representing different views (e.g., marketing, operations, engineering, etc.) is chartered to assess the feasibility of a different organizational design. Their objective is to provide information that will—at least in part—serve as a basis for planning and decision making. By including representatives from different branches of the organization, all with their own unique perspectives, the aim is to increase decision effectiveness. Individuals who participate on such teams are chosen because they are judged to possess a certain expertise. Unfortunately, many design teams are not representative of the range of individuals affected by the business process change. Just as executives are reluctant to make decisions without substantial information about the technical aspects of the system, they should be equally reluctant to make decisions without information on workers' behavior and attitudes toward the organizational change.

Soliciting worker involvement early in the organizational-design process has advantages both to the workers and to the organization. First, workers are experts on their own values and preferences and there is no substitute for their judgments in these matters. Second, by involving affected groups early, alternative designs are less likely to be questioned later. Highlighting the preferences and expectations held by constituents, however, does not make the decision "easier" for the executive who has ultimate responsibility for the enterprise. If anything, a successful design team makes the decision more difficult because it identifies the range of complexities and conflicts that are easily ignored without such input.[3] In short, direct involvement from different groups does not make the executive's decision easier, but it makes a better decision more likely.

Effective worker involvement requires an "interactive exchange" between managers and the workers. The interactive nature of this process implies that worker involvement is more than public relations. Participation is not selling the worker on a particular product or program. Rather, it is honestly and openly soliciting workers' help in the development and selection of alternatives. Group involvement is not a means of achieving a consensus among different groups, but a way to determine preferences and who holds those preferences.

The first step is to realize that there is no single work group. Workers actually separate into numerous groups or "publics." For example, a number of individuals may use a single computer: secretaries primarily concerned with word-processing applications, executives interested in using electronic mail to monitor the status of projects, analysts preparing financial reports with spreadsheets, and programmers. The difference in tasks affects individuals' usage of, and attitudes toward, systems and organizational structures.

Disaggregating workers into more homogeneous groups facilitates the design-team process. When meetings are conducted with a single public—preferably in small groups and on their own turf—individuals may be more willing to discuss their feelings. By documenting the input received at these meetings, it is easier to satisfy other members of the group that their views are heard and considered in the planning process. Finally, by evaluating the input from each group separately, competing needs of workers are highlighted.

Initiating contact with various groups is an important part of worker involvement. However, even with contacts and encouragement, it is necessary to establish mechanisms that facilitate rather than discourage worker input. Meetings and presentations are not settings where people often communicate. Standing up in front of a group is uncomfortable for most people. In such situations, many are intimidated by their lack of expertise. The sterility of input in a formal meeting is in marked contrast to the communication that goes on in the hallways before and after the meeting and at coffee breaks. Much can be done to make meetings less formal so that individuals feel free to express their opinions. Meetings should be small so that people can talk to one another. Facilities should have a number of small rooms so large groups can break up. Plans should be presented informally so that individuals feel free to comment and change the plans (flashy displays and overlays give the appearance that the plan is set even when it is not). Line drawings on paper allow participants to draw modifications and show the audience that their input is important. Seating arrangements that put the worker and the developer together also help to encourage input. Although each of these techniques helps to facilitate worker input, it won't happen on its own. One must make it happen.

The preceding emphasized procedures for encouraging individual participation in a group setting. Group decision making introduces its own unique set of considerations. Groups themselves can take on a life of their own. Therefore, it is equally important to consider the advantages and disadvantages of design teams.

Advantages of Design Teams[4]

Committees and groups have a number of advantages that make their use desirable under certain circumstances (Martino, 1972).

1. The amount of knowledge available in a group is at least equal to the amount of information available to any of its members. And if the group represents a diversity of interests (workers, developers, marketing, planning, human-factors experts), the total information is greater than that possessed by any single member.
2. The number of factors that have a bearing on the issue and that can be considered by the group is at least as great as for any one of the group members.
3. Groups are more willing to take risks than are individuals.

Disadvantages of Design Teams

1. There is at least as much misinformation available to the group as to any one of its members. Although the hope is that misinformation held by a design-team member will be canceled by the other participants, there is no assurance that this will occur.
2. Groups can exert strong social pressures on members to obtain agreement. If the majority view happens to be wrong, those in the minority may find it difficult to modify proposed actions, even if they are right. The probability of a group's decision being in error increases when little historical data can be brought to bear and the decision is based only on opinions.
3. Small-group research has shown that the validity of an argument is sometimes less important than the number of comments for and against a proposed position.[5] Consequently, a vocal minority who actively pursue a line of reasoning may sway a decision, even if their logic is faulty.
4. Reaching agreement in a group frequently becomes more important than a well-thought-out and useful decision. The result of group discussion in these cases represents the lowest common denominator, and although a decision was reached, no one may agree with it.
5. Certain members of a group may have a vested interested in a given outcome. Their objective is to win the other group members over to their viewpoint, rather than reaching a better decision.
6. If the members of a group represent a single subculture within a given area of technology, the entire group may share a common bias. If this bias deviates from the overall goals of the organization, the committee's decision may be inappropriate for the corporation.

Taken together, these observations make it apparent that although group decision making has significant limitations, it is possible to reach better decisions with a committee. Space does not permit a complete discussion of group facilitation techniques; in short, design teams require the use of highly skilled group facilitators to make them useful. In some cases, internal organizational-development resources can be used, if they also have the requisite technical knowledge of information systems.

We now turn to a discussion of the various components of Business Process Analysis methodology. The discussion begins with specification of the various inputs and concludes with a brief description of the outputs and their relevance to management decision making.

Inputs

Workgroup Boundaries

The first form to be completed is the Workgroup Boundary Description (see Appendix A). This form begins the data-collection process by helping you specify the scope of the workflow to be analyzed. The form guides you through the process of labeling the work unit, identifying all of its members, and stating a functional mission. The form also captures the identity of the work units that are upstream and downstream in the value-adding chain. It also aids in specifying the nature of information that flows into and out of the work unit being analyzed. This is a key item in mapping information flows to our organizational health model.

Work Task Outlines

Once the workgroup analysis has been bounded, you need to complete the second data-collection instrument: the Work Task Outline (see Appendix B). This form asks you to specify, in time order, all the major tasks performed in the work group and each subtask that can be identified.[6] It also elicits identification of people responsible for these tasks—identifying a primary social role. This creates a common data dictionary for each person/tasks linked in the other forms. The Work Task Outline can be used to generate a simple graphical image of the workflow (a flowchart of work activities). This step in the data-collection process also specifies the temporal order of the flow of information in the workgroup.

Work Task Description

The heart of the business enterprise is the knowledge of what to do when. This is the contingent nature of information flow in the workgroup. To capture these business rules, some of which are not readily visible to the outside observer, a third data collection instrument is employed. The Task Description Form (see Appendix C) leads you through a series of business-rule specifications based on the order outlined above. Each task is described in terms of the characteristics of the information input to the task (e.g., format, content, and variability). Also shown are the transforms made to the information and the resultant information that is output to the next step in the business process. This enables us to conduct reliability checks across workflows.

This form is quite detailed because it requires the worker to identify the source of business rules (standard instructions, regulations, etc.), all the IF-THEN-ELSE conditions, and quality-assurance procedures. The time element of each specific task is also gathered on this form. If standard scripts are in use, they are also specified.

Work-Role Relationship Matrix

The final data collection application is the Work-Role Relationship matrix (see Appendix D). This form is partially calculated by BPA. Information has already been captured that lists all people in the workgroup and their task responsibility. This information is presented back to the worker for a reliability check. If any changes need to be made, this is the point in the process where those updates occur. This form also collects information regarding who gives direction to whom, and who acts as authority for sources of business knowledge.

Outputs

Use of BPA produces a set of graphical outputs (see Figures 5-2 through 5-5). These are used for discussion material with the workgroup design teams who implement the organizational change process. These workflow diagrams are a clinical diagnostic tool used to highlight redundancies, lack of appropriate feedback channels, and information-flow bottlenecks in the organization. These outputs provide the workgroup with

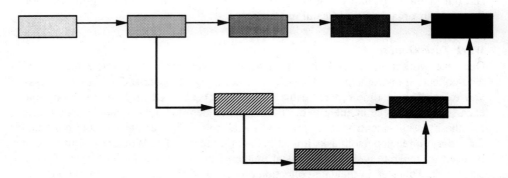

Figure 5-2. *Flowchart of Work Activities*

an ongoing, up-to-date record of standard operating procedures of the group, as well as a listing of functional requirements of each group member.

The following list describes each diagram:

- Flowchart of Work Activities (Figure 5-2). This presents a graphical depiction of the step-to-step work flow. It is a measure of the order in the process.
- Information and Task-Flow Analysis Diagram (Figure 5-3). This chart helps identify redundancies, amplification and deviation paths, choke points, and dead-end information flows.
- Person/Role Relationship Matrix (Figure 5-4). This matrix shows the size, density, and leadership centrality of workers.

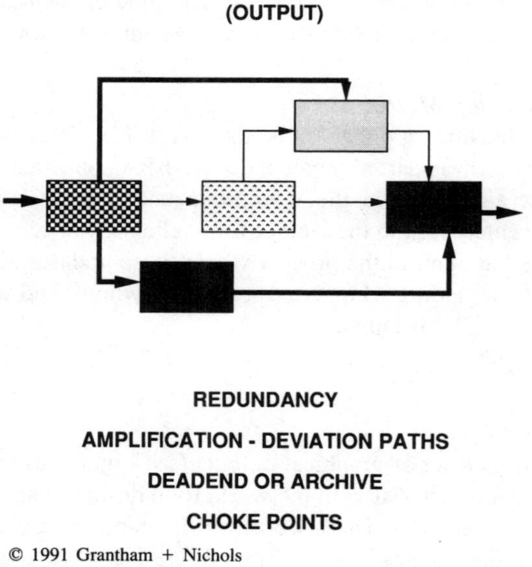

(OUTPUT)

REDUNDANCY

AMPLIFICATION - DEVIATION PATHS

DEADEND OR ARCHIVE

CHOKE POINTS

© 1991 Grantham + Nichols

Figure 5-3. *Information and Task-Flow Analysis Diagram*

ROLES

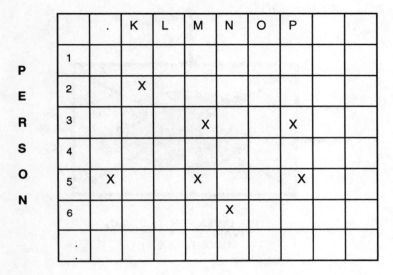

NETWORK DIAGNOSTICS

SIZE
DENSITY
LEADERSHIP

Figure 5-4. Person/Role Relationship Matrix

• Information Flow Characteristics (Figure 5-5). This transform model is applied to each information transform point and presents a temporal view of information flows, variety, and quantity.

Conclusion

The basic advantage of using BPA is the ability of the process to generate a series of analyses and diagrams in which work is made *visible*. This enables design teams to begin the process of changing the way they work to improve organizational efficiency. BPA is the first step in building a simulation model of the business process actually in place in the organization. It has been our experience that the business process reflected in existing documentation is often out of date and does not take into account the changing conditions of the business environment.

BPA is a necessary first step in the incorporation of workgroup computing in the modern office. It is designed to facilitate the collection of information describing the workflow in existing organizations. This process has traditionally been performed through a series of structured interviews with industrial psychologists. We suggest that

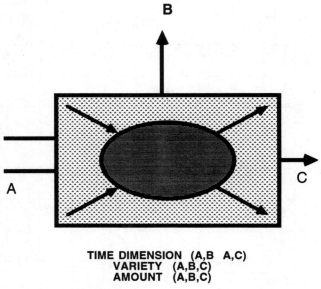

TIME DIMENSION (A,B A,C)
VARIETY (A,B,C)
AMOUNT (A,B,C)

© 1991 Grantham + Nichols

Figure 5-5. *Information Flow Characteristics*

BPA is most useful when combined with design-team techniques to maximize worker involvement in the development process.

BPA can help workgroups identify those sets of tasks that may benefit from automation—and those that would not. It can also facilitate the identification of information bottlenecks and critical-decision points in the business process. Ultimately, BPA becomes the foundation of workgroup computing design and allows workers to be free from the completion of recurring, routine actions. These valuable resources are then available for the more critical, judgmental activities of the workplace.

INFORMATION FLOWS AND ORGANIZATIONAL HEALTH[7]

The output of BPA can be used to construct a "visual metaphor" of organizational functioning. The organizational-functioning model we presented in Chapter 3 can be used as a map—and the data derived from BPA become the points that are plotted on the map. The ability to visualize the relationship among elements of large, complex databases yields new insights into several fields.[8] Recent developments in organizational design and office automation, detailed in this book, are making the visual analysis of workflows possible. We believe that an analytical, cognitive model of organizational functioning can be built upon a BPA depiction of information flows among workgroup members.

The dynamics of organizational functioning can be described in terms of six essential processes (see Chapter 3). Furthermore, each of these subsystems exists within a staged cycle referred to as an Enneagram model. Together, these visualizations portray healthy function in large formal organizations, in both static and dynamic terms. These models can be used to depict the state of an organization, at various points in time, by linking each process to quantitative data taken from monitoring the information flow through BPA methodology.

Introduction

Most applications of visual thinking have been in scientific and technical fields where visual metaphors of underlying processes exist (i.e., molecular chemistry, astronomy). This section of the chapter proposes to extend the use of visual thinking as a tool for the analysis of large, formal, complex organizations. The analysis of such organizations is becoming a critical function for executives in increasingly competitive environments. Historically, such analysis has taken the form of numeric, quantitative reasoning, but those methods appear to be inadequately explanatory for emerging forms of organizations. A new metaphor is required. A large part of the purpose of this book is to make accessible a complex metaphor of organizational functioning.

This discussion is composed of three sections. The first examines the traditional view of organizational functioning as a basis for extending a structural metaphor into a more dynamic form. This new paradigm for organizational analysis is explained in terms of its major components of organizational functioning. The second section describes the current information theory view of an organization—as various systems of information flows. The linkage between organizational process and information system structure is then proposed as a basis for organizational analysis. The last section proposes that this new model presents an opportunity for scientists, researchers, and managers alike to utilize advanced visualization techniques as a methodology of organizational analysis.

Elements of Organizational Analysis

Sociological explanations and descriptions of organizations are concerned with two important properties of organizing behavior: structure and function. Structure refers to measurable, observable patterns of communication that persist over time.[9] Computers not only affect organizations, but—in some ways—are organizations. This is especially true in large, complex, formal organizations where computers are applied in everything from the electronic exchange of memos to the control of heat and lights in the building.

Organizational theories usually explain the structure and function of corporations in terms of authority and power, size and complexity, efficiency and effectiveness, information, technology, and environmental influences. While different theories emphasize different variables at different times, all theories implicitly or explicitly use these constructs to describe organizations. Sociological theories of organizations differ from cognitive and social-psychological theories, in that they concentrate more on general observable trends than on the magnitude of variable relationships. Organizational theories are concerned with identifying consistent patterns of communication between individuals (i.e., structure). The purpose of these theoretical formulations is to provide a framework for comparative analysis of organizations. These traditional theories have been found wanting in explanatory power, as technology has begun to fundamentally alter the time-and-space relationships of work activity.

The structural nature of the workplace is changing. The established industrial order is giving way to more-streamlined ways of work, as noted in the introductory chapter. Flatter organizations, insistence on quality, and self-managing groups are demand forces that require a new generation of software to augment these new organizational styles. The use of electronic forms of symbolic communication is increasing the bandwidth of human-computer interaction. Images, graphs, charts, and iconic symbols are routinely used to facilitate communication. Computing power is moving toward provision of enormous graphical power for the end-worker. One of the most current developments is the use of computers—combined with telecommunications networks—to extend the workplace in time and space. The most important change we will see in computing technology in the workplace will be an ability to separate coordinated work processes and make this *visible* to everyone using the system. Organizational structures are being changed along lines distinct from the typical methodologies referred to above. The salient points of these changes are:

- *Time Shift*. A move from asynchronous, serial processing to parallel work processes.
- *Space Separation*. Decentralization of white-collar work force. Reduction in use of office space by 30 percent by 1995. Reversal of trend to separate the home and office location. Telework centers in exurban areas (see the case study in Chapter 8).
- *Visibility*. Graphical representation of work process in real time. The virtual workplace becomes a reality. Visibility of process allows increased use of simulation of commerce to test impacts of alternative action.

Bennett's Hexad Structure

As discussed in Chapter 3, John Bennett sought to explain systematic functioning of complex organisms by developing multitermed visual models.[10] The model Bennett developed that closely resembles a modern, complex, social organization is called a hexad because it contains six terms or elements. The hexad represents a coalescence of *time* and *space* dimensions of different processes that occur when an organism is evolving. According to Bennett, this structural model formed the essential basis for the dynamic nature of organisms. We have adapted this model in my work with organizational-change efforts as a symbol of organizational robustness. The model has proven to be an excellent diagnostic tool that parallels work done by sociotechnical-systems practitioners (see Figure 3-1). These elements can be defined in a way that allows them to be linked to the flow of information within the organization through use of BPA.

Information-Flow Analysis

The form and function of large, complex industrial organizations are changing as an artifact of increased use of advanced communication technologies. A quotation from a recent analysis of the topic illustrates this point:

Advancements in management information technologies in the past half decade are bringing to organizations forms and functions unanticipated even a few years ago. The revolution in personal communication and computation power is changing organizational roles and tasks and is offering increased effectiveness and productivity to organizational designers who choose to take advantage of technological innovations.[11]

When these changes take place, the empirical question becomes, "What are the patterns of these changes in organizational form and function?" My hypothesis is that these structural forms can be understood as changes in information-flow patterns and are best comprehended as visualizations of these patterns—that is, visualizations of the BPA output.

Network Analysis

Network analysis has been employed in several social-sciences disciplines to provide graphical representation of complex communication structures.[12] Looking at information networks as a metaphor for organizations is becoming more relevant with the development of increasingly dense communication structures.[13] Indeed, the cybernetic model of organizations is quickly becoming a dominant metaphor of analysis.[14]

A network picture of an organization includes nodes, pathways, transformational rules, and form and content as we have discovered with Business Process Analysis. What moves, or flows, through these networks is information in its raw form. Moreover, we may say that it is data that flow; data only become information when viewed *in the context* of the organizational structure. Data are information in the context of the *model* of the organization. Above, we have proposed one model of the organization. We suggest, at this point of theory development, that reliability of the model is more important than validity—which will be determined after empirical testing.

Contrasting Views of Information

To translate our function model of an organization (Figure 3-4) and our process model (BPA) into operational definitions of variables, we must first carefully define information flows. Communication theorists have traditionally looked upon information as an entity—a particle.[15] This view has fit well with database models (i.e., entity-relationship models) and with the management science perspective of variance theory. In some ways, this approach is analogous to the view in physics that sees energy as particles.

The developing view of information is much more process-oriented.[16] Markus and Robey note that in process theories, "outcomes are not conceived as variables that can take on a range of values, but rather as discrete or discontinuous phenomena that might be called 'changes of state.'" This distinction is important to developing a visual model of the organization. Bennett's hexad model is composed of different levels of energy, or discrete states, within each functional element (i.e., growth, focus, etc.). An organization moves from one level to the next as it completes the transit of process described in the Enneagram. Therefore, a process model of organizational information-flows fits conceptually with Bennett's visual images of organic process and structure. The view of information, then, becomes more like a "wave" theory of energy with differing "levels of energy."

Relationship of Process and Structure

Bennett's models can be used to depict the "state" of an organization at specific points in time by linking each functional process to quantitative data taken from monitoring the flow of information in the organization by use of BPA methodologies. Communication networks have many characteristics that can be related to their function and effect upon members of the network: size, connectedness, density, content of communication, form, and reciprocity. If we examine the network literature, in the context of operationalizing the hexad model of Bennett, we find the information-flow analogs shown in Table 5-1.

The need for brevity in this paper prevents an extended discussion of development of these analogs. However, growth is seen as an indicator of scale of communication and number of nodes in the network. It is normalized to control for nonreciprocal communication. Focus, in turn, can be viewed as a measure of nonvariation in categories of communication; one topic of conversation is more focused than five topics. Freedom can be taken as the amount of creation taking place: the development of new topics of conversation expressed as objects, folders, files, etc. Order has to do with the specification and definition of sequence, or scheduling. Identity is a self-referential function, a measure of distinctiveness and recognition of boundary. Network is a measure of communication interaction, or density.

Table 5-1   Dimensions of Organizations and Information Flow Analogs

Organizational Dimension	Operational Defintion	Information Flow Analog
Growth	Measure of Organizational Scale coupled with Rate of Change	Normalized Volume 1st Order Derivative
Focus	Efficiency of Operation Output Variance Reduction	Variation in Output Types Standard Deviation
Freedom	Rate of Innovation Measure of Creative Ability	Creation Rate of "Objects" 2nd Order Differential
Order	Measure of Sequencing of Operational Steps	Degree of Indexing of Objects Log-Linearity: Entropy
Identity	Measure of Uniqueness Boundary Permeability	Self References Degree of Translation
Network	Measure of Interaction Pattern Density and Reciprocity	Density of Communication Ratios of Frequency and Direction

© 1991 Grantham + Nichols

Development of Data Models

Visualization of organizational data has a rich history.[15] The ubiquitous organizational chart is a prime example. While these methods of displaying hierarchical authority structures are adequate for relatively stable, formal organizations, their use is marginal with the development of more fluid, information-based organizational structures. Organizational-redesign techniques[18] employ a variety of means to visually represent workflow, authority structures, and boundary conditions for large, complex organizations.

The use of models to depict data flow is a common technique in computer programming. For decades, flow-charting has been used to clarify the pattern of data flow and of control structures. It is commonly understood that visualizing complex information structures helps clarify the processes that are being automated. These methodologies of using visualization techniques to display complex data have been explicated quite well by demographers. Cognitive psychology has understood for some time that the human brain has an innate capacity to recognize complex patterns and structures when they are displayed in visual fashion. The recent advances in computer technology are allowing us to expand our visualization ability and apply enormous computer power in new areas. The areas that show most promise are those where complex patterns develop over relatively longer periods of time (e.g., weather forecasting and demographics).

Simulation Models

When these two cognitive models (Bennett's Hexad and the Enneagram) are combined, they produce a basis for a visual simulation of the functioning of a complex organization, based upon characteristics of information flow. The relatively static structures of communications patterns (form) are combined with a representation of flow dynamics (process). Historical data of information flows can then be used to test and correct the model. Algorithms of variable relationships can be created from this data. Then, algorithms can be used with simulated data to test hypotheses of organizational functioning and "what-if" scenarios can be constructed to test the impact of various organizational-design decisions.

Tools for Management Analysis

This brief discussion has been intended to extend the use of an industrial engineering tool (BPA) to the dynamic analysis of organizational functioning. The model can be used for diagnostic, analytical, and simulation purposes to aid managers and executives in making practical business decisions. The model is an example of visual thinking applied to a new area of science and technology—organizational analysis. In the future as larger and more interconnected databases are constructed within organizations, visual metaphors will become a standard way of viewing the enterprise—the virtual reality of business.

As organizations expand over greater time and space, models such as this will become a standard way of analyzing function and determining relative success of alternative network forms. Information is rapidly becoming the commodity of service industries. Old models built upon a paradigm of manufacturing goods are no longer adequate to anticipate impacts of environmental or market changes.[19] Distributed databases, wide-area networks, and increased graphical modeling powers are all converging to provide powerful analytic tools. However, these tools are of little use without clearly articulated cognitive models of organizations.

We began this discussion by referring to the shift in time and space dimensions of organizational activity brought about by use of advanced communication technologies. It is my hypothesis that the understanding of *time* and *space* alterations can be more readily comphrehended through techniques of visualization than through more traditional financial models. The cognitive maps presented here provide an empirical model to map information-flows in this context.

Social Roles and Business Functions

All of this discussion is very academic. But what does the business manager do with this while waiting for technology to develop to the point where BPA analysis occurs automatically? There are practical techniques of organizational design that can be used today—built upon the models of the Enneagram and healthy organizational functioning.

But first, we believe it is helpful to return to a central theme of this book to link the theory with the practice. Early in Chapter 2, we presented a model that integrated technology, teamwork, business process, and customers (see Figure 2-1). You must not forget that the principle, and reason, behind planned organizational intervention is to increase customer satisfaction, and—therefore—business performance. Let's stop a minute and examine that assumption: that increased customer satisfaction does correlate with improved performance of the business enterprise.

Relationship Among Employee Attitude, Customer Satisfaction, and Business Success

Figure 5-6 presents the relationship among values, attitudes, behavior, and performance. These relationships are well documented in the social psychology literature.[20] A person's values (e.g., "hard work is purposeful") are associated with attitudes toward work. These attitudes are then correlated with such behaviors as showing up for work on time, staying focused, and obeying directions. It is pretty much a common-sense observation that good workers produce good results. Hard work results in improved business performance.

The point here is that the social role you play in the workplace is related to your attitude and behavior—which in turn affect business performance. But beneath these attitudes are values and beliefs. If the role you play in the workgroup is in conflict with your value-set and belief, your business performances will suffer. That is why it is so important to examine the *social role* played by each worker. BPA has been designed to produce such role-relationship information as authority delegation patterns, network structure, and locus of business expertise.

If you hold a value, or belief, that people need to be closely supervised, you will feel uncomfortable in a fluid, loosely coupled workgroup where authority structures are

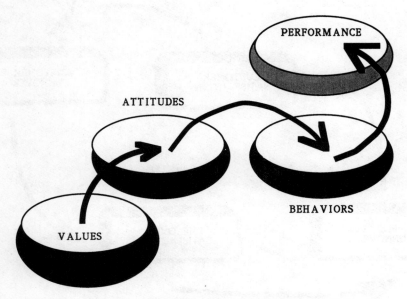

Figure 5-6. Formal Control Systems and Social Control Systems

diffuse. Conversely if you value innovation, creativity, and spontaneous action, a rigid, bureaucratic structure would be inappropriate. Your attitude toward the workplace changes, you don't like it there, you feel uncomfortable, and your behaviors become suboptimum for the work unit.

If we take this analysis one step further we can see how worker behavior is linked to business performance through customer satisfaction. Figure 5-7 is a simple model of the relationship.

The more satisfied that employees are with the work environment, the lower the turnover of employees. From our previous discussion, we would expect that the closer the role/value match, the higher the level of employee satisfaction. Customer satisfaction and employee turnover are linked through the dynamic of improved service—especially in the service industries. Employees with longer tenure are better able to meet customer expectations because of increased knowledge and skill. With increased customer satisfaction, you get decreased customer turnover. Decreased customer turnover leads to increased employee satisfaction because of increased stability and certainty in the work environment.

Although this relationship looks complex at first blush, it is really basic psychology of the workplace. Ask yourself: What were the characteristics of the work environments where you were comfortable? Of the ones that weren't comfortable? The point is that the closer the social role you play at work matches your personal belief structure, the more satisfied you will be with the business environment. This satisfaction leads to behaviors that impact customers and in turn reflect back on your attitude. The relationship between workrole, employee satisfaction, and customers is systemic and linked. Interventions in one part of this system impact all other parts of the organization.

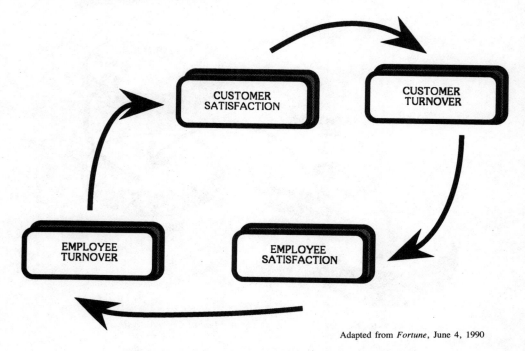

Adapted from *Fortune*, June 4, 1990

Figure 5-7. *Customer Satisfaction and Employee Satisfaction*

Therefore, if you can design an intervention that improves organizational effectiveness, it should translate into customer satisfaction and business performance.

THE SIX STEPS OF PROCESS MANAGEMENT

Relationship to the Enneagram

Business Process Analysis produces a powerful set of data that illustrates where organizational modifications need to be made. Design teams were used to help produce this intelligence. Now the question becomes, "How do we move forward?" The Enneagram can also be used as a model for planning *the process* of organizational intervention. The outer, linear process is a good map for designing an intervention.

Figure 5-8 is the diagram of the outer loop of the Enneagram showing the original Points 1-2-4-5-7-8. Original Points 9, 3, and 6 are removed. Remember that these points are where additional information comes into the process. The six-step process we are explaining here relates to actual work—it is a project plan. The steps in the process have been relabeled with more familiar terms. The first step in the process is assessment, followed by design, and then prototyping. After prototyping, but before action, comes a planning step. The concluding step in the cycle is a system audit or

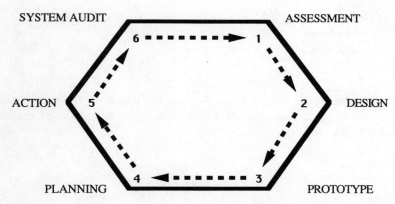

Figure 5-8. Grantham and Nichols Design Process

quality-control review. Then the cycle starts over. This linear process of intervention has many analogs in the sociotechnical design school and represents a general pattern of intervention.[21]

One of the key features of this action model or map is that it is both necessary and sufficient to guide a manager through an organization intervention. Steps cannot be left out, nor should they be completed out of sequence. We will return to this point after describing each step in terms of its purpose, the task at hand, link to other stages, and desired output.

The Six-Step Process—Evolving the Organization

You may want to refer back to Figure 1-3 at this time. Our process of organization intervention is a derived variant of the general Enneagram model. Points 3, 6, and 9 have been deleted from the Enneagram to leave points 1, 2, 4, 5, 7, and 8. We have then renamed these points Stages 1 through 6, respectively. At each stage we offer a reference to linking work at this stage to other stages and points on the Enneagram.

Stage 1: Assessment and Specification

PURPOSE:
To initiate a defined *process* to bring into being, and put into place, an organizational change in business procedure, system, or structure.

TASK AT HAND:
Prepare a description of the required characteristics, functions, and quality of the end product. This stage tests the will of the organization to engage in the process.

LINK TO OTHER STAGES:
Dependent upon management direction, commitment, and vision. View is toward Points 4 and 7 of the Enneagram.

METHODOLOGY:
- Design teams (BPA)
- Executive coaching
- Key-person interviews

OUTPUT:
Documents outlining the *process* to be used and the reason for the intervention (i.e., how this links to an overall plan for the enterprise). High-level design document or "platform"-design modules.

Stage 2: Design

PURPOSE:
To ascertain and integrate the availability of materials and demands of the business environment.

TASK AT HAND:
Produce and outline through experimentation and research a "drawing" of the ideal product (organization), including performance specifications and quality standards. This is a "craftsmanship" activity.

LINK TO OTHER STAGES:
Consensual agreement is required of all impacted parties. View is toward Points 4 and 8 of the Enneagram.

METHODOLOGY:
- Design workshops
- Team-building seminars

OUTPUT:
Specification of market/environment requirements, technology capabilities, and resource allocations needed. A final design document, the "blueprint" for the desired outcome.

Stage 3: Prototype Development

PURPOSE:
To construct a limited-function working model of the desired outcome. This stage is not coupled with ongoing business operations.

TASK AT HAND:
Construction of samples and testing of these against the design and requirements of the market. Prototype is built and tested in a controlled environment to check validity of engineering principles.

LINK TO OTHER STAGES:
The management will to continue is verified at this time. View is toward Points 1 and 2 of the Enneagram.

METHODOLOGY:
- BPA
- Business intelligence analysis
- Customer-satisfaction surveys/testing

OUTPUT:
A well-documented, working prototype in a stand-alone environment.

Stage 4: Implementation Planning

PURPOSE:
To develop a "playbook" on *how* the end product will be integrated into the normal business process and allocate the necessary resources.

TASK AT HAND:
To test the interactions of the prototype against other impacted systems in the organization. Resources of tools, training, and management direction are allocated, tested, and committed to full-scale implementation.

LINK TO OTHER STAGES:
The end product begins entry into normal business. View is toward "scaling up" Point 7 and putting into place quality-control procedures (Point 8).

METHODOLOGY:
- Team-building Workshops
- Organizational-change management coaching
- Communication-skill building

OUTPUT:
A "playbook" for organizational change. Roles, responsibilities, and boundaries identified and rehearsal of hypothetical problem areas. Implementation team has "experienced" the process.

Stage 5: Implementation Action

PURPOSE:
To conduct a staged implementation of the desired results. This stage begins slowly and builds momentum throughout the organization.

TASK AT HAND:
To continuously test the design and method to eliminate wasteful steps and to drive toward economies of scale. Mobilization of resources and coordination of parts of the value-adding streams are carried out. This is the manufacturing step in the process.

LINK TO OTHER STAGES:
This stage is connected to both the Assessment stage (Point 1) and the Planning stage (Point 5). This stage synchronizes management intention and market demand.

METHODOLOGY:
- BPA
- Simulation Modeling
- Systems-engineering workshops

OUTPUT:
End product on organizational scale

Stage 6: System Audit and Quality Control

PURPOSE:
To put in place an ongoing feedback system to monitor deviations of the process from design requirements.

TASK AT HAND:
Check specifications against expectations, both internal to organization (efficiency) and external (effectiveness).

LINK TO OTHER STAGES:
This stage is linked to the perfected design (prototype, Point 4) and the initial design (Point 4). It feeds forward into the next iteration of the cycle because it monitors changes in external forces

METHODOLOGY:
- Business intelligence network
- Customer-satisfaction surveys
- User groups

OUTPUT:
Information relative to match between end-product and changes in the business environment. Also internal forecasting (simulation) model for trajectory management.

Associated Organizational Issues

During each of these steps, certain organizational issues are deliberately raised. Many times, client groups will want to move quickly through a stage that points to the critical issue they have not been able to deal with. Again, it is very important to stress that each stage must be completed before moving to the next, and that no stages can be skipped without endangering the reliability of the entire process. Figure 5-9 displays the major organizational design issue associated with each step.

You can use Figure 5-9 as a guide to assure that that issue is adequately dealt with at each step of the process. For example, make sure that you have specified all resources necessary for production during the prototype stage before moving to planning. One tendency most managers have is to jump from Stage 1 (assessment) right to Stage 5 (action). Failure to determine business needs, resource requirements, and infrastructure lead to disaster in this scenario.

STEP	KEY ISSUE
ASSESSMENT	DIAGNOSIS
DESIGN	BUSINESS NEED
PROTOTYPE	RESOURCE REQUIREMENT
PLANNING	INFRA-STRUCTURE
ACTION	EDUCATION/ TRAINING
QUALITY CONTROL	EVALUATION

© 1991 Grantham + Nichols

Figure 5-9. Design Step and Business Issue

Techniques to Be Applied to Each Step

During the description of each stage, we included recommended methodoligies to be employed. These methodologies are structured opportunities for learning in the organization. They are merely recommendations, and the trained organizational consultant will employ these, or other techniques, based on their experience. Figure 5-10 is a matrix of these recommendations, displayed for each stage of the process.

CONCLUSION

This chapter has covered a great deal of material. Analyzing the internal business process of an organization is part of an overall intervention strategy. This chapter has covered several practical techniques for conducting that analysis. Business Process Analysis was presented as an information-flow modeling tool, coupled with a social-role analysis methodology. This technique was then linked to the concept of presenting a visual analysis of the organization to better grasp the systemic dynamics of organizational functioning. Both these approaches are built upon concepts introduced previously (i.e., Bennett's hexad and the Enneagram).

The remainder of the chapter explained why social roles are necessarily linked to business function by tying the concept back to the Chapter 2 development of a customer-driven representation of the business enterprise. Finally, we explained in detail a process for moving from planning the intervention, based on BPA, to actual implementation. This six-step model is again taken from the Enneagram process and can be applied in numerous situations requiring systemic organizational intervention.

SERVICE	STAGE OF PROCESS					
	1	2	3	4	5	6
COACHING	X			X		X
DESIGN WORKSHOP		X		X		
FOCUS GROUP	X		X			X
TEAM BUILDING		X		X		
BUSINESS PROCESS			X		X	
SURVEYS	X					X
COMMUNICATION SEMINAR				X	X	
SYSTEMS ENGINEERING SEMINAR				X	X	

Figure 5-10. *Method and State of Intervention*

Chapter 5 represents point 4 on the Enneagram model. This chapter has concerned itself with describing "How to Work" in Popoff's analysis. Chapter 6 will focus on the relationship between technology and organizational structure, and moves you toward action with the "Preparation" step. Application of the tools described in Chapter 5 will yield a well-documented working prototype in a stand-alone environment. BPA, design teams, and the six-step model will produce that result. The next step is to look at how technology systems can support and create organizational structures.

NOTES

1. The process grew out of frustration of bringing some reliable order to the software-development process, which was viewed as being a "dark art" conducted with smoke and mirrors. These models were initially tested on software-development organizations, later extended to medical service environments, and most recently to the design of community work centers.
2. This section has been adapted from Vaske and Grantham (1990), ch. 5, and extended to reflect the practical experience of utilizing BPA in the field.
3. See Ives and Olsen (1984).
4. Martino (1972).
5. Cartwight and Zander (1986); Michener, DeLamanter, and Schwartz (1986).
6. Definition of "major" and "subtask" is in itself part of the intervention process. Asking people to label the tasks caused them to question "just what do we do around here?" Therefore I do not try at this point to offer any ad hoc definition—but extract that from the workers themselves.

7. Grantham (1991).
8. See Tufte (1990).
9. Ball (1978).
10. Bennett (1987).
11. Foster and Flynn (1984).
12. Knoke and Kuklinski (1982).
13. Markus and Robey (1988).
14. Morgan (1986).
15. Krippendorf (1986).
16. See Markus and Robey, op. cit., and Taylor and Katambee (1988).
17. Tufte (1983).
18. MacKenzie (1986).
19. Applegate, Cash, and Mills (1988).
20. Vaske and Grantham (1990) discuss the various theoretical models of this relationship in ch. 2.
21. We have used this pattern in diverse endeavors ranging from software development to market testing. It is often helpful to change the signs for each step to match the business environment you are operating in. For example, assessment may become "market research" in marketing or "requirements' analysis" in the software world. However, the general point obtains.

REFERENCES

Applegate, L. M., J. I. Cash, and D. Q. Mills. (1988) "Information Technology and Tomorrow's Manager." *Harvard Business Review*. 66 (Nov.–Dec.), pp. 128–36.

Ball, R. A. (1978) "Sociology and General Systems Theory." *The American Sociologist*, 13, pp. 65–72.

Bennett, J. G. (1987) *The Dramatic Universe*, vol. 2, Claymont, WV: Charles Town.

Foster, L. W. and D. M. Flynn, (1984), "Management Information Technology: Its Effects on Organizational Form and Function," *MIS Quarterly* (Dec.): 229–236.

Grantham, C. (1991) "Visual Thinking in Organizational Analysis." *Proceedings of the Society for Imaging Science and Technology*. San Jose, CA, Feb. 1991.

Ives, B. and M. H. Olson. (1984) "User Involvement and MIS Success: A Review of Research." *Management Science*. 30(1): 586–603.

Knoke, D. and J. H. Kuklinski. (1982) *Network Analysis*. Beverly Hills, CA: Sage.

Kripperdorf, K. (1986) *Information Theory: Structural Models for Qualitative Data*. Beverly Hills, CA: Sage.

Mackenzie, K. D. (1986) *Organizational Design*. Norwood, NJ: Ablex.

Markus, M. L. and D. Robey. (1988) "Information Technology and Organizational Change: Causal Structure in Theory and Research," *Management Science*. 34(5): 583–598.

Martino, J. P. (1972) *Technological Forecasting for Decision Making*. New York: American Elsevier Publishing.

Morgan, G. (1986) *Images of Organizations*.: Beverly Hills, CA: Sage.

Taylor, J. R. and J. M. Katembwe. (1988) "Are New Technologies Really Reshaping Our Organizations?" *Computer Communications*. 11(5), 245–52.

Tufte, E. R. (1990) *Envisioning Information*. Cheshire, CT: Graphics Press.

Tufte, E. R. (1983) *The Visual Display of Quantitative Information*. Cheshire, CT: Graphics Press.

Vaske, J. J. and C. E. Grantham. (1990) *Socializing the Human-Computer Environment*. Norwood, NJ: Ablex.

APPENDIX

WORKGROUP BOUNDARY DESCRIPTION
© 1991 Grantham + Nichols

What is the name of your workgroup? _____

Briefly describe the mission of your group. _____

_____

_____

_____

_____

Please list all the people who work in your group

Person	Job Title	Status (full time, etc.)
_____	_____	_____
_____	_____	_____
_____	_____	_____
_____	_____	_____
_____	_____	_____
_____	_____	_____
_____	_____	_____
_____	_____	_____

Where does the information come from that your group works with? For example, directly from customers or other functional units. If it comes from multiple sources, please identify all of them.

Source	Form of Input (e.g., phone call, memo, form or file)
_____	_____
_____	_____
_____	_____
_____	_____
_____	_____

Please briefly describe your group's final product

_____

_____

_____

_____

Is there a standard format for your product? _____ Yes _____ No
If YES, attach a copy of the format.

Where does your product go? If the product goes to several places, please indicate if it is the original or a copy

Product Destination	Original	Copy
_____	_____	_____
_____	_____	_____
_____	_____	_____
_____	_____	_____

Work Task Outline
© 1991 Grantham + Nichols

The purpose of this form is to build a picture of the actual workflow in your organization. Please take a few minutes and think about how work actually gets done in your group. Please outline all of the major tasks and their components, if appropriate, in the TIME SEQUENCE presently in use.

Major Task: Sub-Task   Person Responsible

1. _____   a. _____   _____
                        b. _____   _____
                        c. _____   _____
                        d. _____   _____

2. _____   a. _____   _____
                        b. _____   _____
                        c. _____   _____
                        d. _____   _____

Repeat for each major task.

WORK TASK DESCRIPTION
© 1991 Grantham + Nichols

Task: _____   Sub Task: _____
Person Responsible: _____   Job Title: _____
===
>> Input <<
Please describe the characteristics of the information which is the input to this (sub) task

Does the information always come to you in the same form? _____ YES _____ NO

If YES, what form is that (please describe)

_____
_____
_____
_____

What is the quantity and frequency of input? (e.g. per day or per hour)

_____ per _____

If the information comes in different forms, what are they and what is the frequency?

Form   Frequency

_____   _____ per _____
_____   _____ per _____
_____   _____ per _____
_____   _____ per _____
===

WORK-ROLE RELATIONSHIP
© 1991 Grantham + Nichols

Person: _____

Task/Sub Task Responsibility:

_____ // _____
_____ // _____
_____ // _____
_____ // _____
_____ // _____

Who does this person take work direction from? _____

Who does this person give work direction to?

_____   _____
_____   _____
_____   _____
_____   _____

Most people are experts at some aspect of the business process they are involved in. What task expertise does this person have?

_____   _____
_____   _____
_____   _____
_____   _____
_____   _____

>> WORK ACTIVITY <<

This section is designed to help you organize the business rules, or guidelines you use to make decisions. For every piece of information that enters this (sub) task you have to do something with it. You may check it for accuracy, perform a calculation, or transform it to another format. For every information flow into this (sub) task please list the following characteristics of your work.

+++

Information Form: _(*ex: Form A*)_____ Data Item: ___(*Loan Amount*)___

Action Performed: _____(*ex: Review and Forward*)_____

Work Rule: _____(*ex: If loan amount is over $20000, THEN send to Joe, or ELSE perform the calculation_*)_____

How long does it take on average, to perform this function?

_____ days _____ hours _____ minutes

Do you use any computer software to accomplish this task? _____ YES _____ NO

If YES, what is the name of the program? _____

If you have a special application program to work inside this package what is it called?

_____

Authority for the Work Rule: (manual or procedure book): _____

_____

If you don't know what to do with this information, who do you ask? _____

_____

How can you tell if you have done the correct action with this information?

_____

_____

Does anyone check your work? _____ YES _____ NO

If YES, who? _____

++

>> Repeat this section for each distinct (sub) task <<

++

>> OUTPUT <<

This section will help you to specify who gets the product of your work and the format that is forwarded.

Please describe the characteristics of the information which is the output of this (sub) task.

Does this information always go out in the same form? _____ YES _____ NO

If YES, what form is that? (please describe)

_____

_____

What is the quantity and frequency of output? (e.g. per day or per hour)

_____ per _____

If the information comes in different forms, what are they and what is the frequency of dispatch?

Form   Frequency

_____   _____ per _____

_____   _____ per _____

_____   _____ per _____

_____   _____ per _____

6

Technology and Organizational Structure

One of the central questions that theoreticians and practitioners alike ask is whether or not the use of technology *causes* changes in organizational structure. Throughout this book we have been developing the idea that any effect on organizational structure is as much a process question as it is an absolute certainty.[1] In this chapter, we focus on those technologies that intervene in the communication process of large, complex organizations.

As you will see, there are no easy, cut-and-dried answers to this question. Communication technologies are benign in themselves. The ultimate impact they have seems to depend on how they are integrated into the ongoing work process. This issue is growing in importance. Today's managers wonder why the promised increases in productivity have not been found to result from greater use of personal computers, local networks, and—most recently—"groupware." We would like to raise a different question: How do you organize (structure) work groups to make the most effective use of available technologies?

The purpose of this chapter is to delve into that question in some detail, building upon the preceding chapters on design process and customer service. At this point, you have followed the consultative process through our method of assessment, design, prototyping, and internal-process examination. Now, it is time to begin designing a structural intervention. In keeping with our sociotechnical approach, we now turn our focus to technology.

142

Plan of the Chapter

This chapter is laid out along the same framework employed earlier. The discussion begins with finding our place in the overall process-model of the Enneagram, specifying learning objectives, and explicitly stating a definition of technology in the organizational context. Next, we survey the history of technology use and organization change, coupled with concrete examples taken from the management literature. We also include a critical review of the current research literature, which points to our estimation of the direction of research and practice. Finally, we conclude with a case study of an attempt to think through the process of structuring a work organization to make maximum use of available communication technology.

Where We Are

This chapter represents Point 5 on the Enneagram model. This is the step of preparation to do work, after we have figured out how to work. This chapter concerns itself with preparing the work site or looking into the possibility of taking the site apart to fix it. The inner process (planning) is moving from Point 5 to Point 7. The quality of work depends on the quality of the foundation laid down for the work. We hope this concept provides you with a perspective to think through the process of diffusing communication technologies into work groups. Instead of "doing it right the first time," we would like to provide an intellectual basis for working through the process in your mind before actually implementing an organization change.

Learning Objectives

The learning objectives of this chapter are quite simple. After reading this chapter, you will:

- Have a explicit definition of communication technology
- Understand the historical co-evolution of technology and organizational form
- Be able to cite examples of organization change associated with technology
- Know what the current and best thinking is concerning this question
- Have an understanding of the most probable trends of technology impacts on organization-design practice.

Definition of Technology

Defining technology is a difficult task. A review of the research literature easily produces a half-dozen definitions. Choice of the definition often influences the conclusions you reach in examining the effect technology has on organizations. Here, we choose to use a rather expansive definition of technology. Technology is much more than hardware, software, and supporting peripheral equipment. In our view, technology also includes ways of thinking about organizational processes. In a sense, there are *mental* technologies. Clearly, a central theme of this book is the elucidation of a "mental technology": the Enneagram itself.

For this reason, technology must be taken to include hardware and software and also extended to include the "wetware" or the mental component of technology. Just as software design influences how you interact with the hardware of computer technology, so does how you—as in intelligent organism—envision an organization influence how you plan to interact with it.

Perhaps the best overview of the expansive vision of technology is given by W. Richard Scott (1992). Scott points out that conceptual clarity is required to understand how technology impacts organizational structures. He argues that "technology, technical systems, task environment, and environment" are analytic concepts with much overlap that often leads to confusion. He shares our view that "technologies" impact organizational processes in several ways, including inputs, transformations, and outputs. He then goes on to further delineate these impacts in terms of materials, operations, and knowledge.[2]

This definition of technology, extended to include operations and knowledge, is critical. Operations are processes—the doing within the organization. Knowledge is analogous to thinking about operations. We feel that there is a correspondence here to the difference between the doing and thinking processes symbolized by the Enneagram. Therefore, we define technology as including the actual material used, a functional definition. But we also see technology as being a process and a mental map of the process.[3]

As an example of this, consider a centralized word-processing operation in a large corporation. When we examine technology, we would go beyond the visible computers and software to include the ways in which they are used and the manner in which that part of the business process was integrated into the whole of the operation. In this way, the Business Process we talked about in Chapter 5 and the mental models we will discuss in Chapter 7 are technologies also.

Scott follows his definition with a set of hypotheses about the expected effect this broad definition of technology can have on an organization. He predicts:

1. The greater the technical complexity, the greater the structural complexity. The structural response to technical diversity is organizational differentiation.
2. The greater the technical uncertainty, the less the formalization and centralization.
3. The greater the technical interdependence, the more resources must be devoted to coordination.

Indeed, we believe that these predictions are becoming evident with the evolution of the business enterprise into the distributed workplace—a theme we return to in the conclusion of this chapter.

HISTORY

A Critical Review of the Literature

Perhaps the most cogent comment found in the published research literature is "Yet after decades of research relating organizational technology to organizational structure, the evidence for technology's influence on structure, is at best, confusing and contradictory."[4] The general impression is that you can support just about any contention of technology effect by selectively choosing references to support your thinking.

This theme has been evident in the literature for almost a decade. In 1984, as personal computers were making significant headway into large organizations, it was reported that "Advancements in management information technologies in the past half-decade are bringing to organizations forms and functions unanticipated even a few years ago.[5] A few years later, the same cry, "Results of studies of the organizational impact of computer-based information systems (CBIS) are contradictory and uncertain."[6] Finally, in 1988, academic researchers begin to ask for explicit statements of assumptions and use of cogent theories in organizational research, noting that 30 years have passed since the seminal publication of Leavitt and Whisler's article in the *Harvard Business Review* (1958), speculating on technology impact on management— with little agreement being reached in the interim.[7]

To the nonacademic person, this seems to fulfill the idea that researchers really don't understand what they are doing. While we would not argue that point here, there is an explanation of why the current research literature offers no clear-cut explanations of technology effects. The major reason is the lack of a unified, underlying theoretical perspective. Every researcher comes at the question from a different set of assumptions and gets different results.[8] Perhaps a better way to approach this question from the viewpoint of organizational-design practitioners is to look at what we know, what we don't know, and what we can speculate that we don't know we don't know.

What We Know

What we know is largely summarized in the propositions contained in this chapter. However, there are some additional points that can be teased from the literature and that are of particular interest to practitioners.

With the introduction of a new technology, certain employees seem to increase their social power and become more central to the decision-making network—that is, those employees who master the technology as it becomes a new way of communicating in the organization. Therefore, early adopters of new technologies emerge over time as the more powerful; late adopters become relatively less empowered. This implies that an intervention coupled with technology diffusion should also concentrate on the development of functional skills to aid in the empowerment process. Further, it appears that centrality in the communication network comes before power is bestowed. This means that the actual change in structure (centrality) comes before it is formalized and becomes socially sanctioned. Function precedes form.[9]

Technology has differential impacts on the level of social aggregation. Individuals, workgroups, organizations, and societies find different impacts in terms of power and status relations and decision making. For example, a technology that promotes empowerment and group cohesion at the organizational level can at the same time disenfranchise segments of society. The pervasiveness of personal computer technology can arguably be seen as improving the quality of work life for thousands of Americans. However, at the same time, there are computer-illiterate populations who are becoming increasingly isolated from the rest of society because of their lack of access to, and knowledge of, these newer technologies. The design implication in this technological effect is to alert practitioners to the unintended impacts. Issues of social equity, we would predict, will become increasingly important to organizational design professionals.[10]

What We Don't Know

What we don't know can be summed up in three broad categories of inquiry, as follows:[11]

- How to conceptualize technology and structure
- How to address specification of a level of analysis
- How to measure change

The conceptualization of technology and structure must be explicit and commonly understood for people to engage in a discussion of the topic. We often find ourselves dealing with a client group who think they are all operating from the same definitions of the organization and technology. Any design process that proceeds without first clarifying these issues is doomed to failure. We hope that some of the discussion in this chapter can serve as a basis for such a clarification, as facilitated by practitioners.

Specifying the field of study, or intervention, is another issue. Again, this may seem to be sophomoric advice to a seasoned practitioner, but it is an issue often overlooked. Systems thinking tells us that the first distinction to be made in any analysis is the bounding of the group under study. Just what are the limits to the group we want to examine? The answer is critically important because communication technologies have a unique effect of spanning organizational boundaries and present a rather difficult problem in placing limits on the impact analysis. Boundaries, which may be quite artificial, must be drawn to keep the intervention on track and defined.

How do you measure change? Do you focus on the individual, on the group, or on society? Do you look at attitudes, behaviors, intentions, or something else? Our favorite example of this conundrum is productivity. How do you measure productivity? The promised increases in productivity have not been documented with the introduction of computing technologies in large organizations. At least, not at the organizational level. However, if you ask most individuals if they are more productive after learning how to use computers, they will usually reply yes and then go on to give several specific examples. One of the most effective services a practitioner can deliver may be to help develop a definition of productivity against which the effectiveness of the intervention can be measured.

What We Don't Know We Don't Know

It is difficult, if not impossible, to talk about what we don't know we don't know. We would like to suggest that a way to start thinking about this issue is to turn the question around. How can individuals, workgroups, business enterprises, and societies organize themselves to take advantage of what capabilities communication technologies offer? We have seen that—consistently—the effects of technology, when observed in hindsight, are explained away as "unintended consequences," or in other words, "we didn't expect that to happen."

We still approach the question from a cause-and-effect perspective. This way of thinking is vacuous in today's world, with ever-increasing rates of change. As we move into the mid-1990s, it is becoming evident that how people organize to work, play, and police themselves can be influenced by the use of modern developing technologies. But what thought is being given to questions of social equity, enhancements of the quality of community life, and cross-cultural communication? These, we think, are the areas that we don't know what we don't know, and they deserve tremendous effort. Practitioners of organizational design, or "changemasters," have a particular responsibility, in our view, to be responsible to clients for the unintended consequences of the interventions they design and implement. Careful thought must be given to what you don't know you don't know.

We now turn to an analysis of the effects technology has had on large, complex organizations. This analysis is by no means exhaustive, but is intended to give readers enough background to proceed with their own investigations.

TECHNOLOGY EFFECTS

We view organizations as intelligent systems capable of learning new behaviors. Organizations interact with their external environment in complex ways based, in part, on how they analyze and synthesize information about the environment. [12] Also in this sense we can see organizations as communities, a theme we will return to later in Chapter 8 on organizational learning. The use of communication technologies helps people experience each other, share perspectives, and develop social bonds. You cannot assess the effectiveness of a communication systems without a clear understanding of its purpose. Technologies can be used to inhibit interaction as well as promote it as we saw in the case study in Chapter 2. Experience with a technology also has an effect. That is to say, simply hooking people together electronically does not automatically yield increases in performance or radical shifts in ways of organizing.

One of the underlying themes of this book is that the use of a socio–technical design approach yields the most utility. Nowhere is this more evident than when we are examining communication technologies. [13] A sociotechnical approach to organizational design presumes a certain type of culture. Cultures that are open and participatory in nature make most effective use of this approach. Cultures shape and define the use of communication technologies according to their match with dominant values. Therefore an examination of technology effects needs to proceed from an understanding of the dominant values expressed (or not) by enterprise leaders and members.

Effects on the Large Corporation

Quite obviously, any change in the way we communicate with one another creates a possibility of changing how we interact in the work unit. However, as we have seen from a review of the literature, there are no consistent findings. But it isn't quite as bleak as saying that the final answer is, "It depends." When we asked noted historians of technology diffusion to give us a bottom-line answer, they outlined five consistent long-term trends of the impact of technologies on large organizations.[14] These five trends are as follows:

1. *Improvements in communication technology lead to increased information flow.* Improvements come in two ways. First, the increase in simple bandwidth allows more data to flow. This is similar to increasing the number of lanes on a freeway. The more lanes, the more cars can travel on the road. Second, improvements can also be in the form of connectivity. Technologies can increase the number of possible members in a network and network density increases. Therefore, the absolute volume as well as the density of the connections may increase.
2. *Improvements in communication technology tend to centralize power and control.*[15] Historically, this is true. Whether this trend will continue remains to be seen. We would like to suggest that a curvilinear effect is becoming evident. Technologies have improved to the point that control can now be decentralized.
3. *Improvements in communication tend to increase geographic decentralization.* The ubiquity of modern telecommunication networks speeds up this process. We are rapidly reaching the point that, for voice and data communication, cooperating workgroups can be located anywhere on the planet. Moreover, such spatial separation is largely invisible to group members. As anecdotal evidence of this trend, we note that the most typical first question in a conversation over a cellular phone link is "Where are you?"
4. *Improvements in communication technology tend to increase the rationality with which an organization's goals are pursued.* The underlying assumption here is that increased volume and connectivity reduce the amount of uncertainty in the business environment. Leaders are better positioned to know what competitive forces are operating and, as a result, become more sensitive to changes in customer behavior, thus presenting the *possibility* of making more rational, calculative decisions, based on goals of efficiency.
5. *Improvements in communication technology tend to increase the pace of organizational life.*[16] Being connected to more and more communication channels does usually increase pace of interaction. Now, we have voice-mail systems, E-mail systems (perhaps more than one), and telephones—all of which can create interruptions in the flow of work. It should be noted that this is not in itself a necessarily positive effect. We have found in our research with telecommuters that in fact lack of interruptions is associated with increases in productivity. It appears that there is an optimum pace of work dependent upon task and individual characteristics.

ORGANIZATIONAL INTELLIGENCE AND DECISION MAKING

In a more contemporary vein, Huber (1990) advances a theory of organizational effect of technologies that relates to an organization's ability to make decisions and gather intelligence. This represents the idea that there is something qualitatively different about recent communication-technology advances that does not allow us to simply extrapolate organizational-design effects from past research.

This idea seems to fit quite well with our approach of taking the modern, complex organization as an intelligent system with inherent learning capabilities. Huber feels that today's technologies (e.g., artificial intelligence, groupware, decision-support systems, etc.) offer the opportunity to directly impact how organizations make decisions and learn. As a result, the emphasis shifts from communication technologies that aim toward increasing efficiency (i.e., the Westrum approach) toward effectiveness. Specifically, he proposes that these communication technologies:

1. Increase variety and number of information sources in the decision-making process
2. Decrease the number and variety of face-to-face decision makers
3. Decrease decision-making meeting time
4. Change distribution of decisions; decisions get made at different levels[17]
5. Increase the variation of decision structures across a population of organizations
6. Decrease the number of organizational levels requited for a given decision
7. Decrease the number of intermediate nodes for communication
8. Store more organizational intelligence in computerized databases
9. Identify problems and opportunities more quickly
10. Organizational intelligence is more reliable, accurate, and accessible
11. Result in higher-quality decisions
12. Reduce organizational action time

The proposed overall effect of these communication technologies then becomes an organization that is flatter in structure, responds faster to changes, and has an improved quality of business decisions. Also, the variety of decision-making structures is increased, which you would expect would also lead to increased innovation. Please bear in mind that these ideas represent a theoretical stand, still subject to testing and observation. There is no guarantee that increasing the use of these technologies will automatically lead to a flatter, leaner, more effective organization. We also know that the primary impediment to these changes is cultural inertia. Business don't always operate on a calculative, rational basis.

Conclusion

The purpose of listing these effects is to give you a sort of checklist of items to consider in systems-design deliberations. Look at these trends and try to project the impact of a specific decision on each, and, in turn, what organizational-design impacts are indicated. Given these overall historical impacts, we now turn to a detailed examination of some examples in which these effects can be seen influencing organizational structural changes.

EXAMPLES OF ORGANIZATIONAL ANALYSIS

Let's examine some contemporary examples of organizational analysis. We have chosen three seminal articles that outline a research approach to analyzing the relationship between communication technology and organizational structure. The first article was written in 1988 and reviews some thirty years of work in this area from a business perspective. The second looks at how an organization's structure helps relate to the larger environment. In the third article analyzed below, a communications perspective asks the question, "How do organizations process information?"

Tomorrow's Manager

In 1958, Harold Leavitt and Thomas Whisler predicted that information technology would allow organizations to become flatter, more responsive, more centralized. Thirty years later, this still hasn't happened. Why? The simple answer is that complexity has increased, and—as a result—we are seeing more centralized control but with decentralized decision making. Certainly, companies are downsizing to cut out middle management, but not in response to technology capability—they are downsizing to cut costs. The form of organization seems to be changing into a team-like structure that bands together for particular projects and then dissolves. Structures are becoming more flexible and dynamic. All this has certainly been encouraged by available technology, but not directly caused by it. The article by Applegate, Cash, and Mills[18] concludes that the coming challenge is for managers to learn how to manage the process of introducing technology into business. The shift is from simply reacting to these forces, to being in control of them.

Environmental Linkages

What is the relationship between modes of communication, the communication environment and organizational structure? This question has been repeatedly asked without a definitive answer. In 1973, when David Conrath[19] first posed the problem, we were beginning to see personal computers enter the office. The intervening years have seen voice-mail, widespread E-mail, and now cellular phones and fax machines come into business. The conclusions Conrath reached in 1973, however, seem to be just as valid today. For example,

1. The pattern of written communication follows from formal authority structure.
2. Telephone communication follows from the workflow structure.
3. Face-to-face communication is influenced by physical proximity.

These relationships are now expanding when we can use telecommunication to substitute for differences in time and space. Face-to-face conversation can be accomplished through two-way video. However, Conrath's points remain important. He suggested that we really don't know how to measure some of these complex ideas and that future research should begin with detailed observations of how people actually use the technologies and, most importantly, for what purpose.

Information Processing

According to Daft and Lengel,[20] there are two dimensions of communication that are related to organizational structure: uncertainty and equivocality. Uncertainty is actually an absence of information. It is the difference between what you know and what you need to know to perform a certain task. Today's business environment is characterized by a high degree of uncertainty, both internal and external to the organization. Equivocality is a related measure of communication but refers to the existence of multiple interpretations of what is going on. A situation has high equivocality when everyone thinks something different is going on. Daft and Lengel's contribution to our thinking is that they feel particular organizational structures can help solve communication problems in this 2 × 2 framework of information requirements.

For example, in a situation of high uncertainty and high equivocality, people tend to gather data and constantly negotiate the meaning of the data. This requires a rich media environment and a high degree of face-to-face contact—a team structure. At the other extreme, a situation with low uncertainty and low equivocality would be characterized by routine collection of objective data and numerous formal reports—a traditional hierarchical structure. The point is that there is a basis for designing organizations consistent with what they need to do with information. Therefore, an organization's environment, its information-processing needs, and technology provide some design guidance for the practitioner.

NEW MODELS OF TECHNOLOGY AND ORGANIZATIONAL IMPACT

As you have seen, the traditional academic literature looks at technology impacts in a linear, causal fashion. It views technology as a cause of structural modification in large, complex organizations. A focus on such issues as complexity, size, and degree of formalization is the typical approach. This analytic paradigm has served us well in the past. However, it is our belief that fundamentally different forms of organizations are now being created in an evolutionary climate. Analytic paradigms are no longer adequate for us to understand the ecology of interaction in organizations.

In Chapters 3 and 5, we proposed that modern organizations can best be understood in terms of their internal information-flow patterns. Further, we have outlined a model of those flows, based on Bennett's work, to analyze these properties. At this point, we would like to take that approach one step further and move into the realm of the organizational design practitioner. What intellectual tools, what mental models can you use when you are called in to consult and advise a client who is experiencing organizational change?

A New Way of Looking at Organizations

We believe an effective, simplifying heuristic is to view organizations as containing three levels—or, more appropriately, spheres—of work. In the activity level, products, or services, are produced and distributed. In the administrative level, different activities are coordinated. In the policy level, general direction is set. These spheres of influence roughly correspond to direction (policy), distinction (administration), and definition (activity), which can be mapped to the Bennett model.

Each of these spheres has a core issue, a characteristic set of processes, and a system of organizing. These processes and systems form unique patterns of action and

		ACTIVITY	ADMINISTRATION	POLICY
C O R E	**I S S U E**	WHAT EFFICIENCY RESOURCES TOOLS COMPLETION	HOW CONTROL METHODS STATUS QUO SURVIVAL	WHY EFFECTIVENESS THEORY CREATION RENEWAL
	P R O C E S S	PRESENT FAST COOPERATION	PAST TRANSLATION COORDINATION	FUTURE SLOW COLLABORATION
	S Y S T E M	FACTS "INTRA" INFORMAL NETWORK	RULES "INTER" FORMAL NETWORK	CONTEXT EXTERNAL "META" NETWORK
	P A T T E R N	CIRCULAR TEAMING HETERARCHY	VERTICAL TASK-FORCE HIERARCHY	HORIZONTAL FAMILY MOLECULE
O P T I M U M	**F U N C T I O N**	ACTIVATING ANALYSIS FUNCTION WORK	NURTURANCE RESTRAINING BEING HEART	UNIFY HARMONY SYNTHESIS WILL SPIRIT
	T O O L S	PRODUCTIVITY TOOLS WORDS NUMBERS GRAPHS	DATABASE PUBLISHING COMMUNICATION WORKGROUP	MODELS SIMULATION EXTERNAL LINKS ENTERPRISE

Figure 6-1. *Organizational Level Functions*

have optimal functions associated with them. Further, each sphere has a set of communication tools that most effectively promotes its functioning.

Figure 6-1 is a diagram of the relationship of the two factors—sphere of work and defining characteristics. We believe this simple model provides an organizational map that the practitioner can use in organizational design. Before discussing each block within the model, let's look a little more closely at the spheres of work.

The basic trend in organizations today is to decrease the number of hierarchical levels of power relationships. The three spheres of work—activity, administration, and policy—represent a minimum set of necessary levels of an organization in the traditional sense. Executives set policy, middle managers coordinate action, and nonmanagement people do the "work" of the enterprise. The first step in a technology-impact analysis is to understand where you are in the organization—within what sphere of work. You can best do this by looking at the core issue of your client organization.

Core Issues

The core issue for the activity sphere is, "What are we doing?" These people are concerned about efficiency, resources, and getting things completed. Administrators are concerned with, "How will we get it done?" They are characterized by control issues, methods of work, and maintaining the status quo. Administrators are interested in survival. Policy makers look at the question, "Why are we doing this?" Their concerns center around issues of effectiveness, creation of new abilities for the organization, and renewal.

Process

Activity is about the present, is fast paced, and looks for cooperation.[21] Administrators, on the other hand, engage in a work process that looks to the past for guidance, translates information from policy into activity direction, and tries to coordinate activities. Policy makers look to the future, are usually slow to react, and foster a sense of collaboration.

System

Activity systems are based on facts—knowable and observable. Within this system, group communications are key; the informal social network manages power and status relations. The next sphere (administration) works from historically based rules, across-group communication occupies most of the time, and the formal network structure is used to shape behaviors. At the policy level, systems center on the context of linking the organization to larger wholes, such as communities and markets. The "meta" network of business and professional associations or community service dominates.

Pattern

The basic pattern of action at the activity level is circular, with people being organized as teams with hierarchical (network) power structures. Examples are the sports team, military platoon, religious diocese. Administrators tend to organize around vertical power dimensions, group into cross-disciplinary task forces, and rely on hierarchy to establish order. Policy makers form up around horizontal principles with equality a goal. The ideal type here is the family or kinship model, which seems to be emerging into a molecular formation.

Optimal Function

The optimal function of the activity sphere is action, or initiating action; it is very functional. Administration is a restraining force that tends to impede action but is concerned with nurturance. The policy sphere functions to unify the others, activating and restraining forces through a process of reconciliation, of looking for synthesis. This level is the spirit of the business enterprise.

Tools

Productivity tools are found most prevalent at the activity within the activity sphere. Examples are software products that manipulate numbers, words, and graphs. Administration uses databases and boundary-spanning communication tools, such as electronic mail. Policy makers use modeling and simulation tools emphasizing linkages across organizational boundaries.

Conclusion

The basic conclusion that we draw from this heuristic is that you must design communication technologies to fit the needs of the organizational unit you are serving. The needs will differ depending on core issue, process, systems, patterns, and function. We offer this template as a diagnostic tool for the practitioner to begin analyzing the requirements of the organization. A modeling-tool package is almost useless at the activity level. The kind of communication tool needed to support the informal social network and that required for the formal structure would vary greatly. You need to understand the environment you are operating in before you begin the technology design or implementation process.

THE FUTURE

As we hope is clear, the equation is much more complex than merely using a technology to improve organizational efficiency. We believe that a fundamental shift, equal in scope to the industrial revolution, is occurring. While such technologies as E-mail and voice-mail systems may first help people do what they do faster and with increased precision, the ultimate impact is unintended. For example, Finholt and Sproull (1990) report that electronic groups actually can foster group identity and playfulness within the work environment. This seems to fly in the face of conventional wisdom that electronic communication *always* inhibits social interaction.

Modern communication technologies are more than things—they are artifacts of our culture.[22] They have the power to redefine social roles in the workplace, home, and community. Ultimately, they also have the potential to redefine political-power relationships across large boundaries. The dramatic change in the relationship between the United States and Japan can be traced in large part to the Japanese development of tighter communication networks after World War II.

On the forefront of this shift is the arrival of teleworking and telecommuting. This is much more than shifting the location of physical work—it is a driver of community change. Our research indicates that people who engage in this new way of working find increased satisfaction with everyday life, offer more service to their communities, and experience less stress. Our vision of future impacts of technology on work organization centers on the emergence of electronically distributed work communities.

Electronically-Distributed Work Communities

Whereas the industrial revolution attracted workers away from home-based community settings to central locations, the current proliferation of personal computers and asynchronous telecommunication technologies is reversing the trend. A new brand of work, termed telework, is emerging that allows employees to utilize electronic communication for working in locations away from a central office, often from their own homes. Evidence suggests that the trend toward incorporating telework into organizational policy is escalating due to the pressures of urban gridlock, unavailable housing, national fuel shortages, and clean-air legislation. This escalation is resulting in a radically different type of work community.

One of the greatest influences on work life was this attraction of workers to central sites away from home-based communities. In contrast, during the information revolution, one of the more significant influences on work life was the distribution of work over time and space (Hiltz & Turoff, 1978). Now, with the proliferation of personal computers and asynchronous communication technologies, the process has come full circle. Technologies supportive of a new work style—a style some have referred to as telework[23]—are providing the mechanism to distribute the work community away from centralized locations and in many cases back into the home. Although the diffusion of these technologies is in its infancy (Kraut, 1987), there is ample evidence to suggest their increasing acceptance. It is our contention that technologies that distribute work communities back into the home will have a substantive impact on the work life of the employees who use them and on communication patterns in the organizations in which they are incorporated.

Distributed Work Communities

Organizations are changing form, driven by a variety of environmental pressures (Applegate, Cash, and Mills, 1988; Drucker, 1988). As researchers have sought to understand the influence of this change on how employees work together (Conrath, 1973; Daft and Lengel, 1986; Markus and Robey, 1988), they have focused on physically co-located employees engaged in productive action.

It is this—physical co-location of organizational members—that is changing, however. Forces are causing companies to distribute their resources as they move production capacities from expensive, high-rent locations to more cost-efficient sites. At the same time, new communication and information management technologies are evolving to facilitate the distribution of information-processing abilities. Whereas the computing facilities of ten to fifteen years past resided in highly centralized environments, the evolution of computer technology in organizations today is creating a structure in which computing power is shared among the nodes of local-area and wide-area networks, a structure in which the "network is the computer" (Verity, 1990).

This distribution of computer power is also facilitating the distribution of work activities among people across time and space (Johansen, 1988, 1990). Electronic mail, computer bulletin boards, teleconferencing, voice mail, and facsimile machines, to name a few, are emerging technologies that dissolve the barriers imposed by geographic distance (Hiltz and Turoff, 1978) and temporal separation (Huff, Sproull, and Kiesler, 1989). Organizations are transforming from highly consolidated centers into what Kling (Kling, 1987; Kling and Scacchi, 1982) referred to as the "web organization." The recent development of interest in computer-supported cooperative work (e.g., Johansen, 1990) is another manifestation of the trend toward the increased mediation of human communication by computer systems in web organizations.

A natural extension of these technologies has also allowed the residence to become a remote site for work. In this sense, the trend toward increasing spatial and temporal separation of home, community, and workplace is being reversed (Mokhtar-ian, 1990), as is the breakdown in community organization that was brought about by separation of home and workplace (Fisher et al., 1977). Furthermore, as the cost-benefit ratio for relying on telework shifts due to precipitous drops in computer costs and soaring increases in energy and housing, more people will be substituting electronic movement of information for physical movement of themselves.

As the work community becomes distributed across offices and into the home, the social psychology of people's relationships to the distributing technology needs to be better understood. Previous research, for example, has indicated that computer mediation of interpersonal interaction can change group structure and affect the decision-making process of the group (Rice, 1984). We contend that technologies supporting electronically distributed work will create further changes and will radically alter patterns of interaction among workers, especially as the "web" of the organization extends into the home. Computer-based systems of communication are socially complex (Kling, 1987), and there are many important issues that require basic scientific investigation (Attewell and Rule, 1984).

The History of Telework

Some segment of the population has always been involved in work away from a central location. These people have typically been home-based entrepreneurs, site-independent professionals, individuals with disabilities, or those who work at home to save on child-care costs. Many white-collar workers have used the home to supplement their office work, either to finish work started at the office or to earn additional income.

During the energy crisis of the mid-1970s, commuters were confronted with the prohibitive costs of traveling by car to and from work over long distances. In response, some high-technology organizations began allowing their employees to access their computers from home via remote terminals over telephone lines. This practice led to a particular brand of home work termed "telecommuting" (coined by Nilles et al., 1976). The early promise of telecommuting led some to propose a vision of the future in which large numbers of employees routinely elected to remain at home full time, conducting the affairs of their work remotely from their own "electronic cottage" (Toffler, 1980).

During the 1980s, several companies experimented with the concept of telecommuting in the form of pilot programs, informal endorsements, and formal policy changes. IBM, for example, initiated a program to supply its employees with computer hardware for use in supplementing their office work with work at home. Early evaluations of the programs[24] indicated that participants felt generally positive toward the notion of using computers at home and many expressed a desire to use the technology more than they had.

Not all programs met with employee approval, however. Some were initiated to cut company costs by offering home workers lower pay in exchange for the "privilege" of working at home. In an atmosphere of exploitation, unions soon became involved in fighting the concept of telecommuting and were instrumental in limiting its practice among low-skilled clerical staff. Other sociotechnical obstacles were also encountered in the widespread acceptance of telecommuting. Managers balked at not being able to see their supervisees directly and reported a loss of control over employees' productivity. Teleworkers themselves complained that staying at home for extensive periods of time deprived them of desired social contact and informal communication with their colleagues.

In spite of these obstacles, telework has continued to evolve as an attractive alternative to office work for at least some people, and the concept is expanding to be more than just calling the office from home on occasion. In part, this evolution has been facilitated by the development of cost-effective computer communications that, when coupled with rising transportation costs, have encouraged people to substitute movement of electronic communication for movement of themselves (Mokhtarian, 1990). In fact, among the high-tech companies of California's Silicon Valley where traffic congestion is endemic, informal approval of telecommuting is necessary to attract and retain many talented employees (Olson, 1987). As an added incentive, companies in many regions (especially in California) are receiving pressure from air-quality management legislation to permit telecommuting as a viable option for improving air quality (Mokhtarian, 1991).

What appears to be emerging in the diffusion of telecommuting technology, then, is not a wholesale acceptance of full-time home work but an "evolution" toward more flexible organizational structures to permit telework, along with other work options, when needed to meet organizational and employee needs (Pratt, 1984, 1988). This trend is leading to what Gordon (1987) described as the emergence of "hybrid" organizations designed to support changes in lifestyle and to meet multiple member needs. There is some evidence (Handy, 1989) that this trend toward new organizational forms is already occurring. Handy describes several alternative forms of working (i.e., the shamrock,[25] federal,[26] and triple-I[27]) that are being adopted in the United Kingdom that allow workers and managers to be increasingly separated in time and space.

The flexibility inherent in the structure of hybrid organizations allow companies to adapt to changing environmental and social demands. It was the use of flexible work strategies and telecommuting in the San Francisco Bay Area, for example, that minimized the impact of massive traffic congestion following the collapse of the Bay Bridge and Oakland Cypress Structure during the Loma Prieta earthquake of 1989

(Furger, 1989; Langberg, 1989; Levander, 1989; O'Connor, 1989; Siegel, 1990). Computer industry experts (Saffo, 1991) predict that telework would provide an opportunity "for entirely new kinds of companies to emerge, with distributed business structures uniquely suited to the opportunities presented by telecommuting infrastructures." We believe that this confluence of forces provides a special research opportunity to examine empirically an organizational form in its development.

What We Know About Telework

A significant portion of research in the area of telework has taken the form of descriptive research concerning the demographics of the telecommuting work force or development of telecommuting managerial policies. In an extensive review of that literature, Kraut (1989) reported that motives for telecommuting varied widely and that the individual effects of working away from the traditional office varied as a function of job classification and perceived economic tradeoffs. From this research, we know that overall more men than women work at home, principally because they use the home for part-time work or overtime work related to a primary job, while more women work at home to the exclusion of all other employment (Pratt, 1988). In terms of job engineering, we know that high-skill, high-status professional telecommuting jobs have been designed to enhance employee satisfaction; while low-skill, low-status clerical jobs are offered to cut overhead and labor costs and often disregard issues of employee morale (Tomaskovic-Devey and Risman, 1988).

Empirical research on the social-psychological aspects of telecommuting, however, are more suggestive than conclusive. Most studies claim that teleworkers are generally satisfied with working away from the office, and a few have made claims that telecommuting boosts productivity. It must be remembered, though, that most of this research was conducted on volunteers in telecommuting pilot programs for whom satisfaction would be expected, given the self-selected nature of the sample and the novelty of the program. At least one study suggested that full-time telecommuters are at risk of feeling socially isolated and experiencing job burnout. Although another study reported similar feelings of isolation among participants in informal telecommuting programs, it also reported that on some occasions telework actually *improved* employees' coworker relationships (see Olson, 1987). This latter study did not reach conclusions on why the effect would occur and for what kinds of employees, however, and typifies the incompleteness of the early literature.

There is evidence that telecommuters are selective in the type of work they do at home versus the type of work they do at the office, with work in the office made up of social, interpersonal tasks (meetings, interviews, etc.) and work at home reserved for purely cognitive functions. Data supporting that notion suggest that employees communicate face-to-face and by telephone more in the office than at home. This is not say that employees who work at home do not communicate with their colleagues, however. The same data indicate that employees who work at home communicate more by electronic mail than by other channels. Thus, employees are still fulfilling communication needs but are doing so in another, more controlled and asynchronous, channel.

In sum, little is understood about the social-psychological impacts of telecommuting as a substitute for work conducted in a typical business setting. Most survey samples have been taken from employees already in telecommuting programs and suffer from self-selection biases. Important questions need to be answered concerning selection of appropriate employees for distributed work, work-task selection, and management controls. Of particular concern to managers is the effect telework has on employee morale and the change in informal interaction patterns in the work environment. Closely coupled with these concerns are questions about power/status relationship changes between employers and supervisors and among the social network of employees themselves. Tomaskovic-Devey and Risman (1988) report that managers' fear of losing control has the paradoxical effect of limiting telecommuting options for clerical staff while increasing telework options for professionals.

The emergence of telework, we believe, is the first evidence of a changing work environment that has profound social implications. It is the manifestation of the "atomization of the economy" first predicted by Birch (1987). The impact is not so much on existing forms of organization but on the emergence of new structures of working social networks (Taylor and Katambwe, 1988). The major gap we find in the literature is an understanding of the intervening relationships between telecommuting technologies, attitudes, and behaviors within the context of newly emerging organizational structures, structures made up of a flexible mixture of office and home work environments. We suspect that a balance between task orientation and the socioemotional aspects of workplace interaction is being significantly shifted by adoption of telework technologies in American government and business.

Motivation to Use Telework

We believe that the substitution of telework for office work is a strategy used by employees primarily to cope with life stresses such as those posed by childcare problems, traffic congestion, and other emergencies, but secondarily to control access to the self, a process referred to as privacy regulation. The former set of motivations has already been explored in the descriptive literature on telecommuting; the latter, best described by Altman (1975), refers to the tendency of individuals to seek privacy when social stimulation is disruptive and, conversely, to seek social stimulation when privacy is undesirable. We contend that the principles of privacy regulation aptly apply to individuals who use telecommuting technologies, especially asynchronous messaging facilities such as E-mail and voice mail, as tools for controlling social input. That is to say, apart from coping with external pressures, employees will use telecommuting as a way of giving themselves privacy when they wish to be alone and their needs for affiliation are low.

Satisfaction with Telework

We contend that an employee's satisfaction with telework is dependent on perceptions of self-efficacy regarding the technologies. As described by Bandura (1977), individuals maintain personal perceptions of their own abilities to carry out actions, termed percepts of self-efficacy. They match those perceptions against the probability of a positive response from the environment for successfully completed actions. Specific emotional responses are elicited by the manner in which percepts of self-efficacy are matched against environmental expectations as illustrated in Figure 6-2.

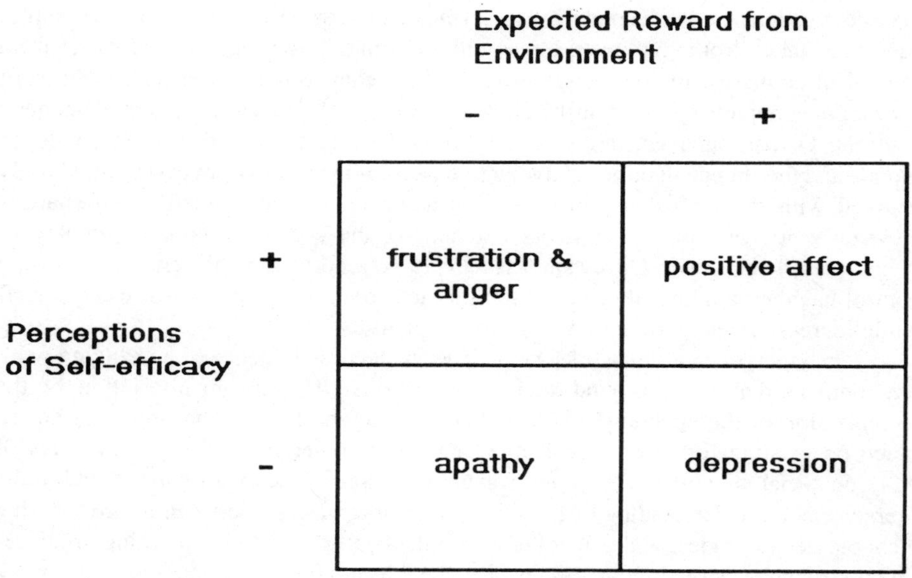

**Expected Reward from
Environment**

	−	+
+	frustration & anger	positive affect
−	apathy	depression

**Perceptions
of Self-efficacy**

Figure 6-2. Self-efficacy

From the figure, many of the self-selected telecommuters who reported satisfaction in previous studies undoubtedly fell into a category of feeling confident in their own abilities to perform work at home *and* expected positive recognition from the organizational environment (the upper right cell). On the other hand, indignation felt by exploited clerical staff was probably the result of a clash between feelings of self-efficacy ("I can work at home successfully") and a recognized lack of reward or selective punishment from management ("I am being paid less and respected less by my supervisors," the upper left cell). Cases not reported in the literature but possibly just as disruptive are instances of lowered self-esteem for individuals who recognize that they could be rewarded for telework but do not have the wherewithal (self-management skills, equipment, computer savvy) to work successfully in an electronically distributed community (the lower right cell). Finally, the more ubiquitous case has to be the one for which telework is simply not an issue: the employees don't know how to make telecommuting work for their job, and even if they did, it would not be supported by management anyway (the lower left cell).

The work of Bandura and others points to a solid linkage from perception of efficacy and control to employee satisfaction. Roskies, Liker, and Roitman (1988) reported from qualitative interviews (N = 60) that confidence in one's ability to control new technologies differentiated those who perceived themselves to be "winners" or "losers" in the technological-change process. A similar tradition exists within sociology in the form of an interactional theory of emotional states (Kemper, 1978). This perspective has not been extended to a work environment. It appears that these two traditions of research (those of Bandura and Kemper) intersect around the issue of self-perception of efficacy (Bandura) and power/status relationships (Kemper).

Temporal Aspects of Employee Behavior

Relying on a perspective outlined previously by one of the authors (Hesse, Werner, and Altman, 1988), we expect that telework will have a specific impact on the temporal qualities of workflow and communication. In particular, we anticipate that one effect of using asynchronous technologies away from the office will be to decrease variability in the duration and frequency of communication behaviors. Social interaction in the office primarily takes the form of face-to-face communication, is frequently spontaneous, is cued by chance encounters, and is influenced by nonverbal dominance/submissiveness cues. In the absence of these characteristics, we expect that communications among teleworkers will appear more planned and regulated and will tend to be more uniform in scope. We also expect that because cognitive-task demands in relation to social coordination demands fluctuate near deadlines (Gersick, 1988), the frequency of staying home to complete a task for part-time telecommuters will vary across the phases of a project's life.

Communication Patterns

Research in the area of computer-mediated communication has a lot to offer for understanding the impact of telecommuting technologies on employee behavior. At the interpersonal level, data suggest that as communication becomes restricted to a textual channel (as when communicating via E-mail), it loses important nonverbal and contextual information, frequently resulting in disinhibited behavior. In some contexts, this disinhibition may lead to more candid communication, but in the context of a frustrating event (e.g., Hesse, 1989), may lead to aggressive interpersonal responding (see also Kiesler et al., 1985). At the organizational level, computer-mediated networks influence decision making by giving greater voice to minority input (Siegel et al., in press) and by promoting upward communication of negative information (Sproull and Kiesler, 1986).

Those technologies that rely on computer mediation should have the effect of increasing input from peripheral and otherwise isolated members. Assuming from the literature that teleworkers are themselves susceptible to isolation, we would expect that teleworkers who effectively use asynchronous technologies should communicate more effectively within the organization. We should also expect that those individuals who prefer an introverted work style will express greater satisfaction from using asynchronous technologies than those who have an extroverted work style. This anticipated effect should help to clarify the earlier, mixed findings on differential benefit from telecommuting. Finally, we would expect that the content of electronically mediated communication, in general, will be more candid and will convey more negative information upward through hierarchies, with either beneficial or detrimental results depending on the circumstances.

Organizational Effectiveness

The organizational-effectiveness literature points to technology being viewed as a central intervening force linking attitudes and behavior within the firm. Recent theoretical work (Huber, 1990) posited that availability, and access to, advanced communication technologies creates increased information accessibility, leading to changes in organizational design (structure) and ultimately to improvements in effectiveness of the firm in terms of intelligence development and decision-making capability. Also, Burkhardt and Brass (1990) found in an empirical study of technology diffusion that rates of adoption of new computer-mediated communications technologies led to status and power differentials emerging as a function of rate of adoption and positions of end-users in their business-based social networks.

Further, we find that managerial competence and perceptions of control were reported to be intervening variables between employee characteristics and job performance (Storey, 1987). Similarly, from pilot work performed by one of the authors (Grantham, 1991), we know that managers' acceptance of telecommuting was related to perceptions of control over subordinates' work. Applying the model of self-efficacy, managers who feel self-efficacious in their ability to manage telecommuters and to use the technologies themselves (even from the office, rather than from home) will be more effective managers of teleworkers in the long run. Imagine a scenario where an employee stays home to work but is unreachable because all he or she has is a telephone that is always busy. In such a case, if the manager has no other channel for reaching the employee, a breakdown in communication would be expected to subvert the manager's sense of control and effectiveness and would ultimately reduce both the manager's and employee's productivity. In another scenario, the effective use of an asynchronous communication channel—electronic mail, a facsimile machine, even call waiting—would be enough to facilitate the supervisor's sense of managerial efficacy and to avert frustration.

Conclusion

In short, we believe that developing an understanding of how electronically-distributed–work communities will influence aspects of employees' work lives and the effectiveness of the organizations to which they belong is an important issue for organizational designers as well as technologists. We outlined several areas that we felt would contribute to this goal. First, we applied the concept of privacy regulation—a theory suggesting that individuals control access to the self by alternately blocking and inviting social stimulation—to understand when it is that employees feel motivated to use telecommuting as a work option. Second, we suggested that employees' satisfactions with telework is dependent on perceptions of self-efficacy in using the related technologies. Third, we proposed that the use of telecommuting will lead to changes in temporal aspects of employee behavior, specifically in the frequency and duration of communication. Fourth, we predicted that asynchronous communications technologies, such as electronic mail, would help telecommuters feel less isolated and would stimulate input. Fifth, we posited that the effectiveness of an organization implementing telecommuting as a policy is largely dependent upon its ability to encourage the use of appropriate communications channels among its members.

This is perhaps one of the most exciting aspects of developing organizational change. We are beginning to see public policy being formulated on the premise that telework is an emerging viable option to increase American competitiveness. In California, where environmental quality is a highly-charged political issue, local government regulation now levies fines on large corporations that do not incorporate some of these alternative ways of working into their normal business operations.[28] The use of technology to promote the growth of alternative organizational forms has moved beyond the boardroom decision-makers and entered the halls of community governments, state legislatures, and finally Capitol Hill. This is a very exciting area for practitioners to become involved in, over the next few years. But only if they approach it from a sound understanding of how technology influences organizational self-design, and with a clear model of the intervention strategy they will employ.

Enough of our predictions for the future. Let us now turn to a case study in which we applied the ideas outlined here to help a senior manager make a major decision about restructuring a large information-systems–development organization.

CASE STUDY

Background

This case involves a large telecommunication company whose executives wished to make it more responsive to a changing environment with more competitive pressure. It was clear for some time (three to five years) that the current bureaucratic, hierarchical organizational form wasn't working. Customer satisfaction was slipping, morale was low, and time to complete projects was out of control.

One of the chief executives commissioned an organizational-design group to prepare a series of alternative organizational forms that would increase the responsiveness of his software-development function, while maintaining tight cost control and promoting the use of new, developing technologies. The team was composed of 15 people with expertise in organizational design, systems theory, software development, and systems analysis. The study took approximately six months to complete and was conducted in relative secrecy to avoid creating adverse organizational-climate conditions.

It was envisioned that the "ideal software factory" would be more than a production house. It would be a grouping of teams that are both independent and interdependent. The high-performance team we had in mind can be likened to a sports team, more specifically, a basketball team. This metaphor was very apt because it symbolized a highly integrated, interdependent work unit with a single purpose but a multiplicity of roles for every member. No prima donnas, only team players sacrificing individual status for team purpose.[29]

Intervention Strategy

Our strategy was to play the role of staff advisor with no particular self-interest in mind. However, that proved to be difficult because this was an internal intervention. We attempted to use the current metaphors of change evident elsewhere in the organization, thus adapting to the corporate culture as it existed. What follows is excerpted from the draft planning documents, with changes made to preserve the anonymity of the client.

Tracing out a path to get from here to there is really that—tracing out a path. We attempt to set a compass direction in this section, not outline each step along the way. We assume that change is a process and that there are many paths to the same goal. We propose starting out in a general direction with constant awareness of the need to assess progress and redirect trajectory as dictated by internal and external environment influences.

Our plan for getting us there is intended as an architectural rendering. The picture isn't fully colored in, yet. We have some paints and brushes and a piece of canvas in front of us. However, we need to work together to give shape, substance, and color to the final picture. The one fact we feel quite certain of is that it will be the group of artists who bring this idea into being. It will be the people, with their diverse values, interests, and abilities, that will make the Software Company be born. No set of tools, administrative procedures, or structures will make it happen—it will be the souls of those who come together in the spirit of creative activity that will be the key.

Whatever option, if any, is finally chosen, it will be necessary to more completely sketch out this vision before any action takes place. There can be no rush to judgment with an effort of this magnitude. A time of clear and orderly thinking will be needed. The value of first developing capability before action needs to be exploited. With these caveats in mind, we now try to outline a path forward to achieve the goal of developing a new software development organization for Waldo Corp. that will make us a viable, profitable, world-class telecommunications entity.

Our orientation to designing "a way to get there" is sociotechnical. The sociotechnical perspective on fostering organization change was developed at the Tavistock Institute in the 1950s as an outgrowth of the Human Relations movement within organizational theory. The basic tenet of this perspective is that people can only come to realize their full human potential within organizational work structures when they realize that both technology and social factors co-evolve and recursively influence each other.

This perspective is particularly relevant in a software development organization because the people in the work setting are *planning, designing,* and *creating* technological tools for others to use. We believe that the new *development group* will not just improve the way people build software, but will also alter the way in which people work in Waldo Corp. When tool or technology begins to alter this basic fabric of the workplace, we must adopt a particular sensitivity to the interaction between technology and sociology: this is the sociotechnical approach.

People don't voluntarily change their behavior (especially if work-related) unless they can find some personal value in the change. Cognitive anthropology tells us that work imparts life meaning to people. When you begin to shift that meaning, there must be a motivation attached to it so that people can personally answer the question, "What's in it for me?" Just as you cannot legislate attitudes, you cannot impose change in cognitive meaning by management dictate. Change takes time, is intertwined with the other parts of a person's life, and must facilitate growth, or it won't be successful.

More importantly, movement from one stage to another is not a discrete, step-function process. There is a transition between each of the stages that has many bumps in the rug. You can't engineer movement from one stage to another in lockstep for everyone in the process. William Bridges (1988) maintains that the transition is the key thought here. What we need to do is to manage the transition from one stage to another. Ending one stage to begin another is difficult. Kubler-Ross outlines a series of steps common to people's emotional experience of change: denial, anger, bargaining, and acceptance. People can be expected to go through this same series of emotional events when change comes to the workplace. Therefore, introducing change requires an understanding and empathy towards this experience. We need to recognize that it is going to happen and some will move through it faster than others; some will never complete the transition from one place to another.

Recommended Solutions and Rationale

The teams' suggested solutions were prepared in the form of suggested alternatives and rank-ordered according to a process of examining critical factors. Although this approach appears to be overly simple and analytical, it was chosen to keep within the bounds of existing decision-making processes.

Comparison of Alternatives

The above discussion of critical-success factors serves to isolate those few character-istics of a software-development organization that can be evaluated to ascertain likelihood of acceptance or failure of the endeavor. These factors are people, teamwork, work structure, leadership, management system, and transferability. In addition, there is a cultural view of the workscape that can be shown to be associated with successful high productivity organizations. Even if all critical-success factors are complied with, an attempt to build a new, evolving, high-productivity culture can quickly die if the culture does not have characteristics of legibility, coherence, and open-endedness.

In preparing this analysis, we have examined a number of possible options for implementing a high-productivity software-development organization within the Waldo Corp. information systems community. We have sought out options in terms of change management strategies and past experience we have had with change such as the Total Quality Management process. Although our list of options is not exhaustive, we believe it represents a sufficient range of options to point us in a direction for change—in short, a specification of direction.

We feel that there are six basic structural options, as follows:

- *Business Atom:* A small, self-contained business unit with shared values, displaying relative autonomy. It focuses on external customers, virtually self-contained resources, has control over internal allocation, and is accountable based on profitability. The ideal is very close to an independent business unit, but still maintains a concept of holographic identity with the parent organization. It does not incorporate the idea of "management boards" or deliberately structured output feedback loops.
- *Gradual Shift:* This concept centers around the overall movement of the entire Waldo Corp. IS community to new methods, ways, and practices of developing software. Everything moves at once through the use of wide-based training, redeployment of key personnel across existing organizational lines, and new efforts at all levels of management to coordinate and systematize software-development processes.

- *Component Move:* In this view of change to the ideal end-state, discrete components of the process are shifted in different parts of the organization at different times. For example, an effort to standardize the way in which requirements analysis is done would be sponsored by a change agent. At some later time, the same change process would be implemented with Quality Assurance and on and on until the entire community had shifted its way of developing software in all critical aspects of people, work, technology, and management.
- *One-Group Trial:* This is a classic organization-development strategy. One existing group within Waldo Corp. would be chosen to begin developing software in a new fashion. The entire group would be trained, coached, and evaluated as a "test case" of the efficacy of the new methodology. The group would remain within the existing organizational context and be closely monitored. Results would be in terms of pre/post comparison of past performance to current.
- *New Group:* In this scenario, a new group is constructed—from the ground up—by selecting and redeploying assets throughout the company to a new reporting structure and unit. This option poses great administrative difficulties in implementation. The group would be carefully "architected" and would be focused on output products, not process.
- *Subsidiary of Waldo Corp.:* This option would entail the construction of a new independent business unit of Waldo Corp. to develop and build software for use by Waldo Corp. It would essentially be structured the way any normal, unregulated business would be. It would be a venture-capital approach using Waldo Corp. as a seedbed.

Analysis

Figure 6-3 displays the structural alternative against the critical success factors (CSF) we have identified. The ratings are categorical in terms of our evaluation of high, medium, or low congruence of the alternatives to selected CSFs. We will briefly discuss each model before presenting a recommendation.

The Business Atom concept shows high chances of success on the dimensions of people, teamwork, leadership, and transferability. Basically, this is due to its ability to select, train, and reward people in any way that is effective; it could build upon success without causing the baggage of past organizational failures. However, the Business Atom's ability to structure internal work is seen as medium in mapping to our ideal model. Its focus on external customers may make it more driven to production of software that meets immediate needs and sacrifices long-term viability. This same point gives the Business Atom a medium management-system rating, basically due to its lack of management boards.

The Gradual Shift strategy shows a low rating in almost all categories. This model of change would be very slow and pretty much mimic past attempts at unifying and systematizing software-development efforts within Waldo Corp. The major impediment in the Gradual Shift is the continued existence of current organizational problems and lack of standards across functional organizations. In fairness, however, this shift strategy would probably be the easiest to digest because of the slow pace. Component Movement shows many of the same characteristics as the Gradual Shift

	People	Teamwork	Work Structure	Leadership	Management Systems	Transfer-ability
Business Atom	H	H	M	H	M	H
Gradual Shift	L	L	L	L	L	M
Component Move	L	M	L	L	L	M
One Group Trial	H	M	M	M	L	L
New Group	H	H	H	H	H	H
Subsidary	M	H	H	H	M	M

Figure 6-3.   *Critical Success Factors*

because it is, in essence, a discrete-entity model of change. Production processes are changed and emphasized in this model; thus its ability to deal with specific "people" issues of high productivity are not well addressed. This is the robot approach—plug them in on the assembly line and, eventually, the whole will have changed. The major problem here is the lack of attention paid to integration across components of the software-development process.

A One-Group Trial approach has a lot of intuitive appeal. It ranks high on the people CSF because it would offer new opportunities and attention to its members. The medium ratings on the other dimensions come from some realization of the Hawthorne effect. The closest analogy to this model is the current *Brightstar* project. The lack of high rankings on the CSFs stems from the necessity to still totally embed this group within an existing administrative structure (i.e., performance evaluation, training, office space, etc.). So, even though a trial might be conducted, it would be tethered to the Waldo Corp. system via an administration umbilical cord.

Constructing a New Group within Waldo Corp. shows uniformly high ratings in all categories. Other examples exist of this tactic proving successful when you want to fundamentally shift how things are produced and accomplish the goal in relatively short timeframes. The Macintosh Group in Apple is the classic example. Although the freedom to experiment with structure to promote productivity is necessary to obtain CSFs, it does have a potential downside that is immediately apparent. We have rated this approach as being high on the transferability scale, but realize that there can be a danger in being too unique, different, or away from the pack. The corporate immune system could attack with a vengeance. We still evaluate this potential as high, given the visible upper-management support for the overall vision of a new software development paradigm in Waldo Corp.

The last option we analyzed was the scenario of building a subsidiary company of Waldo Corp. to accomplish the function of software development. This approach is being adopted within Ameritech in centralizing all development at the corporate level by combining resources from the telecommunications industry. This option has high potential in terms of teamwork, work structure, and leadership largely because it could build from the ground up, similar to the Business Atom or the New Group in Waldo Corp.

However, we rated its ability to deal with the people issue somewhat lower, because it would be structurally distinct from the people who would use the products it developed. In a similar vein, separation across a corporate boundary to the unregulated part of the business would incur some looseness in management-system coupling (feedback loops) and pose problems later on in terms of transferability back into the mainstream of Waldo Corp. business.

When we consider all the comments together, it quickly emerges that three of the six options demonstrate relatively high chances of success, if their implementation is carefully evaluated and tracked: the Business Atom, New Group in Waldo Corp., and the Waldo Corp. Subsidiary. In order to isolate one of these, we need to consider each of them in light of the criteria we have chosen to describe a culture of high productivity (i.e., legibility, coherence, and open-endedness).[30]

None of the options varies in terms of its legibility of workscape because all three have the potential to construct themselves in whatever image they want. Coherence here refers to a mapping or close cultural coupling with the parent organization and the users of the developed software. In this dimension, the New Group emerges as distinctly different from the other options. A Business Atom would be a separate company within Waldo Corp., and the Waldo Corp. option would be very similar outside the company.

Therefore, the New Group promotes more coherence with the culture in which its products will be embedded: Waldo Corp.'s Information Systems. On the other hand, in terms of open-endedness, the New Group is at a disadvantage compared with the other options. Growth, change, and evolution are more difficult in a constrained environment than in an open one.

Recommendation

Our overall recommendation is that Waldo Corp. adopt the model of constructing a New Group within the existing company to design, develop, and test new methods of software production as detailed in the first section of this book. We feel that this option, at this time, entails the highest chance of success in augmenting the present, existing information-systems structures within the company.

However, we do offer the caution that even though this recommendation poses the greatest chance of success in terms of congruence, it faces a danger of not developing sufficient adaptability to a rapidly changing software-development environment. That is, the gestation of this concept is best done within the womb of Waldo Corp. Later growth and maturity may be best placed in a more open-ended environment.

One last caveat to this recommendation is to identify criteria that may be indicative of the failure of the organization to develop. In a positive vein, the New Group's continued ability to attract top talent and maintain high morale, and the expressed interest of other development groups, would be seen as evidence of success. Alternately, if personnel churn rates become very high, restriction of funding occurs, and excess time is required for administrative tasks (say over 20 percent of the effort), then these could be taken as indicators of impending failure.

Conclusion

We have developed the outlines of an implementation plan in this section of the analysis. We have specified a context within which to bring a new software-development organization to life within Waldo Corp. as being the adoption of the sociotechnical perspective. Further, we have outlined a number of Critical Success Factors that need to be met in order to produce a work culture of high productivity within this organization. We also have detailed a pathway to make this happen, a set of general tactics if you will.

In conclusion, we have analyzed a number of structural options based on our vision of the ideal software-development organization and Critical Success Factors. That analysis, coupled with a cultural-audit view, led us to recommend developing this organization as a new entity within Waldo Corp. We offer a cautionary note that this pathway is optimum at this time, but the inherent dynamics of the software arena beg continued attention to other structural alternatives.

Postmortem Analysis

Executives in Waldo Corp. chose not to implement any organizational changes based on this analysis. There is no rational explanation for this failure to act. In retrospect, the design team was able to garner some information as to why the intervention effort failed—or was not attempted.

The recommendations ultimately presented conflicted with deeply held social values on the part of the company executives. A high value was placed on control, monitoring of activities, and process at the expense of results. The New Group concept was very threatening to the people with power. Empowerment and human-resource development were held as public goals, but when faced with a chance to act on those values, the management team balked and retrenched into the old organizational form. One anecdotal comment from a senior executive was quite telling. "You mean," he asked of the presenting team, "that under this plan I wouldn't be able to walk out my door and see these people working?"

The ultimate secret to success of a new organization will be the people who are brought together to form it. Finding the people with the "right stuff" will be *the* key management task. The right people will undoubtedly be a combination of talents and personality types who blend together with a uniqueness not found in most traditional organizations. A synergy of diverse people will be needed. Hiring the "right stuff" is possible by using competency-based assessment methods (Hendrickson, 1987) and an awful lot of intuition. Management didn't want to bring in proven outside talent, but instead wanted to utilize people with proven success in the old system—risk-adverse and compliance-oriented.

There is no one strategy for successful change management. The best counsel we have received stresses the necessity for fundamental concern for people, constant adaptation, and focus on the power of the context or the cultural surround. Change within existing culture is more difficult than creation of new environments because of the inertia of existing rituals and myths. However, no change takes place totally outside this context; therefore, we need to be very alert to the power of the symbols—or strategies—we choose to use.

The most basic of these attitudes is that change designers are empowering others to change. They are facilitating a process, not making it happen. The old saying that if you give a someone a fish, they can eat today; but if you teach them how to fish, they can feed themselves always is true here also. Change designers are empowering people to change; and change is an ongoing process that will continue even after the designer has moved on.

Building a new organization and spreading this innovation throughout a large corporation can be expected to take on the same general form as any social innovation. The literature on diffusion of innovation is replete with examples from agriculture to office automation in which the adoption of new ways follows a knowable pattern. Change is cumulative over time. It begins slow, is quickly adopted by a few (around 10 to 15 percent), then moves rather quickly through the majority of a social group and finally slows again with the last 15 percent of the population. Technically, this pattern is known as a logistic curve. The point here, however, is that change designers need to focus their effort on the vast majority of people in the middle of the curve who are neither the first to adopt nor the last. The early adopters will change anyway—some may even have to be slowed down (the zealots). And the last, slow-adopting group may never accommodate to change, no matter how much effort is expended.

Realizing that the bedrock key to success will be the human factor, we feel that implementing change in a way that gives maximum support to development of human capability is the right pathway. People will need time to adjust to change, find relevance, and feel secure in their own abilities before they can venture forth into a very dangerous business environment. The soul of the new organization can best be nurtured within the protective shelter of Waldo Corp., where energy is devoted to developing capability. *Then a parting—a letting go—will be required so that a new organization can be born with the capability—and will—to succeed.* It was a realization on the part of upper management of the necessity of this parting that doomed the change effort.

NOTES

1. F. E. Emery and E. Trist (1960), "Socio-technical Systems," in C. Churchman and M. Verhulst (eds.), *Management Science, Models and Techniques.* vol. 2, Pergamon: London.
2. See Scott (1992), Table 9-1.
3. Another view of this effect is to see technology as a socially constructed reality, in which individuals assign meaning to technologies, which in turn influences their selection, use, and valuation. See Sproull and Goodman (1990), "Technology and Organizations: Integration and Opportunities," in Goodman and Sproull, op. cit.
4. Barley (1986), quoted in Burkhardt and Brass (1990).
5. Foster and Flynn (1984).
6. Leifer (1988).
7. Markus and Robey (1988), op. cit.
8. Differences in both ontology and epistemology result. Er (1989) outlines these as ontological differences of whether reality is objective or socially constructed. From an epistemological view, there are positivism and antipositivism, which translates into whether inquiry is for predictive purposes or simply for "understanding." This two-level dichotomy yields at least eight different ways to approach organizational analysis—resulting in eight possible conclusions from the same case, dependent upon your location in this philosophical map.
9. Burkhardt and Brass (1990).
10. See Er (1989), for an extended discussion.
11. Fry (1982).
12. See R. Westrum and K. Samaha (1984), *Complex Organizations: Growth, Struggle and Change,* Prentice-Hall: Englewood Cliffs, NJ.
13. See for example E. Trist, "The Evolution of Sociotechnical Systems as a Conceptual Framework and as an Action Research Program," in A. H. Van de Ven and W. F. Joyce (eds.) (1981), *Perspectives on Organizational Design and Behavior,* Wiley: New York.
14. We would like to thank Professor Ronald Westrum, Eastern Michigan State University, for comments and insights into this process. Specifically, his views as outlined in "The Historical Impact of Communications Technology on Organizations," Working Paper no. 56, *Institute for the Study of Social Change,* Purdue University, 1972. Although this analysis may seem somewhat dated, we are aware of nothing in the current literature that contradicts Westrum's conclusions.
15. We note this trend here because, in our experience, many large organizations have a relative paucity of communication technologies compared with competitors in their sector. Therefore, as communication technologies enter the workplace, they may first serve to centralize control and later begin to permit decentralization.
16. See Table 2-2. Pace of communication is a primary effector of productivity. When pace rises to the level of frequency interuption, productivity declines.
17. This may seem somewhat paradoxical. Huber feels that centralized decision making becomes decentralized and vice versa. As we have seen in the literature review, it is largely a matter of what level of aggregation you choose to look at.
18. Lynda Applegate, J. I. Cash, and D. Q. Mills (1988), *Harvard Business Review,* Nov.–Dec., pp. 128–136.
19. David W. Conrath (1973), "Communications Environment and Its Relationship to Organizational Structure," *Management Science,* vol. 20 (4–11), pp. 586–603.
20. R. L. Daft and R. H. Lengel (1986), "Organizational Information Requirements, Media Richness and Structural Design," *Management Science,* vol. 32 (5), May, pp. 554–571.
21. See Chapter 2, especially Table 2-1, for a more detailed discussion of this difference.
22. That is, they embody our collective perceptions of status, role, and power.

23. Telework has been defined in numerous ways and, in many cases, has been used synonymously with "telecommuting." Mokhtarian (1991) offers the definition we find most cogent in the context of the proposed studies: *work done by an individual while at a different location than the person(s) directly supervising it.*

24. The American Institutes for Research was instrumental in providing some of the early program-evaluation work for IBM (see Rubin, 1982).

25. As described by Handy, the shamrock organization is composed of three parts corresponding to the leaves of the shamrock. The first part is the core of the organization: the essential workers who plan strategy, monitor markets, and oversee production of goods and services. The second part consists of the contract workers and the outsource workers we know today who will make up the bulk of the organization. The third part is made up of the part-time and temporary workers who are brought in as needed. The core part of the organization will remain in the same place, but the rest of the organization can be spread out and connected electronically.

26. The federal organization is a grouping of loosely affiliated companies or groups who bond together for a single purpose. They are all small but leverage their value-adding functions by coming together for specific short-lived projects. The common form today is the general joint venture, but extended to include several companies. This form could turn into the shamrock over time.

27. The triple I organization is more of a philosophy than a structure. It stands for Intelligence, Information, and Ideas multiplied one against the other to yield added value (p. 141). Intellectual property becomes the central economic good. All organizations will begin to realize this and try to capture those workers who are specialists in these fields. Triple-I tasks are not bound by time and place; therefore, they become the primary focus of the distributed organization. The organization's assets, measured in these terms, can be linked together through time and space electronically.

28. Proposition 15; Air Quality Management Districts set fines of up to $25,000 per day for companies in non-compliance with reducing the number of average vehicle miles travelled by their employees.

29. Leavitt, 1987.

30. See Gibb and Akin (1986).

REFERENCES

Altman, I. (1975) *The Environment and Social Behavior*. Monterey, CA: Brooks/Cole Publishing Company.

Altman, I., and B. Rogoff. (1987) "World Views in Psychology: Trait, Interactionist, Organismic, and Transactionalist Approaches." In *Handbook of Environmental Psychology*. Ed. D. Stokols and I. Altman New York: Wiley, pp. 7–40.

Ambrosio, J. (1988) "Software in 90 Days." *Software Magazine*. 1 (Jan. 8): pp. 34–35.

Applegate, L. M., J. I. Cash, and D. Q. Mills. (1988) "Information Technology and Tomorrow's Manager." *Harvard Business Review*. 66 (Nov.–Dec.), 128–36.

Attewell, P. and J. Rule. (1984) "Computing and Organizations: What We Know and What We Don't Know." *Communications of the ACM*. 27:1184–92.

Bandura, A. (1977) "Self-Efficacy: Toward a Unifying Theory of Behavioral Change." *Psychological Review*. 84:191–215.

Birch, D. L. (1987) "The Atomization of America." *Inc.*, March, 21–22.

Brass, D. J. (1985) "Technology and the Structuring of Jobs: Employee Satisfaction, Performance, and Influence." *Organizational Behavior and Human Decision Processes,* 35:216–240.

Bridges, W. (1988) *Organizations in Transition.* W. Bridges and Associates 1(1).

Burkhardt, M. and D. Brass. (1990) "Changing Patterns or Patterns of Change: The Effects of a Change in Technology on Social Network Structure and Power." *Administrative Science Quarterly,* 35:104–127.

Conrath, D. W. (1973) "Communications Environment and Its Relationship to Organizational Structure." *Management Science,* 20(4) Dec. Part 2, 586–603.

Daft, R. L., and R. H. Lengel. (1986) "Organizatonal Information Requirements, Media Richness and Structural Design." *Management Science.* 32(5):554–571.

Drucker, P. (1988) "The Coming of the New Organization." *Harvard Business Review.* Jan.–Feb. 45–53.

Er, M. C. (1989) "A Critical Review of the Literature on the Organizational Impact of Information Technology." *IEEE Technology and Society Magazine,* June, pp. 17–23.

Finholt, Tom and Lee S. Sproull. (1990) "Electronic Groups at Work." *Organizational Science.* 1(1):41–64.

Fischer, C., R. Jackson, C. Stueve, K. Gerson, L. Jones, and M. Baldassare. (1977) *Networks and Places.* Free Press: New York.

Foster, L. W. and D. M. Flynn. (1984) "Management Information Technology: Its Effects on Organizational Form and Function." *MIS Quarterly,* Dec. 229–236.

Fry, Louis. (1982) "Technology-Structure Research: Three Critical Issues." *Academy of Management Journal.* 25(2):532–552.

Furger, R. (1989) "Quake Effects May Alter Work Patterns: Firms Seek Alternate Work Arrangements to Ease Traffic Problems." *InfoWorld.* Oct. 30.

Goodman, P. and L. Sproull. (1990) *Technology and Organizations.* San Francisco, CA: Jossey-Bass.

Gordon, G. (1987) "Corporate Hiring Practices for Home Workers: Who, Why, How Many and What Does It Mean?" *Proceedings of Conference on the New Era of Home Work: Directions and Responsibilties.* Washington, D.C.

Grantham, C. E. (1982) *Social Networks and Marital Interaction.* Palo Alto, CA: 21st Century.

Grantham, C. E. (1991) *Managerial Attitudes Towards Telecommuting.* Northern California Telecommuting Advisory Council technical report. San Francisco, CA.

Grantham, C. E., and J. J. Vaske. (1985) Predicting the Usage of an Advanced Communications Technology. *Behavior and Information Technology.* 4(4):327–335.

Handy, C. (1989) *The Age of Unreason.* Cambridge, MA: Harvard Business School Press.

Hendrickson, J. (1987) "Hiring the 'Right Stuff'." *Personnel Administrator.* Nov.: 70–74.

Hesse, B. W. (1989) "The Effects of Future Interaction and Specified Locus of Frustration on Male Participants' Aggression Within a Computer Medium." *Dissertation Abstracts International.* 50(6-B):2669.

Hesse, B., L. Sproull, S. Kiesler, and J. Walsh. (1990) *Computer Network Support for Science: The Case of Oceanography.* Manuscript submitted for publication.

Hesse, B., C. Werner, and I. Altman. (1988) Temporal Aspects of Computer-Mediated Communication. *Computers in Human Behavior.* 4:1–19.

Hiltz, S. R., and M. Turoff. (1978) *The Network Nation: Human Communication via Computer.* Reading, MA: Addison-Wesley.

Huber, G. (1990) "A Theory of the Effects of Advanced Information Technologies on Organizational Design, Intelligence, and Decision Making." *Academy of Management Journal.* 15(1):47–71.

Huff, C., L. Sproull, and S. Kiesler. (1989) "Computer Communication and Organizational

Commitment: Tracing the Relationship in a City Government." *Journal of Applied Psychology*. 19:1371–1391.

Johansen, R. (1988) *Groupware: Computer Support for Business Teams*. New York: Free Press.

Johansen, R. (1990) *Leading Business Teams: How Teams Can Use Technology and Process to Enhance Group Performance*. New York: Addison-Wesley.

Joreskog, K. G., and D. Sorbom. (1984) *LISREL VI User's Guide*. Mooresville, IN: Scientific Software.

Kemper, T. D. (1978) *A Social Interactional Theory of Emotions*. New York: Wiley-Interscience.

Kiesler, S., and L. Sproull. (1986) "Response Effects in the Electronic Survey." *Public Opinion Quarterly*. 50:402–413.

Kiesler, S., D. Zubrow, A. M. Moses, and V. Geller. (1985) "Affect in Computer-Mediated Communication." *Human-Computer Interaction*. 1:77–104.

Kling, R. (1987) "Defining the Boundaries of Computing Across Complex Organizations." In *Critical Issues in Information Systems Research*. Boland and Hirscheim. Eds. New York: John Wiley and Sons.

Kling, R., and W. Sacchi. (1982) "The Web of Computing: Computer Technology as Social Organization." *Advances in Computers, 21*. New York: Academic Press.

Kraut, R. E. (1987) "Predicting the Use of Technology: The Case of Telework." In *Technology and the Transformation of White-Collar Work*. R. E. Kraut, Ed. Hillsdale, NJ: Lawrence Earlbaum.

Kraut, R. E. (1989) "Telecommuting: The Trade-offs of Home Work." *Journal of Communication*. 39(3):19–47.

Langberg, M. (1989) "Rerouting the Bay Area economy: Quake to Shift Way We Work, Get There." *San Jose Mercury News*, Oct. 23, pp. C1 C9.

Leifer, Richard. (1988) "Matching Computer-Based Information Systems with Organizational Structures." *MIS Quarterly*. March, pp. 63–73.

Levander, M. (1989) "Home Is Where the Work Is." *San Jose Mercury News*, Nov. 13, pp. D1 D7.

Leavitt, D. (1987) "Team Techniques in Software Development." *Datamation*. Nov. pp. 78–86.

Leavitt, H. J. and T. L. Whisler. (1958) "Management in the 1980s." *Harvard Business Review*. 36:41–48.

Marsh, H. W., J. R, Balla, and R. P. McDonald. (1988) "Goodness-of-Fit Indexes in Confirmatory Analysis: The Effect of Sample Size." *Psychological Bulletin*. 103:391–410.

Markus, M. L., and D. Robey. (1988) "Information Technology and Organizational Change: Causal Structure in Theory and Research." *Management Science*. 34(5):583–598.

Mokhtarian, P. L. (1990) "A Typology of Relationships between Telecommunications and Transportation." *Transportation Research* 24A(3):231–242.

Mokhtarian, P. L. (1991) "Defining Telecommuting." Unpublished manuscript. University of California-Davis, Department of Civil Engineering.

Myers, I. B. (1986) *Gifts Differing*. Palo Alto, CA: Consulting Psychology Press.

Nilles, J. M., F. R. Carlson, P. Gray, and G. Hanneman. (1976). *The Telecommunications-Transportation Tradeoffs: Options for Tomorrow*. New York: Wiley.

O'Connor, R. J. (1989) "Quake Gave Us Needed Jolt to Get Serious about Telecommuting." *San Jose Mercury News*, Oct. 29, p. F1.

Olson, M. H. (1987) "Telework: Practical Experience and Future Prospects." In *Technology and the Transformation of White-Collar Work*. R. E. Kraut, Ed. Hillsdale, NJ: Lawerence Earlbaum.

Pratt, J. H. (1984) "Home Teleworking: A Study of its Pioneers." *Technological Forecasting and Social Change*. 25:1–14.

Pratt, J. H. (1988) "Socio-Issues Related to Home Based Work." In *Handbook of Human-Computer Interaction*. M. Helander, Ed. North-Holland: Elsevier.

Rice, R. (1984) *The New Media: Communication, Research and Technology*. Beverly Hills: Sage.

Roskies, E., J. K. Liker, and D. B. Roitman. (1988) "Winner and Losers: Employee Perceptions of Their Company's Technological Transformation." *Journal of Organizational Behavior*. 9:123–137.

Rubin, D. (1982) *Research on the Long Term Effects of Home Terminal Use*. AIR Technical Report #24901-FR-12/82. Palo Alto, CA: American Institutes for Research.

Saffo, P. (1991) "Future Tense." *InfoWorld*. Jan. 7, p. 49.

Schmeideck, R. A. (1978) *The Personal Sphere Model*. New York: Grune and Stratton.

Scott, W. Richard. (1992) *Organizations: Rational, Natural and Open Systems*, 3rd Edition. Englewood Cliffs: Prentice-Hall.

Siegel, J., V. Dubrovsky, S. Kiesler, and T. McGuire. In press. "Group Processes in Computer-Mediated Communication." *Organizational Behavior and Decision Processes*.

Siegel, L. (1990) "More Workers Able to Avoid Traffic as Telecommuting Becomes More Popular." *The New York Times*, Jan. 22, p. B1.

Sproull, L., and S. Kiesler. (1986) "Reducing Social Context cues: Electronic Mail in Organizational Communication." *Management Science*. 32:1492–1512.

Storey, J. (1987) "The Management of New Office Technology: Choice, Control and Social Structure in the Insurance Industry." *Journal of Management Science*. 24(1):43–62.

Taylor, J. R., and J. M. Katambwe. (1988) "Are New Technologies Really Reshaping Our Organizations?" *Computer Communications*. 11(5):245–252.

Tomaskovic-Devey, D. and B. J. Risman. (1988) *Organizational, Managerial, and Employee Constraints on the Technological Reorganization of Work: The Case of Telecommuting*. Paper presented at the 1988 American Sociological Association Annual Meeting.

Toffler, A. (1980) *The Third Wave*. New York: Marrow.

Vaske, J. J. and C. E. Grantham. (1990) *Socializing the Human-Computer Environment*. Norwood, NJ: Ablex.

Verity, J. W. (1990) "Rethinking the Computer." *Business Week*. Nov. 26, pp. 116–124.

Williams, F., R. E. Rice, and E. M. Rogers. (1988) *Research Methods and the New Media*. New York: The Free Press.

7

New Models of Thinking

This chapter begins the final phase of the book. Readers have now moved through skill development and business analysis to understanding how to integrate today's technology into their present organization. This chapter leaps to developing increased personal capability to deal with an increasingly uncertain future. The chapter returns to a theme begun in Chapter 1, namely, "We need to learn how to do business differently." One of the best ways to learn how to do things differently is to have more than one mental map of how to do things. Western culture is steeped in causal thinking: this action leads to that end. It should be quite obvious to you, at this point, that this type of thinking does not offer much explanatory power in today's business environment.

Managers need more mental tools than they currently have. As you will see later, this idea is based on the need to have a requisite variety of mental models. The cyberneticians tell us that you always need to have more mental tools than you need to use so that you have a choice among options. Without choice, everything is determined and consciousness is not required.

The Texture of Organizing

Organizations do not exist as stand alone objects in our life. They are connected to other organizations, are made up of individuals, and are becoming increasingly complex. They have an almost indescribable texture:

Texture itself is viewed analogically as a weave or web of interacting elements that resists operational definition. It is a tacit quality of the field of social action that, by definition, must remain beyond the grasp of explicit statement.[1]

Thie texture of an organization is its connectedness in action. There is no inside or outside, no top nor bottom. The texture is what surrounds us when we are acting in the organization. One way to look at this is to envision a crossword puzzle. The texture of that puzzle is the entire pattern that emerges "as we fill it in."

The explicit order of an organization is what we commonly see. However, it comes from a deeper, more implicit order—a potential. This potential is the texture of the organization. Until now,[2] we have discussed largely the explicit order of organizations—their plans, actions, movements, customers, and technology. We now are shifting to an analysis of the implicit order—the potential locked up in the minds of its members and embedded in its collective intelligence. What we need is a way of talking about this texture as the root of all orders that may become explicit. That is the purpose of mental models: to give us a common language to talk about the potential patterns of structure that exist in all organizations. Figure 7-1 depicts the connection between values, thinking, and doing. This chapter is intended to expand the range of thinking tools, especially systems thinking. Values certainly underlie the thinking that leads to doing. Judgment takes place in the thinking process and is colored by the variety of mental models a person has. Increasing the number of mental models you have can lead to a new understanding of relatedness and connectedness in any organization.

The important point is to realize here that we don't always have such models of organizational texture. Further, the difference between what is possible and what currently exists defines the gap we must bridge in organizational interventions. We

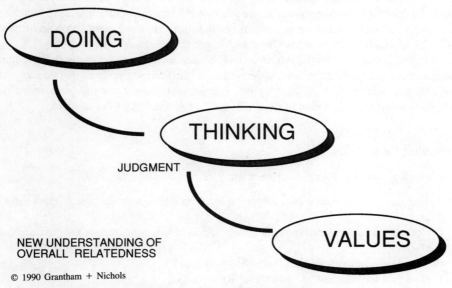

© 1990 Grantham + Nichols

Figure 7-1. Mental Technology To Deal with Cultural Diversity

will return to this distinction in the section below regarding generative rationality. For now, let it stand that organizational texture is the implied, unmeasured, and almost invisible quality of an organization that delineates its boundaries.

Plan of the Chapter

Chapter 7 follows the standard pattern of discussion and example we have developed throughout this book. The introduction is meant to set the stage and present the field of a larger view of organizations, extracting the underlying pattern from the minutiae of everyday activity. We have chosen three new mental models to explore. The first, general systems theory, has been increasingly employed to understand the complexity of today's business enterprise. Next, we briefly discuss the Viable Systems Model as a way of moving from static models to more dynamic ones. Finally, we revisit the idea of generative rationality[3] as a means of actually creating greater potential in our ability to think about organizations.

The final part of the chapter outlines the rationale behind using visual models of organizations to do assessment and testing. These visual models are an extension of systems thinking and are a very recent development. This background is followed by another case study, presenting the results of using visual modeling and computer simulation to analyze the potential effects of management decisions on an organization.

Where We Are

This chapter represents Point 6 on the Enneagram—another energy-input point. The first energy input was purpose; the second, customer need. This chapter on mental models is concerned with new energy in the form of increased mental capability of the practitioner. In the doing process, we are moving from structural issues to learning as a organizational process. In order to make that transition, we need some additional tools. In short, these tools are ways of looking at the world around us.

In the previous six chapters, we have discussed systems, systems theory, and models of organizations from various perspectives. This chapter pulls all that conceptual material together in a way that focuses our mental energy on the core ideas of cybernetics, viable systems, and dynamic and visible images of organizations.

Learning Objectives

The learning objectives for this chapter are:

- Appreciate the relevance of different mental models on formulating intervention strategies
- Understand what General Systems Theory is and how it contributes to organizational analysis
- Be knowledgeable about the Viable Systems Model
- Understand the concept of Generative Rationality
- Be aware of the psychological basis for using visual systems models

- Comprehend the importance of computer and communications technology integration
- Have experience with dynamic modeling as an intervention technique

The first step in this process is developing new models of viewing the world. The scientific literature has variously referred to this as a "paradigm shift," right- versus left-brain thinking, etc. We would like to present to you some evidence of contemporary thinking of new mental models of organizational analysis that cover both the old paradigms and the emerging ones. First, we offer an overall view of systems thinking. Next, we explore a more traditional, rational analysis of organization—extended into the development of a creative rational model. The "right brain," symbolic approach is next. It is followed by an attempt to integrate these new mental models in exploring a concrete application of cybernetics.

SYSTEMS: CLOSED, OPEN, AND EVOLVING

There are many approaches to systems analysis of organizations. We have talked about a number of these before, especially in Chapters 5 and 6. We have compiled an extensive bibliography for this chapter that can lead you to more resources (see Bibliography). It is not our intent here to provide a basic tutorial on systems theory. We assume that you can do, or have already done, that yourself. What we want here is to elevate our thinking to see the systems pattern in systems thinking. That is, what is the overall pattern to systems approaches to organizations?

The more traditional approach to systems thinking has been to see organizations as closed or open systems. Given this choice, we can then look for feedback loops, communication links, and patterns of interaction. The developing thinking about systems, however, is to move from this highly mechanical model to one showing how the form of the organization can actually change and evolve. R. L. Ackoff's work in the 1970s and early 1980s sought to give purpose a place in systems thinking. This purpose, or guiding principle, of a system then allowed for a richer analysis of everyday activities. If you know what the compass setting is for an enterprise, it becomes easier to understand the multitude of individual activities within it.

However, as practitioners we know that this general direction, or vision, for an organization is often not known or well understood. Also, we know that not everyone shares in that vision, even if articulated. The problem for us, then, is how do we reconcile these images of organizations as systems of activity with differences in purpose? The best way to do so is to develop a higher-level model of organization that incorporates traditional systems thinking with the emergent approach of purposeful activity.

Systems Viewpoints

Michael Jackson,[4] a British cybernetician, has boiled all of this down into a fairly simple two-dimensional model. The idea behind the model is to give people a new "mental map" of systems theories on which they can place various organizational intervention strategies. This allows them to see which techniques are most appropriate given the nature of the systemic issue being managed.

RELATIONSHIP

(AGREEMENT ON OBJECTIVES)

		UNITARY	PLURALIST	COERCIVE
S Y S T E M	MECHANICAL NATURE PROCESS ORIENTED	Operations Research Quantifiable Systems Engineering *Manage Scarceness*	Appreciative Inquiry *Manage Conflict*	Intentional Systems *Manage Conflict*
L E V E L	SYSTEMIC NATURE PERMEABLE BOUNDARIES	Viable Systems Socio-Tech Contingency Theory *Manage Complexity and Uncertainty*	Strategic Assumption Surfacing and Testing (SAST) *Manage Interpretation*	Critical Systems Heuristic *Manage Decisions about which group's interests are to be served*

after D. Jackson, 1988

Figure 7-2. *OD Technology Matrix*

The horizontal axis of the model breaks systems analysis into two categories: either mechanical-process-oriented or more systemic, with permeable boundaries. Process-type organizations are usually seen as a physical goods production model or in the extractive industries. Newer organizations that are characterized by intense information processing are the ones that move us into the realm of interpenetrating boundaries, with examples such as financial and administrative services.

The horizontal axis signifies the manner in which agreement on objectives is obtained in the organization. Unitary agreement occurs when all members of the enterprise have common agreement on what the problem context is. Situations in which there is some difference in opinion based on enlightened self-interest can be seen as pluralistic. When the only way problems are defined is through the exercise of power, we have a coercive relationship among actors in the enterprise.

This 3 × 2 matrix allows us to identify the central systems issue that characterizes each of these situations and the corresponding intervention approach usually employed. The implication, of course, is that the use of the inappropriate mental model of intervention—given the characteristics of the situation—would lead to inappropriate results. Let's examine each cell in order.

Mechanical–Unitary

The central management issue is managing scarceness of resources and market. Operations research with its attendant statistical-analysis and systems-engineering works in this environment. The Business Process Analysis technique we discussed in Chapter 5 is an example of this intervention strategy. You may note that this is the goal state of the Total Quality Movement. When you have unitary agreement of business objectives and a mechanical production process, you can use statistical-analysis and systems-engineering processes to achieve incremental improvements.

Mechanical–Pluralist

The issue is management of conflict, usually within the systems themselves. Getting everyone on the "same sheet of music" is the presenting complaint. Here, interventions such as appreciative inquiry work best. Appreciative inquiry[5] is an interactive experience facilitated to help people develop an affective bond with one another. Some of the suggestions given in Chapter 2 on how to improve communication would be an example.

Mechanical–Coercive

Again, the issue of managing conflict is central. However, the shift is the management of conflict with the external environment. This usually happens when market share begins to slide, or when significant changes in the business climate occur. Intentional systems interventions work well here. These are interventions based on establishing some highly structured thinking processes in the organization, along with continuous examination of "purpose." There is a double loop here. If management has to coerce its members into agreement on objectives, any intervention, especially a highly structured one, will probably not succeed.

Systemic–Unitary

The issue is the management of complexity and uncertainly usually created in the market environment and brought into the organization. There are several approaches that can work in this situation. The viable systems model, sociotechnical approaches, and use of contingency theory are appropriate. This book is an example of these systemic-unitary approaches. But note that the base condition of successful intervention is a common agreement of the problem, situation, or goal. That assumes healthy, open communication, clearly articulated vision, and highly visible business processes. These are rare conditions in today's business environment.

Systemic–Pluralist

Here, the issue is management of interpretation of business condition. Leaders know they don't know what's going on. Everyone has a different opinion and no action can take place until some people have agreed on a definition of the situation. Strategic-assumption surfacing and testing[6] is a useful intervention. These are techniques to operationalize C. W. Churchman's ideas of strategic planning. They are designed to "surface" the underlying assumptions people hold about market, environment, work process, and security.

Systemic–Coercive

Management of interest groups is the issue. This is a very political environment, where management is attempting to balance forces to form coalitions and some consensus. Imposition of an external agreement is often the dynamic. Critica systems heuristics[7] is a method to help people decide what they "ought to do." This enables critical reflection upon organizational purpose without any unwarranted assumptions. This approach is relatively new and depends on using an "emancipatory" approach. This is the level of critical systems thinking in which the analysis of the business enterprise becomes explicitly linked to community and social action.

PRACTICAL APPLICATION OF SYSTEMS APPROACHES

Again, this classification scheme is meant to provide another mental model of what occurs in organizations undergoing change. We have found that being able to label the process and draw a picture of where the organization is can be a powerful tool in making the process visible and manageable. Most corporate executives (at least in the United States) are highly analytical people and respond positively to figures and charts. The model developed by M. C. Jackson can be a very useful guide when helping a client organization select the most viable approach to use in the change process. As consultants descend on an organization seeking help, what appears to be lacking is some overall, generalized change model. There are different tools of change. Each has its place and time. The difficulty is selecting when, where, and what to use based on some decision process rooted in reality. We believe that Jackson's model, and McWhinney's to follow, are good examples of the general mental-models of change strategies.

Generative Rationality

Classical theories of organizational functioning, such as the bureaucracy of Max Weber, are based on a rational[8] model of human behavior. Economists have extended this model of action and called it contingency analysis. The basic assumption about human behavior that underlies these models of thinking is that people make conscious choices in behavior.[9] These choices are assumed to be based on a rational gain/loss kind of logic, where each individual seeks to maximize his or her gain. Recent scholars have begun to extend the definition of rationality to incorporate a view of creative, generative behavior.[10]

The more traditional type of rationality is called calculative rationality. This type of decision making is usually found in production environments, where the standards for acceptable behavior and the methods for accomplishing tasks are based on the efficiency goals. Such environments tend to be relatively stable, promote standardized operating techniques, and have established procedures for implementing change.[11] In organizations where things are relatively stable and all input and outputs can be easily identified, this type of decision making is very effective. However, in dynamic environments in which uncertainty and/or equivocality is high, a different type of rational decision making is required.

The other type of rational thinking is called generative rationality. Perhaps the best example of generative rational thinking is chess strategy. The basic moves are clearly defined and restricted. However, the combination of those moves is almost endless and depends on the pattern of interaction between the competitors' moves. The individual-piece movements actually can be seen to generate new patterns of interaction. There is a rational, systematic process operating, but the results are often unpredictable and unique.

Historically, we have applied calculative rationality to organizational analysis. Analyze the financial statements to assess health, use sales figures to forecast production demands, and hire workers based on standardized-test scores of psychological batteries. We are finding that a new type of rational thinking can be helpful. The systems-analysis case study that concludes this chapter is an example of calculative rationality. A small set of basic, unchangeable rules (or relationship definitions) is used in different, unpredictable combinations to present a model of system functioning. It is rational, in the sense that the basic rules are known and invariant; but it is generative, in the sense that the permutations of the results are unlimited.

So how does this idea of generative rationality help extend our tool kit of mental models? First, it gives the opportunity to say that the final outcome of any given analysis is not predestined. Second, it says that at the start we must make very clear the basic rules by which the analysis will proceed—we establish the logic up front, and it does not change. An example of this would be to agree upon the different weights of importance that may be assigned to several factors, *before* collecting data. Another example is the use of this generative rationality to develop products. We may agree on the process to be followed and strictly adhere to that process. We could make a rule that says each iteration of the product must be subjected to testing with potential customers and that their evaluations would be the basis for the next design cycle. We have put in place a "rational" process of development, but cannot necessarily predict the exact form of the final output.

Paths of Change[12]

The last category of mental model we would like to explore moves us from the logical and systemic to the symbolic. If generative rationality serves to extend left-brain thinking, and cybernetics informs whole-brain thinking, then right-brain thinking can be amplifed with symbolic analysis. We have chosen the recent work of Will McWhinney as the best contemporary illustration of this approach.

McWhinney's basic thesis is that the pathways that organizations embark on to generate change have patterns to them. Further, these patterns have a linkage to underlying views of reality. That is to say that different people, and groups of people, have different reality pictures. These differences can give rise to conflict, and it is important to realize that conflict is an inevitable social reality itself. McWhinney's four realities are: unitary, sensory, mythic, and social (see Figure 7-3).

Locating yourself and your journey toward change on this map involves two questions: (1) Does the change move things toward being more alike or more different? Alike moves toward monistic; difference, toward pluralistic. (2) Is the cause for change external or intentional? External drives toward determined; intentional toward free will. The point in being able to anchor oneself in this framework is that the change process itself is a pattern of movement from one of these locations through some to a final place. McWhinney's model has several levels of complexity. Each of these realities has a number of characteristics attached to it.

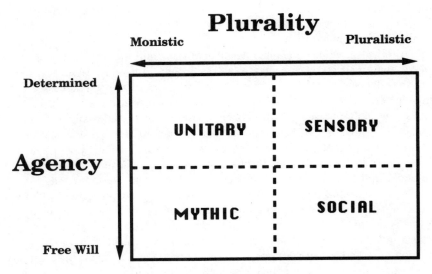

Figure 7-3. Realities of Change

Looking at this map, we can see just how complicated different realities can become. When you enter an organization, you can start to tease out their ethos by listening carefully for statements, or better yet, symbols of what realilty they operate within. Questions about testing for reality and how changes are made are often very revealing. When one applies this map in real situation, one sees that most formal organizations today are operating out of sensory or unitary realities. Both are very deterministic and are associated with leadership characteristics that value analysis and facts.

The implications, then, are that if you are engaged in helping an organization move toward a different goal than it currently is seeking, you can start to lay out a pathway with markers to tell you where you are. Figure 7-4 is really an outline of what outcomes you can expect in attitude shifts associated with change. For example, if you were trying to help move a culture from sensory to mythic, you would set up reward structures to promote exercise of will instead of efficiency goals.

How Change Occurs

McWhinney proposes that there are two basic patterns to organizational change embedded in his model. These basic patterns can be extended and reduced—but remain the same. Educed patterns of change neglect key elements and can become ineffective. Elaborated pathways can build incredible amounts of capability, but require much more time and effort. The two main paths of change are revitalization and renaissance.

Revitalization is the path that begins in a unitary reality and moves first to the mythic, then to the social, and finally to the sensory before returning to the unitary. This is the pattern of change found in Western democratic revolutions and organizational transformations. It is a top-down strategy and moves from an analytic mode to

Quality	Sensory	Social	Unitary	Mythic
The Source	Nature	The Other (in relation to me)	Logos—The Truth	The Self
What is it (Onta)	Objects—things	Feelings, expressed interpersonally	Ideas and principles, articulation of laws	Symbols
Cause of it	Efficient	Intentionality	Formal	Exercise of will
Relations	Things act on each Other	Connect via processes of valuing	None—no separation	None
Test of Reality	Observability—direct or indirect	Feelings/values	Consistency with the truth	None
Source of Information	Senses	Self engaged with others	Direct experience of oneness, deduction from rules	Oneself
Moral Judgment	None, no values	Concern for values held by others	None, no alternatives acceptable	Total responsibility, others are not recognized
Changes by	"Going with" the environmental imperative	Social Interaction, no inherent stability	Interpreting ideas in accordance with principles	No change, just creation
Operates in	Necessity	Openness	Certainty	Identity
Seen in	Creature comforts, science	Social exchange, organizing	Mathematics, law, devotion	Play, creating, leading
Comes from	Environment	Society	Culture	Person

Source: Note to come

Figure 7-4. *Characteristics of Change*

a participative one. The process begins with an awareness of problems by upper management and flows through the organization, getting buy-in and support. Masculine forces (yang) initiate the process and it becomes more feminine (yin) in its later stages.

Renaissance begins in the unitary, moves to the sensory, then to the social, to the mythic, and returns to the sensory. This is open-systems planning and community redevelopment. It begins with a sense of loss of meaning and a realization that the forces that once held the group together and gave it identity are no longer strong enough to continue. The pattern is reversed from the previous mode of change. It begins with a participative mode and ends with an analytic mode. Loss of meaning is sensed first, the framework of reality is destroyed, and a new core is established leading to a new cultural reality. It begins as feminine and ends as masculine.

These pathways of change are highly elaborated by McWhinney and can serve as an excellent roadmap for change. The central point is that there *is* a pathway; it must be covered; there are no shortcuts. Anyone who has experienced profound personal change knows this. However, most executives are under tremendous pressure to obtain quick results and don't see the utility of spending the time to transverse the intermediate steps along the way. McWhinney's paths of change give some cognitive structure to a highly symbolic process.

Viable Systems Model

There are several variations on the application of cybernetic principles to the analysis of organizations. One of those that we find with the most utility is called the Viable Systems Model (VSM) and was developed by Stafford Beer over a long time-period.[13] In general, cybernetics extends the classical information theory of Shannon and Weaver[14] to the flow of information within an organization.

Key principles are information feedback loops, attenuators, amplifiers, and filters. Cybernetics builds upon this base and incorporated some new, key ideas. The salient ideas are:

- *Recursion:* a level of organization that contains all levels below it. Patterns of organizational interaction can be embedded in technology and made visible.
- *Requisite Variety:* existence of numerous options for thought and action. Technology can be used to examine the potential impact of these various options.
- *Homeostasis:* internal stability of enterprise environment. Communication systems provide feedback throughout the system.
- *Self-Referential:* a system's ability to maintain an identity, repair itself, and be aware of itself. Histories of its operation are maintained in readily accessible databases and archives.

Basic Building Blocks

Beer takes these basic building blocks and constructs a general model of complex organizations that acts as a diagnostic map. The key to an organization's "viability" is the maintenance of its identity. For Beer, purpose is simply "what an organization does." The basic parts of this model are environment, operations, and management. Figure 7-5 is a diagram of this model.

In Beer's conceptualization, organizations consist of five levels of activity nested within one another. You might think of it as a series of boxes within boxes, but with each having the same general characteristics. These common characteristics are information-channel connections to the environment and to one another. Each portion of the model has three elements: management, operations, and environment. For any system within the overall structure, there must be connections between its relevant management, operations, and environment.

Beer calls his levels of analysis *systems*. They are simply numbered One through

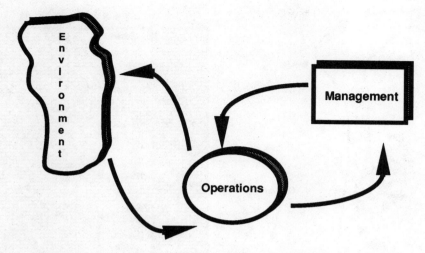

Figure 7-5. Basic Viable Systems Model Elements

Five and begin at the activity level we described in the last chapter.[15] Each system has a core management issue and is characterized by its unique focus on different activities that a viable system must incorporate. The implication here is that if an organization is missing one or more of these "systems," it is by definition not viable and will cease to have a unique identity over time.

Systems Within Systems

Figure 7-6 is a schematic of the overall Viable Systems Model showing the relationships among the systems. The lines connecting the elements are information channels. Notice that each System One is connected to various levels of the environment. Also, each System One contains within it a miniature model of the System Three, Four, Five cluster. Each of the information channels contains a two-way linkage, as well as attenuators and amplifiers we have deleted from the diagram for the sake of simplicity.

SYSTEM ONE.

This is the level of production. This is the base activity of the enterprise—be it production line, food gathering, or housecleaning. This is the level where we say the "real work" gets done. The key management issue is one of managing complexity. Moreover, it is the management of environmental complexity in which the entire organization exists. Many signals are coming at the organization and they bombard System One continuously. System One is connected with information channels that embed attenuators (to dampen flows) and amplifiers (which multiply inputs). This is equivalent to first-line management and workers.

SYSTEM TWO.

This system is charged with managing a state of homeostasis between Systems Ones. This is a coordination and balancing function. This process is managed through

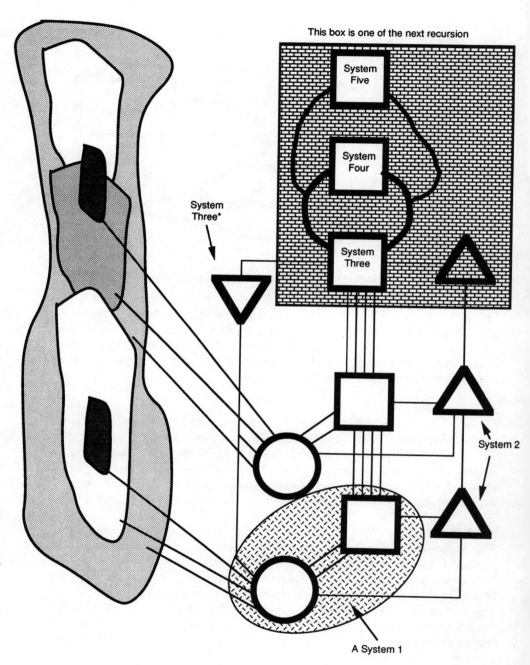

Figure 7-6. *Viable Systems Model Levels of Analysis*

establishment of accountabilities and reporting upward in the organization. Critical issues for this system are local regulation among operations and the dampening of oscillations around some sort of ideal limits. This is the first level of system in the VSM, where information crosses unit boundaries; therefore, channel capacity[16] and transducers[17] are included in the information links. This is roughly the same as our depiction of middle-management functions.

SYSTEM THREE.
The central task here is to manage the internal "here and now." This is where the limits to oscillation[18] are set. This system sets rules and makes resource bargains with System Ones based on information it receives from System Two concerning oscillation. There is some component of autonomic action introduced by this system, but only within the limit it established. System Three-A serves an internal-audit function by comparing "values" against expectation. This is the first specialized level of senior management where overall enterprise-responsibility is found—vice presidents.

SYSTEM FOUR.
The key management task here is looking outside and toward the future. Some would call this the planning function—but only as it is connected to the environment and can envision the future. It is linked to System Three through tight feedback loops that settle the issue of balancing potential against actual capacity of the organization. It embeds a model of itself and the system being analyzed. Here we find research and development, market research, and corporate planning activities. Most enterprise failures occur here, when System Four fails to test its anticipated actions against a model of correct overall functioning.

SYSTEM FIVE.
System Five concerns itself with managing identity and sustainability of the enterprise. This is the ultimate arbiter of questions and the wellspring of sense of purpose. Systems One, Two, and Three struggle to maintain homeostasis; Systems Four pushes toward new directions. This basic organizational tension must be reconciled. System Five does that—or, at least, should.

This is the system of leadership responsible for developing and articulating vision. This system contains a unique element that Stafford Beer has termed *algedonic*. By that, he means that this is the structural location where signals coming from System Ones are sensed to be alerting danger—a signal to wake up! Many contemporary corporations can be seen to be deficient in their ability to process algedonic signals. This is equivalent to the board level of corporations.

Application of the VSM
When you review the central tasks that each system in the VSM is supposed to be responsible for, it seems to make sense that all of them need to be happening in a successful organization. VSM makes visible those mysterious organizational processes that are ingredients of viability. An interesting exercise is to take something in the popular management press, such as Tom Peters' *In Search of Excellence,* and map his qualities of excellence to the VSM.

A strong point of the VSM is its use in identifying the information-flow links among elements of an organization. A quick check concerning the existence of these can prove to be a powerful diagnostic. For example, what would happen if System Three-A were not present in an organization? This internal audit feedback loop from corporate to operational unit is usually the province of the accounting corps. It is easy to predict what would happen if there were no financial audit procedures in place in an organization.

Let's take another example. System Two is supposed to dampen out oscillation among System One units. What happens when this function is missing? Simply put, upper management finds itself managing the day-to-day operations of the firm and not concerned with setting policy based on other input concerning the future. The company gets too close to the trees to see the forest and can go bankrupt or lose market share quickly.

Perhaps the most glaring problem today in American business is the lack of a clearly defined System Five. This top-level system needs to incorporate a model of the entire system, develop and articulate a vision, and—overall—give a sense of purpose while responding to signals of alarm and pain.

The utility of the VSM, as with any other mental model, is to provide the practitioner another tool to use in helping client companies develop a clearer understanding of what's going on. One of the best examples of how to use the VSM in organizations has been articulated by Barry Clemson.[19] Although these ideas have been articulated by Beer and others, they have not come into common use because of their inherent complexity. Our work has been aimed at moving beyond this conceptualization to the creation of business decision-aiding tools that embed these ideas, in ways that are more understandable by managers. A good way to do so is to make these VSM patterns visible.

VISUAL THINKING AND INFORMATION FLOWS

Cognitive Basis for Approach

Modeling of an organizational process has traditionally been done through financial modeling. The advent of the spreadsheet in the mid-1970s ushered in a whole era of examining the impact of alternative courses of organization action. However, those models assumed that all important processes of the firm could be reduced to cash-flow equivalents and displayed in two dimensions. As we have outlined above, there are at least two other well-developed theoretical schools of the nature of the driving aspects of an organization: viable-systems technology and generative rationality. So why even bother to develop advanced ways of thinking about how the firm functions and can be modeled?

Dur and Bots (1991)[20] offer three cogent reasons, as follows:

1. Organizations develop over long time-spans and much knowledge about functioning is tacit knowledge, not reflected in past financial records.

2. Organizations allow for many points of view—which are continually negotiated.
3. Organizations often grow rapidly so that no one individual can have a reliable picture of the entire organization at any one time.

Modeling of organizational processes can overcome these problems by making the tacit knowledge explicit, can relate various vantage points, and can provide a cognitive bridge between complexity and the rationality of discrete parts of the organization. From a psychological perspective, modeling helps managers "surface" assumptions about behavior and do that in a way that makes these assumptions visible. When these otherwise-hidden assumptions are made visible, they are more easily interpreted, modified, and agreed upon.

Lastly, the interactive discussion process by which the model is constructed allows people to step back and get the big picture and not be bounded by their everyday experience and limited scope. The technique we use involves between five and seven executives and a trained facilitator in order to construct these models. The facilitator's job is to question executives about how their business works and then to use computer software to build a model of this process. The model is shown to the executives, and another series of inquiries specifies parameters of the variables. This procedure continues through several iterative loops until everyone is satisfied that the computer model is a valid reflection of how the business really works.

Going about this task is not easy. It is best attempted when guided by experienced facilitators who can manage the conflict, interpretation, and political interests involved. The process must promote active participation of all involved because we are trying to capture all of the variety existing in the minds of participants—maximum requisite variety. It is also necessary to represent all points of view (i.e., world views) without initial regard to consistency of all parts of the model.[21] The techniques should also be aimed at reducing the cognitive distance between current mental models and reality, by, for example, asking such questions as, "Are you sure that's the way marketing and operations think about each other?" This causes the real mental-models that people are using to surface and does not let any of the participants assume they know what others are thinking.

The next part of this process is the one that adds a time dimension. Static models are good for looking at one point in time—but business is an activity over time. Dynamic modeling must make explicit use of time dimensions. In this case, we usually refer to linear time as a first iteration. It is also helpful to have a time-scaling feature that allows you to extend the analysis over long time-periods to examine relative short-range and long-range impacts.[22] Further, you must be able to specify the sequence of events in this time domain. In Chapter 5, we outlined our view of Business Process Analysis, which can be used as a template for this sequencing activity. The modeling technique must permit—even encourage—investigation of the model from different viewpoints. This can have a very playful aspect, when participants in the process mentally "walk around" the model, "get inside it," and examine it from all angles while communicating among themselves what they see, are experiencing, and believe to be true about their organization.

Current Approaches

Organizational simulation has been around for some years and takes many forms. However, we are now beginning to see a dramatic surge in its use as a management-analysis technique. This has been brought about by increased computer capacity that allows dynamic simulation using graphical interfaces, rapid processing for real-time analysis, and networked personal computers so that many people can experiment with the same model over separations in time and space. The main modeling techniques are as follows:

- *Discrete-event simulation.* Models both objects and processes at one point in time
- *Systems analysis.* Input, output, and control features model with no explicit time reference
- *Conceptual data model.* Graphic description of data structures
- *Data-flow model.* Information-system design model looks at data in system
- *Organizational charts.*
- *Process model.* Business Process Analysis is an example
- *Mathematical optimization.* Operations-research perspective
- *Spreadsheet models.* Based on financial data
- *Equation simulation.* Dynamic, closed systems models.

Linkage to Previous Work

We introduced dynamic modeling earlier in Chapter 3. We believe that visual analysis of information flows in organizations will become a standard, accepted business practice within ten years for successful business firms.[23] Tools are becoming available and interfaces to computers are evolving rapidly, especially with virtual-reality techniques. We now have the capacity to construct a dynamic model of an organization that links hard variables, such as financial data, to softer variables such as levels of trust and commitment. These modeling processes meet all the requirements for adequacy outlined above in the discussion of Dur and Bots' work. This chapter is intended to push our thinking into this new realm of mental models. We have taken the work in Chapter 3 on information flows and organizational dimensions and constructed a complete equation-simulation model, using commercially available software. We have included a case study in this chapter that demonstrates how this dynamic modeling approach can be used to increase business effectiveness.

SYSTEMS THROUGH TIME: SIMULATION MODELS

Before we launch into the case study of organizational simulation, two more conceptual elements must be put into place. First, what technologies are arriving that make this approach practicable? Also, what is the most elemental process underlying the use of dynamic modeling?

At this point, we have discussed several different conceptual models that can be used to describe organizations (i.e., the VSM and computer modeling). We have also set out an overall template to look at organizational interventions taken from Michael Jackson and, finally, a new way of seeing change processes from McWhinney. These are all parts, or conceptual tools, that can be used in the organizational assessment and analysis phase of interventions by organizational-design practitioners.

Technology Integration: Computers–Telecommunications and Education–Entertainment

Several technologies are integrating themselves in a way that makes real-time simulation possible and engaging. In the past, we have had large mainframe computers, complicated algorithms, and paper output of numerical data to simulate processes. These have been expensive, and the results hard to interpret—especially in a holistic, nonquantifiable manner. We believe technologies are emerging that make this new type of systemic analysis possible (see Figure 7-7).

Telecommunications and computer software have been coming together for some time now. It is almost impossible to distinguish where computers leave off and telecommunication systems begin in the public network today. Education and entertainment have not been considered a "technology" until recently. The emergence of multimedia, virtual reality, and "edutainment" has changed this. Music TV programs

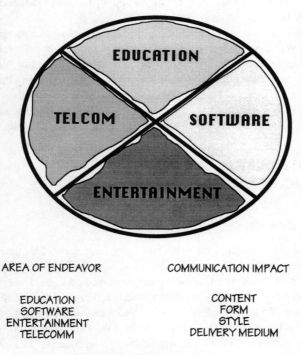

AREA OF ENDEAVOR	COMMUNICATION IMPACT
EDUCATION	CONTENT
SOFTWARE	FORM
ENTERTAINMENT	STYLE
TELECOMM	DELIVERY MEDIUM

Figure 7-7. *Technology Areas*

now do news segments; classrooms employ videos with cartoons to illustrate points. In McLuhan's terms, the medium is truly becoming the message. How we communicate a message is equally as important as what the message is. The "how" has referred to a channel of communication in the past, such as print versus electronic media. But now we are seeing video segments on personal-computer screens, easy interchange between voice and text, and complete interactive control of games and education in virtual-reality systems. All these technologies are now coming together, enabling us to experience each other more directly by increasing the bandwidth of our communications and letting us have control over which mediums are used.

We believe that educational technologies really are the content of the technology. Education (increasing your capability) is the "stuff" of the technological base—it is the texture of the organization. Software is the form of the technology, the general structure. Software by itself is nothing—rather like a virus, it needs a host to interact with in order to be noticed. It is simply a set of instructions that get converted into reality through computation. Entertainment is clearly the style of the communication. Animated characters, use of high-fidelity music, and blending of visual and audio images are advancing quickly. Telecommunication is the delivery medium. How the communication gets from originator to consumer.

We have a natural grouping of technologies that allow us to manipulate (and design) communications. We can change content, form, style, and channel. These abilities can in themselves become powerful tools of intervention. Communicating a vision from leaders, providing high-fidelity feedback from customers, and adding value to product with built-in instructions are only a few of the ways these technologies can be employed by design practitioners.

In this chapter, we have presented a wide array of new conceptual models of organizations. We have increased your requisite variety considerably. However, bringing these ideas down to reality in application is equally important. We have selected a case-study example of the use of dynamic organizational modeling that also uses our idea of healthy organizational functioning to illustrate how some of these models can be helpful to the practitioner. The ancillary learning in this case study is that computer technology itself can be used to help learn about organizations—not only affect them.

CASE STUDY: SIMULATION OF BUSINESS PROCESS

Organizational Modeling

As mentioned before, traditional models of organizational functioning have been limited to financial and statistical analysis. This way of simulating possible scenarios of business is very helpful when the processes are based on cash flows, balance sheets, and income statements. The advent of computerized spreadsheets changed the way in which managers made many decisions. They had a tool to examine possible effects of business decisions before they wer actually made. "What-if" analysis became a standard tool of business managers. However, not all business processes fall into the category of financial analysis.

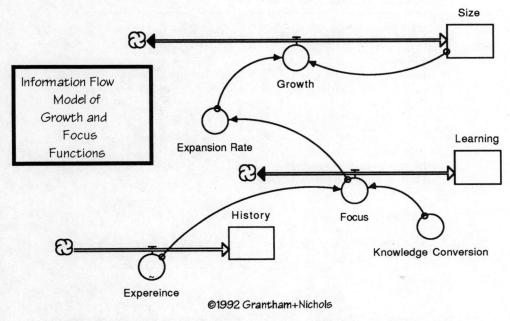

Size

Growth

Information Flow
Model of
Growth and
Focus
Functions

Learning

Expansion Rate

History

Focus

Knowledge Conversion

Expereince

©1992 Grantham+Nichols

Figure 7-8. *Information System Flow Model Growth and Focus Functions*

The business environment is becoming more complex, dynamic, and sensitive to impacts from outside firms, regulatory agencies, and markets. In order to fully understand today's complexity, managers need to look at feedback loops, time-lagged effects, and "softer" variables that can't be easily translated into dollar measures. Management science has also discovered that people can often comprehend very complicated numerical relationships visually. Truly, a picture is worth a thousand words—or a few dozen spreadsheets.

Software tools are becoming available that enable business leaders to quickly and easily model these complex processes and display the results in a visual dynamic format.[24] Figure 7-8 is an example of a simple business model that relates firm growth to organizational learning rates.

The boxes in the model represent reservoirs where quantities, such as learning and size of the organization, are collected. The circles stand for valves that control rates of flow. These valve symbols indentify variables and control points. Arrows are pipes, and the little cloud outlines are boundaries of the model. This model states in explicit form that we assume that an organization's ability to focus on production process is a function of its experience modified by a knowledge-conversion factor. Further, a firm's expansion rate is assumed to be a function of this learning and ability to focus. Finally, size is determined by this expansion rate. Once we have diagrammed this process, the software automatically generates the mathematical equations that relate

Table 7-1   Dynamic Model Code Listing

History(t) = History(t–dt) + (Experience)*dt
INIT History = 5

INFLOWS:
Experience = GRAPH(TIME)
(1, 0.5) (2, 0) (3, 3.5) (4, 9) (5, 14.5) (6, 17.5) (7, 25) (8, 30.5) (9, 39.5)
  (10, 50) (11, 56) (12, 65.5) (13, 69.5)
Learning(t) = Learning(t–dt) + (Focus)*dt
INIT Learning = 0

INFLOWS:
Focus = Experience*Knowledge_Conversion
Size(t) = Size(t–dt) + (Growth)*dt
INIT Size = 100

INFLOWS:
Growth = Size*Expansion_Rate
Expansion_Rate = .1*Focus
Knowledge_Conversion = –.1

---

all parts of the model. Table 7-1 is a partial listing of the code generated by constructing this model.

For a typical graphical output for this model, see Figure 7-9.:

The interpretation of this model is that as learning decreases over time (curve

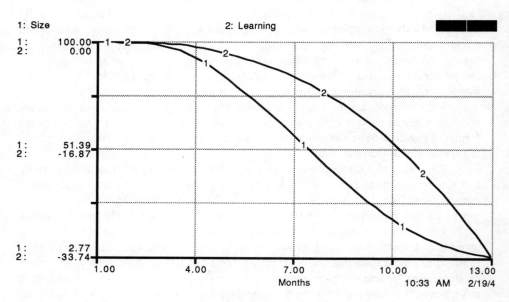

Figure 7-9. Dynamic Modeling Output

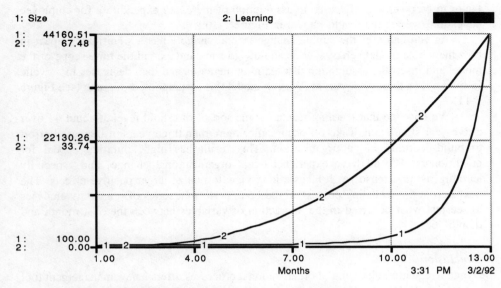

Figure 7-10. *Model Output with Positive Education Assumption*

2), there is a corresponding decline in firm size (curve 1). The power of this modeling technique is that you can instantly return to the model, change the assumptions that underlie its relationships, and rerun the simulation to compare projected results of those decisions. For example, if we return to the model and change the knowledge-conversion

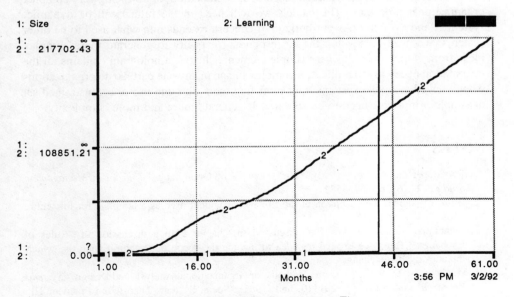

Figure 7-11. *Learning Function over Time*

factor to be positive, reflecting an assumption of increased expenditure for employee education, we get the results shown in Figure 7-10.

As you can see, the simple change in one variable has a significant impact in how the whole model behaves. We can now go back and extend the time-scope of the model and insert the assumption that learning increases and then decreases in a cyclic fashion over a three-year period. We can model this assumption as a graph (see Figure 7-11).

We now see that learning reaches some sort of threshold level at about 44 over a five-year simulation. Take-off occurs after more than three years of increased effort to build learning in an organization. This result has high, intuitive appeal for practitioners. We all have experienced that organizational change, and especially learning, is time-sensitive. It takes a long view to realize larger positive effects. The next step in the modeling process would be to perform a series of sensitivity analyses to see just what occurred in the interaction of variables between the 31st month and month 46.

Conclusion

Dynamic equation modeling of organizational processes offers a new management tool to examine the effects of a range of management initiatives in today's complex business environment. Tools are now available that allow this simulation process to occur on the desktop. Further, the real value to this process is to make implicit assumptions about organizational behavior explicit, model them over time, and finally to make this process visible to participants so that they may conduct the natural negotiation-process among themselves as purposeful managers.

Our mental capacity to model these complex systems is built up with a number of rather simple submodels that are capable, in combination, of mimicing very complex organizational processes. The models we will need in the future will be dynamic, systemic, and evolving. As our horizon of concern extends into what used to be other systems, we need to develop the corresponding capacity to generate more complex ideas from combinations of very simple elements. Just as a hologram contains all the information necessary to replicate a complex image in any one part, so do organizations when viewed as viable systems. Our modeling tools, through use of a constrained set of simple primitives, need to be able to self-generate more and more complexity.

NOTES

1. R. Cooper and S. Fox (1990), "The 'Texture' of Organizing," *Journal of Management Studies,* 27 (6), pp. 575–582.
2. With, of course, the exception of the Enneagram model used as a template for this entire book.
3. Generative rationality was first discussed in Chapter 2 in a discussion of "Rules of Exchange." Here, we expand the idea to include the scope of structural analysis, which includes dyadic exchanges.
4. M. C. Jackson (1988), "Systems Methods for Organizational Analysis and Design," *Systems Research,* vol. 5 (3), pp. 201–10, and (1985) "Social Systems Theory and Practice: The Need for a Critical Approach," *Intl. Journal of General Systems,* vol. 10, pp. 135–151.

5. G. Vickers (1973), *Making Institutions Work,* Associated Business Programmes: London, and (1983) *Human Systems are Different,* Harper and Row: London.

6. R. O. Mason and I. Mitroff (1981) *Challenging Strategic Planning Assumptions,* John Wiley: New York, and I. Mitroff and J. R. Emshoff (1979), "On Strategic Assumption-Making: A Dialectical Approach to Policy and Planning," *Academy of Management Review,* 4, pp. 1–12.

7. W. Ulrich (1983), *Critical Heuristics of Social Planning,* Haupt: Berne.

8. Rational, in this context, means making decisions based on a knowable, observable logic. The rules of logical analysis are articulated, such as symbolic logic, and rules are invariant across situations.

9. The contrasting approach to this has been the development of the "human relations" or Theory Y approach to analysis. This countervailing theory assumes that people don't always do the "rational" thing but sometimes act in accordance with more emotional motivations.

10. R. Westrum (1984), *The Effect of Electronic Communications Technologies on the Large Corporation: Basic Theoretical Framework,* Corporate Information Management, Minneapolis: Honeywell.

11. Vaske and Grantham (1990), pp. 118–19.

12. Will McWhinney (1992), *Paths of Change,* Sage: Beverly Hills, California.

13. Beer's first book on the topic appeared in 1959 (*Cybernetics and Management*) and was extended in *Decision and Control* (1966), *Brain of the Firm* (1972), *The Heart of the Enterprise* (1979), and most recently, *Diagnosing the System* (1985).

14. C. Shannon and W. Weaver (1949), *The Mathematical Theory of Communication,* University of Illinois Press: Urbana, Illinois.

15. See Figure 6-2.

16. The amount of information transmitted in a unit of time.

17. Encoding and decoding of information—a source of "noise" in the system.

18. Oscillations in cybernetics terms refer to the movement of some activity to levels above and below its set target. Sales figures that range widely around sales quotas would be a good example.

19. Barry Clemson (1984), *Cybernetics: A New Management Tool,* Abacus Press: Tunbridge Wells, England.

20. R. C. J. Dur and P. W. G. Bots (1991), "Dynamic Modelling of Organizations Using Task/Actor Simulation," *Proceedings of the Second International Working Conference on Dynamic Modelling of Information Systems,* Washington, D.C., July 18–19, 1991, The American University, pp. 15–35.

21. This often involves just getting the picture up in front of people *before* asking how different sectors of the model impact one another.

22. In Chapter 2 (Table 2-2) we discussed the various impacts of different ways of viewing time. Please cross-reference.

23. Standard in situations where integrated cross-functional strategic planning is practiced. See Chapter 8 on the learning organization.

24. This model was constructed using IThink™ software from High Performance Systems in Nashua, NH.

REFERENCES

Ackoff, R. L. (1984) *A Guide for Controlling Your Corporation's Future.* New York: John Wiley & Sons.

Ackoff, R. L. (1981) *Creating the Corporate Future: Plan or Be Planned*. New York: John Wiley & Sons.

Argyris, C. (1965) *Organization and Innovation*. Homeward, IL: R. D. Irwin.

Bertlanffy von, L. (1962) "General Systems Theory: A Critical Review." *General Systems*. 7: 1–20.

Bertlanffy von, L. (1986). *General Systems Theory: Foundations, Development, Applications*. New York: George Braziller, Inc.

Boulding, K. (1956) "General Systems Theory: The Skeleton of Science." *Management Science*. 2: 197–208.

Buckley, W. and A. Rapoport. (1968) *Modern Systems Research for the Behavioral Scientist*. Chicago: Aldine.

Churchman, C. W. (1983) *The Systems Approach*. New York: Dell.

Churchman, C. W. (1987) *The Well-Being of Organizations*. np:Intersystems Publications.

Cummings, T. G. (1986) "A Concluding Note: Future Directions of Sociotechnical Theory and Research." *Journal of Applied Behavioral Science*, 22(3): 355–360.

Ermeng, C. (1987) "The Impact of Information Technology on Organizations." *Journal of Systems Management*. 38(4): 32–36.

Gray, W. (1982) *General Systems Theory and the Psychological Sciences*. np:Intersystems Publications.

Glasers, S. and M. I. Holliday. (1980) "Organization as Systems." *Human Relations*. 33(12): 917–928.

Hall, A. D. and R. E. Fagen. (1956) "Definition of a System." *General Systems*. 1: 18–28.

Hudson, M. H. (1980) "The Organizational System." *Journal of Systems Management*. 31(7): 37–40.

Kast, E. and J. E. Rosenzweig. (1985) *Organization and Management: A Systems and Contingency Approach*. (4th ed.) New York: McGraw-Hill.

Kast, F. and J. E. Rosenzweig. (1972) "General Systems Theory: Applications for Organization and Management." *Academy of Management Journal*. 15(4): 447–455.

Kidder, T. (1981) *Soul of a New Machine*. Boston: Atlantic, Little, Brown.

Martel, L. (1986) *Mastering Change: The Key to Business Success*. New York: Simon and Schuster.

Sanker, Y. (1988) "Organizational Culture and New Technologies." *Journal of Systems Management*. 39(4): 10–17.

Smeds, R. (1987–88) "The Role of Computerized Information Systems in the Development of Organizational Structure." *International Studies of Management and Organization*. 17(4): 90–104.

Taylor, J. C. (1982) "Integrating Computer Systems in Organization Design." *National Productivity Review*. 1(2): 218–227.

Turkle, S. (1984) *The Second Self: Computers and the Human Spirit*. New York: Simon and Schuster.

Zuboff, S. (1984) *In the Age of the Smart Machine*. New York: Basic Books.

Schoderbeck, Peter P., C. G. Schoderbeck and A. G. Kefalas. (1990) *Management Systems: Conceptual Consideration*. 4th Ed. Homewood, IL: Irwin.

8

The Learning Organization

In the last chapter we stressed the use of new models of thinking as a key tool for individual capability development. We will return to this theme of individual development as a cornerstone of the change process in the final chapter. However, at this point, we would like to consider team learning, or group development. A management team, or any other for that matter, can be—and usually is—composed of many intelligent, talented people. But that does not guarantee business success. What forces enable a group of people to combine their intelligence and motivation in a way that the capability of the whole exceeds the sum of the individuals? This is a key question in a global, competitive environment in which the ability to collaborate becomes a key skill.[1]

To this, we would also add the ability to collaborate faster, at higher, more energy-efficient levels for ever-larger purposes. In the United States, this push toward collaboration can generate an advantage because of our multicultural heritage. As a result of history, Americans, by and large, have learned how to collaborate across racial, ethnic, and religious lines. Obviously, there is a potential disadvantage in a loss of English-language skills in education, which we have begun to witness already.

As we have outlined before, many new technologies supposedly designed to facilitate groupwork and development of teams are becoming available.[2] Our experience is that technology, by itself, is not a sufficient reason to move groups of people in the realm of high-performance teams. The really effective processes have been developed in the field of organizational design over the past 30 or so years. This chapter reviews several of those organizational approaches as adjuncts to currently available technology. It is our contention that there is a rich history of these techniques, often overlooked by technology designers and developers.

Such ideas, techniques, and methodologies have come to be known as "organizational learning" procedures. One could argue about the pedagogical differences between individual and group learning, but that is not our purpose here. We ask you to accept the premise that the learning process applied to a group or organization is sufficiently different from individual application to require an expanded view of the process.

The center for these innovations has been M.I.T. and its program of Systems Thinking and Organizational Learning. You have seen glimpses of these techniques before in our discussions of mental models (Chapter 7) and technology and organizations (Chapter 5). Ray Stata, the CEO of Analog Devices, has elegantly captured this process by describing his own experiences in using the "organizational learning" perspective.[3] Stata posits that the major restraint to improved management effectiveness is a lack of innovation in management style. He has found that, by using organizational learning as a compass, teams can indeed develop group ability far in excess of their historical levels of performance.

Organizational learning occurs when people engage in a joint process that stresses sharing of insights, knowledge, and mental models and builds on past experience and knowledge. Technology can be used to clarify assumptions, speed up communication, and construct histories of insights and catalog them. Let's examine each of these key characteristics of organizational learning.

Insight-sharing often comes through use of facilitated conversation about the process that people experienced when they came to some realization, idea, or novel solution to a problem. We have used the technique with managers to trace the history of problem solution. Others in the groups benefit from seeing the pattern someone else used to come up with a new idea. The same is true with sharing knowledge: what you know is most effectively passed on when a fact can be placed in the context that the recipient understands.[4]

Building on past knowledge and experience is more difficult than one would assume. In order to build upon past learning endeavors, they must be accessible. There is a tremendous amount of knowledge in any business. It is usually carried around in the heads of the workers. During the 1980s, we saw a flurry of activity around the development of expert systems as a way to capture this precious asset and make it accessible to others. However, as our pace of change increases, even computerized business libraries are difficult to use.

We believe that this capture, preservation, and access to previous learning is an area that deserves emphasis in the near term. For example, as companies downsized, they in effect discharged a vast amount of organizational learning. In one case, we discovered that outgoing workers had failed to document the location of very expensive physical assets of the company because of the short time allowed for this process. In the past, the workers were always there and they could be called up and asked a question. But now they are gone, and so is their knowledge. Some chemical companies, for example, are having to relearn basic production formulas and processes. When the company was asked to install a new service, they discovered they didn't know where their assets were and had to replace the lost ideas with new ones—a very expensive process. If you bury your treasure and don't make a map of its location, and then eliminate the burial party, the enterprise suffers a tremendous cost for not retaining its learnings.

How does all this learning theory relate to business effectiveness? The simple answer is through *time*. Time to adjust to new conditions, time to beat competitors to market, time to develop new products. Organizational learning enables quicker and more effective response times of the enterprise to its environment. Learning itself occurs as a function of time. This is one of Stata's key findings. The time to reduce mistakes by half seems to be fairly constant, and is reduced through organizational learning. That is to say that learning takes time—it can't be rushed—but once the process is started, it seems to feed on itself, and groups get better quicker. Again, this point is echoed by Reich, who feels that once you embark on a process of continuous learning, it may be impossible for others to catch up because you are always getting better at a faster rate.[5]

Lastly, Stata reports that organizational learning is best practiced with the aid of an outside facilitator who works on building the communication among team members and is able to challenge assumptions held by managers.[6] Therefore, this chapter is devoted to an exploration of the idea of organizational learning as an outgrowth of systems thinking and mental models and predicated upon the need for business enterprises to respond quicker to environmental changes.

Plan of the Chapter

This chapter begins with looking at establishing organizational learning as an institution within businesses. First, we make a distinction between education (learning) and training. Next, we discuss the classical formulations of how to do organizational learning as an intervention process and briefly review current practices of key actors in this area of practice. As we mentioned earlier, there are concrete organizational costs to not moving in this direction. We discuss these costs and then give an overview of two emerging theoretical approaches that we feel have much promise.

The chapter concludes with a discussion of why organizational learning is becoming a key, competitive, leverage point for global enterprises. As a case study, we include some developing work that looks at how organizational learning can, and indeed must, become fully integrated with the core planning processes of successful organizations. The case study is based on recent research with executives of Silicon Valley high-technology firms.

Where We Are

This chapter represents Point 7 on the Enneagram. This chapter is intended to look at getting better at getting better. We are moving from Point 6, which we used to emphasize individual development, to creation of group capability. To recap our path so far, we started by looking at the purpose of organizational intervention, moved to creating good communication as a foundational idea, and then in turn, looked at techniques of design, customer service, process improvement, structural change, and—finally—mental models.

We are now beginning to close the development loop. We have amassed quite a number of tools to look inside and outside the organization. The last chapter began the final learning process by presenting new cognitive capabilities; this chapter takes that process to the level of group integration. The following, final, chapter will return to the idea of self-improvement as a conclusion.

Thus, this chapter connects organizational learning with communication ability. We believe that, at this point in the Enneagram process, you can begin to see the systemic connections between the points of the process because this is the first chapter that allows you to reflect on material previously covered. You may want to refer back to Figure 1-4 at this time to check where we are in the thinking and doing processes of development.

Learning Objectives

The learning objectives for this chapter are:

- Understanding of the organizational learning perspective
- Appreciation of the distinction between education and training
- Knowledge of the components of the organizational learning process
- Familiarity with the intellectual development of the perspective we are advocating
- Knowledge of emergent approaches to organizational learning
- Recognition of how organizational learning may be integrated into strategic planning processes

This chapter is where we hope that the pieces will start to fall into place. Your previous reading has been replete with facts, figures, new models, diagrams, and rich case material. But how does it all relate to practical application? All the ideas in the world are not worth much unless they can be applied to practical problems. Organizational learning is where this material comes together. Introduction of technologies creates opportunities for positive change. Increasingly, we have to look at systemic solutions to business problems, and we are being propelled into the twenty-first century without adequate conceptual tools to learn how to change faster than our business and political environment. Getting better at getting better—quicker is the theme of this chapter.

CONTINUOUS LEARNING AS AN INSTITUTION

Our basic thesis is that if a business enterprise is to become a learning organization, then learning as a process needs to become a permanent feature. It needs to be institutionalized. Institutionalizing any process significantly impacts how enterprises are managed, budgeted, and planned. First, changes to long-term behavior must be made with reservations regarding its cost. We all know that in relatively tough times one of the first things to go out of the budget is the allocation for training. Learning organizations don't operate this way.

This part of the chapter begins with a description of what we think a learning organization looks like. Then we spell out the often-misunderstood distinction between training and education, review the current literature, and close with a brief discussion of how to begin creating a learning organization, and the cost of not developing this organizational mode.

Definition of Organizational Learning

There are many definitions of a learning organization. The concept goes back at least to 1978.[7] In the field of organizational development, there is a tendency to develop a "theory of the decade," where a number of approaches get relabeled to reflect a current trend. In some respects, organizational learning has suffered this fate in the late 1980s and early 1990s. This is unfortunate because there is a cogent core to organizational learning that distinguishes it from other approaches to development.

The key characteristics of the organizational learning approach are:

- Perspectives are seen as constantly changing. Looking at your organization in different ways is a normal, healthy practice. Change is anticipated. Change is a forward-looking view, not a simple reaction to the environment.
- Employees are characterized as inquisitive, flexible, and self-motivated. Intrinsic reward is a central feature. Individuals are engaged in self-development and like to learn. Risk-taking and experimentation are encouraged.
- Management is measured and rewarded on how it encourages workers to continually improve themselves and the organization.
- Information is routinely collected, analyzed, and made readily accessible to all employees. The process of intelligence collection, analysis, and dissemination is built into the organization's structure. Both internal and external knowledge systems are integrated.
- Boundaries between internal and external are permeable.[8]
- Learning takes place at several levels—learning and learning how to learn.

The organization becomes a student of its environment and uses its employees as parts of the learning system. Learning does not happen by accident—it is designed. As you see in the case study in this chapter, this type of organization is not the norm of United States business. However, in cases where learning has been institutionalized, distinct competitive advantages have been discovered.

Many times, we have had clients who ask, "How will we know when we get there?" Well, the first answer is, "When you stop asking if you are there." However, there are some key indicators we look for that indicate a commitment to organizational learning, as follows:

- Between 5 and 7 percent of gross receipts are devoted to employee development.
- More than 3 percent of employee time is spent on direct learning.
- Human-resource management is integrated into the strategic planning process.
- Capability improvement is available to all employees.

Learning organizations are holistic entities. It is difficult to quantify and measure this characteristic. The Institute for the Future has compiled a list of characteristics of learning organizations.[9] Learning organizations are sometimes called high-performance

Table 8-1   Dimensions of Learning Organizations

Characteristic	Reactive	Responsive	Proactive
Time Orientation	Past	Present	Future
Thinking Style	Task	Possibilities	Conceptual
Planning Process	Extrapolate	Market Share	Global
Management	Control	Coordinate	Facilitate
Structure	Fragmented	Hierarchical	Matrix
Employee Perspective	Self-Preservation	Work Team	Corporate culture
Motivation	Extrinsic	Internal	Personal Values
Communication	Downward	Lateral	Feed Forward
Change	Resistant	Incremental	Planned
Power	Centralized	By position	Empowering
Learning	Experience	Experiment	Mastery
Systems	Segmented	Bureaucratic	Entrepreneurial
	First Wave	Second Wave	Third Wave

*Adapted from Martin (1990) Institute for the Future

organizations and fourth-wave companies. Table 8-1 is an adaptation of the Institute for the Future dimensions.

As you can see, these characteristics are global in nature and have an implicit value in them—that being a learning organization is good and is a goal to strive for. In truth, becoming a learning organization is not an appropriate goal for every business. Becoming a learning organization is simply another tool in the kit bag of the organizational development specialist.

The Distinction Between Education and Training

Education is not training. Organization learning is about education. It is important to make this distinction. Earlier, we suggested that successful, developing companies need to devote between 5 and 7 percent of gross receipts to employee development. This does not include skill-based training. Sending everyone to class to learn how to use a spreadsheet program is helpful but is not directly aimed at creating a learning organization.

There are several levels of learning, which can be called first-, second-, and third-order.[10] First-order learning really amounts to obtaining facts and definitive answers to explicit problems. Second-order learning is developing a set of additional skills to think abstractly and be able to think systemically. Third-order learning involves the realization of changed value-sets and a deep questioning of assumptions about human behavior and meaning. In a business environment, this becomes a process of questioning, "What business are we in?" "How are we different from our competitors?" and "Where are we going?"

The field of organizational development has traditionally focused on second- and third-order learning systems. This focus will increase in importance as organizations realize that gains in productivity and effectiveness expand exponentially with second-

and third-order learning. The changing paradigms of business make it necessary to develop the ability to adapt more quickly as the discontinuous change effects discussed by Handy are experienced. We are reminded of an old French proverb that goes (paraphrasing):

Come to the edge, come to the edge
They came to the edge
We pushed them off and
They flew

This point of experiencing the possibility of step-function change is important because it begins to help managers change their priorities. Cutting the training budget is one solution because you can see that it has immediate short-term impacts. It is also relatively easy to recover from, because of the short cycle times of developing and delivering training programs. However, education is different. Education is cumulative, experiential, and long term. Interrupting an educational process requires a different method of re-engaging. In our experience with adult, returning, college students, we find that they require significant time to simply settle back into the process. We have also seen the same thing occur when an organizational intervention process (i.e., education) stops and then starts again in a few months.

Therefore, one of the first steps in creating a learning organization is to get commitment from executives for a long-term process, with supporting budget and dedication of resources. A test of will is required to initiate a successful process. We have been witness to many large-scale attempts to create second- and third-order learning that failed. Ultimately, they failed because the third-order learning began to shift fundamental beliefs. When this happens, the stability and security of the old order begins to crumble. Repeatedly, we have seen that initiating a change process destabilizes an organization, and therefore needs to be managed with third-order change controls.

Important Works in the Field

There is a rich literature on organizational learning. We would like to briefly review three key works that may serve as a starting point for readers who want to delve deeper into this area of organizational development. The first work, by Argyris and Schon, is a classic that first coined the term "organizational learning." Argyris' work on double-loop learning brought legitimacy to the idea in the business world as, currently, Senge's work is becoming the theory of the decade. For the serious student of learning, this is a starting point; for others, it is intended to bring awareness of another perspective on managing the change process created by the introduction of new technologies.

Organizational Learning: A Theory of Action Perspective[11]
Argyris and Schon were the first to codify the intervention perspective of developing a learning organization. This grew out of their groundbreaking work with large-system change. The earlier approach of conducting action research began to move toward an educational model in the early 1970s with incorporation of Gregory Bateson's work

on deutero-learning and double-binds.[12] Double-binds are situations where players are engaged in a "game" but cannot discuss the rules. These are paradoxical situations. They are often found in organizations where the written rules and unwritten rules are different. (Consider a sign that says "Don't Read this Sign.")

Argyris and Schon start with identifying situations where paradoxes are created and use these as opportunities to shift belief-systems. Their classic examples are directions given to workers such as the following:

1. Take initiative	1. Don't violate the rules
2. Think of the organization as a whole	2. Don't cross into others' areas of responsibility

These are situations where organizational learning can occur. The organization can learn first of all that these paradoxical situations lead to ineffective business practices and create stress.

Intervention in such situations can be accomplished in several ways. One clever technique is to survey, or talk to, subordinates and superiors about the normal cultural rules of behavior. Quite often, these conversations can reveal paradoxical norms of behavior. No change will take place until these double-bind situations are made visible. The role of the interventionist becomes one of surfacing and clarifying these specific situations.

The field of organizational learning has gone much beyond these early formulations but it all began with the explicit recognition that organizations could learn to work differently. Organizations, like individuals, could be taught to examine their most basic assumptions about the world around them, their own behavior, and most recently, the behavior and feelings of their customers.

Double-Loop Learning[13]

Argyris begins his article with the words, "By uncovering their own hidden theories of action, managers can detect and correct errors." This article is similar in content to the Organizational Learning book authored with Schon, but placed in a business context. At the heart of any learning system is the ability to test, reflect, and correct behaviors, theories, or actions. What Argyris calls for is the development of action-feedback loops in organizational structure so it can monitor its own activities and correct aberrant behaviors.

Single-loop learning is much like a simple feedback system found in a thermostat. It detects errors and moves the system back toward homeostasis. Double-loop learning occurs when the system can begin to question what temperature the thermostat *should* be set at. The organization becomes self-reflective about *what* it should do. In most circumstances, organizations can operate very effectively in single-loop learning mode. However, when some radical change in either its internal or external environment occurs, it can become highly dysfunctional.

It is in these times of radical shift that double-loop learning becomes a survival skill, not just a nicety. The governing theories of action and operation are based on valid data, free and informed choice, and constant self-reflection and testing of assumptions. The primary inhibitors to double-loop learning are vague and inconsistent communication patterns. When these are coupled with cultural barriers to questioning the validity of information, the organization is put in a double-bind situation.[14] Effectiveness decreases, but no one is allowed to question why. A vicious negative feedback loop is established and things go downhill rapidly.

Argyris contends that building learning organizations must start with clear communication, have good designs with alternatives, seek out valid internal and external information, and develop the ability to make informed choices and monitor effects of action. If you refer back to Chapter 1, you will find in our Enneagram model many of these same steps.

The Fifth Discipline

A very popular book on organizational learning at this writing is Peter Senge's *The Fifth Discipline*. In this book, Senge sums up all that he and his M.I.T. team learned in working with clients to create learning organizations. The heart of the matter is that Senge believes that there are five key development areas that must come together to foster the learning organizations. We will briefly describe each of these. However, we suggest that the interested reader refer to the original source. Senge's rich descriptions and examples make for good reading.

PERSONAL MASTERY

Personal mastery is more than competence and skill. It involves a true dedication to one's life work. The approach a Zen master or a skilled craftsman takes toward his work is an example of personal mastery. It certainly has a skill component along with a spiritual part. But true personal mastery goes beyond that to a state of consciousness about your engagement with a business enterprise. Work becomes much more than activity to gain reward; it becomes joyful in its own essence.

MENTAL MODELS

Senge argues that we need new ways of looking at the world in order to create a learning organization or, for that matter, to really become significantly more effective. Our previous chapter on mental models was devoted to this topic. An addition to that discussion is making an explicit difference between what is being said and what people are thinking. Often, our mental model of what is going on is different from what we are expressing. Decreasing this differential between implicit and explicit mental models is a task to be worked on in the learning organization.

SHARED VISION

It is obviously difficult to get an entire organization moving toward the same goal if they are not operating out of the same shared vision. We would expect the thinking to include developing a shared understanding of purpose—both individual purpose and enterprise purpose. This task of building shared vision usually falls to leaders, but also has a part in which followers need to interact with leaders to ensure that they are in sync with the changes in the leaders' vision.

TEAM LEARNING

Dialogue, discussion, and practice are tactics Senge promotes as avenues to creation of team learning. Learning within a group structure is often difficult for American business people. Our tradition has been individual learning and individual leadership for direction. Learning as a team, and especially collaboration, is often initially experienced as somewhat strange. Typical organizational interventions, such as team building, can be used to work on this core discipline of the learning organization.

THE FIFTH DISCIPLINE
Senge's fifth discipline is best captured in the "Laws of the Fifth Discipline." Among them are the following:

1. Today's problems come from yesterday's "solution."
2. The harder you push, the harder the system pushes back.
3. Behavior grows better before it grows worse.
4. The easy way out usually leads back in.
5. The cure can be worse than the disease.
6. Faster is slower.
7. Cause and effect are not closely related in time and space.
8. Small changes can produce big results—but areas of highest leverage are often the least obvious.
9. You can have your cake and eat it, too—but not at the same time.
10. Dividing the elephant in half does not produce two small elephants.
11. There is no blame.

These eleven simple statements capture the essence of a core thinking ability for the learning organization. They may seem simplistic at first, but upon close examination, you will find that they come from hard experience and require that you suspend much of the kind of thinking managers traditionally use. These are useful as koans for a learning organization.

Creating the Learning Organization

Creating a learning organization is not an easy task.[15] If you carefully re-examine Table 8-1, you will note that moving from more traditional organizational thinking to a learning model implies a shift in culture and, more fundamentally, a shift in belief systems. McWhinney has called this movement "third-order learning."[16] First-order learning is collecting facts and data; second-order learning is developing skill at the process of learning. Third-order learning is a change in perspective, belief systems, and underlying assumptions about human behavior. Third-order learning is the most difficult, time-consuming, and fearful.

However, there are some basic guidelines you can follow to help enterprises become more of a learning organization. For example, we believe quite strongly that the entire process of managing human-resources needs to become a central part of setting enterprise wide strategy. Acknowledgment of the central importance of people as learning resources is a necessary first step in building a learning organization. Making use of all available technologies to speed learning and reduce its cost is important, also. Organizational intelligence systems need to be made integral parts of the organization's technical infrastructure.[17] This is more than simply recording a lot of information in an archive. Information needs to be turned into intelligence by cross-referencing and opening access to the data. Additionally, use scenario planning and simulation techniques to allow employees to experiment with different ways of doing business.

Our own approach to developing increased learning capability has been outlined earlier in dealing with Strategic Customer Service. This process starts with intervention targeted at building communication capability. This is followed by carefully defining customer expectations and looking at inherent internal processes. The last step is concerned with building continuous improvement capability into the organization. This last step is really about constructing a learning organization. We suggest you refer back to that section of Chapter 4.

One of the current techniques for creating learning organizations is the use of Senge's *microworlds* concept. Microworlds are computerized business environments that simulate a real-world situation.[18] The computer modeling we described in Chapter 5 is an example of a microworld simulation. In this environment, decision makers take control of a fictitious company, playing the roles that they fill in real life. However, unlike the real world, managers are free to experiment with policies, strategies, and different processes without having to experiment on an ongoing enterprise. These simulations have the capability of increasing learning speed. Microworlds can also help people quickly see the differential effect specific management strategies have—if the computer is programmed accurately.

> Microworlds, which have the potential to deepen and accelerate learning in a wide variety of management situations, are developed from a relatively small number of generic structures that recur in all kinds of business situations. An example of a generic structure is burden shifting, which occurs whenever remedies appear to improve a problem in the short term but actually shift attention away from fundamental corrections.[19]

A variant on the microworlds technique is an extension of the old "in-basket" business simulation. This approach is called Looking Glass® and simulates a 20-person, senior management group in a glass factory.[20] The concept is to give students or managers an experience of integrating planning, leadership style, delegation, and subordinate supervision tactics.

In sum, all these tactics of helping people create a learning organization seem to be headed in the same direction. Simulating a business enterprise in a relatively protected environment and using trained facilitators accelerate the learning curve. Not that every possible business situation can be simulated, but theory says that enough can, so that what used to take several years of on-the-job experience can now be compressed into several weeks. These simulations are becoming the laboratory of organizational design.

The Cost of Unlearning

There is a cost associated with becoming a learning organization. We are reminded of the cheers of "quality is free," which led many managers to embrace a change methodology—really believing it would cost them nothing. Any change costs—it costs in time and effort. Yes, ultimately, you can amortize those costs over time and see that it pays off in a business sense; but, initially, you need to be ready to absorb the additional cost of learning, training, slow decision processes, and loss of key personnel.

So if the costs are so great, why embark on the journey? We believe there simply is no choice if you want to remain competitive in a global, dynamic economy. There is a price to be paid for not becoming a learning organization, and it is very large. It is measured in terms of market-share percent lost, write-offs, write-downs, and loss of the priciest of intangibles such as reputation and ability to attract what every company hires—only the best and the brightest. Figure 8-1 is a diagram of the cost/time relationship of developing a learning organization. As you can see, costs rise rapidly as implementation kicks in and don't begin to decrease for about 18 months. Then as you reach a two-year point, the costs go below previous expenses and you begin to recoup the investment.[21] There are a couple of key observations to be made from this curve.

For one, change takes time. You can't expect to significantly shift people's beliefs and habits in a few months. How long does a college education take? How long does it take for artists to become truly proficient in their work? There are many examples around us showing that fundamental change takes long periods of time. You can easily overspend when you attempt a reorganization effort. The optimum is obtained by using an organizational model to analyze and simulate the control of change. The fallacy of change is that you can put more resources behind it and speed up the process.

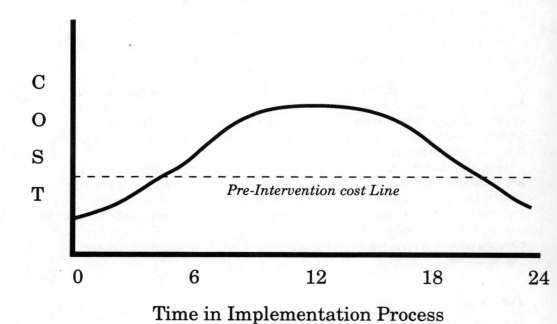

Time in Implementation Process
(Months)

Figure 8-1. Cost versus Time of Developing a Learning Organization

Nonsense. There is a basic, built-in time lag that has to do with learning rates of people and acceptance of change in work life. We believe this cycle takes somewhere between 18 and 24 months of continuous effort.

Costs ramp up quickly, as normal work slows and a higher percentage of time is spent managing the change process. People often say they don't have time to educate, or even train, the workforce because of the press of business. This implies that companies may have to consciously sacrifice some profit-growth in order to position themselves for the long run by developing a learning organization. This takes courage. The hope is that you can effect the change and reverse the profit decline before governance boards demand ceasing the effort. If these costs and time elements are known, they can be planned for in advance. Most often, no planning takes place, and management gets very nervous as they see rising costs and—at first—slower production. Presenting a reasonably long-term view is a key responsibility of the organizational designer on the front end of the intervention.

The initial costs of managing this change process come from the necessity to unlearn old ways of doing business. Developing new ideas and beliefs doesn't happen in a moment. It takes time and effort to unlearn old habits. There are several theories of how this process takes place. Various unlearning models represent different opinions about unlearning, as follows:

1. The *extinction* model, where old behaviors are not rewarded and new ones are. This takes several budget cycles to become apparent.
2. The *replacement* model, where you substitute new for old. This only is effective in later stages of change when organizational momentum is on your side.
3. The *exorcism* model offers a time for a cathartic experience and sudden change. These are often only effective for short, crisis periods of time. A longer-run institutional process needs to be put in place behind this unlearning experience.
4. The *salvation* model, where new leadership is brought in to shake things up. This often depends on a messiah leader to be effective. Hard to manage.

Recently, new models of unlearning have come forward that offer some practical advice of how to structure an organizational learning process to avoid the pitfalls of traditional models. The most current of these is called parenthetic learning. Technically it is defined as "the cognitive expulsion of elements from a set because of enhanced understanding of characteristics that define the set, thereby reducing its size.[22] In translation, this means that by expanding the scope of activities in an organization and coming to see it in more systemic terms, you can help people take certain dysfunctional behaviors out of their repertoire of behaviors.

Fundamentally, it means helping managers become conscious of the negative impact of their old ways of behaving on the entire organization. This process can be helped along by creating a nonthreatening climate and

1. Intervention directly focused on the behavior, not the person.
2. Using a third party to reinforce focus on action, not person.

Again, this incurs a cost—the cost of unlearning.

We are learning more about learning every day. The learning styles that allowed memorization and individual style need to be changed. This change in style for both individuals and organizations is costly, but well worth the effort in the long run. We now turn to an examination of two specific new models of learning and conclude with a discussion of why new industrial policies may encourage the organizational learning process.

NEW MODELS OF LEARNING

As the topic of organizational learning has begun to catch on as a legitimate management strategy, so has the development of learning theory. What once was thought to be a rather dry, esoteric topic left to psychological learning theorists has burst forth in to the light of day in corporate America. Given the review of the organizational learning theory above, we would now like to turn to two developments in learning theory that we believe may well inform organizational design practitioners.

The first is a recent review of three fields of study not normally associated with one another: learning, work, and innovation. The article by John Seely Brown and Paul Duguid was prepared at the Institute for Research on Learning, a research think-tank funded partially by Xerox, where Brown is vice president of the Xerox Palo Alto Research Center. The second article is the result of many years' research at Carnegie-Mellon University into the relationship between various factors and successful industrial research and development.

Both articles begin to bring us full circle from where we began this discussion in Chapter 1. The artificial distinction between home, workplace, and schoolhouse is no longer a viable view for corporate America. This entire book has an underlying theme that integration of workplace and community is being brought about by technologies that increase connectivity across time and space. Also, this trend of integrating work and community runs counter to what we have experienced, at least in the United States, for over 200 years. This makes the transition to a new way of working very difficult unless we can learn new ways of learning.

Communities of Practice

Brown and Duguid[23] begin their discussion of integrating work, learning, and innovation by pointing out that current research shows that the way people really work is vastly different from what is contained in formal job descriptions and procedure manuals. This seems to be a commonsensical conclusion. However, there are several implications to this finding. First, maybe organizations really don't have an accurate record of their core work processes available in documented form. If this is true, then the pleas of organizational learning proponents to make this knowledge accessible as a condition of learning may fall on deaf ears. Secondly, this finding implies that a precursor to any group learning experience is a clear, careful analysis (and documentation) of what the business process really looks like.[24]

The second major point made by the authors is that they find that much learning and innovation takes place in informal "communities of practice." These are the communities that naturally grow up around work practice as it evolves in the day to day experience of people. We all have had the experience of asking, "Who around here knows how this is supposed to work?" That informal community of practice is often not revealed in the formal analysis of organizational charts and manuals. If, as Brown and Duguid contend, much effective learning occurs in these informal groups, then the delivery of learning systems to users must be developed in a nontraditional, nonhierarchical fashion. We happen to agree from our own experience that these communities of practice are the nexus of the social network within organizations. Once identified, they can become powerful communication avenues for the diffusion of innovation within an organization. In fact, they are the unseen and often unplanned-for power points that disrupt the easy introduction of new technologies.

Their findings, we believe, argue strongly for the development of open communication systems and communications-based interventions to promote organizational learning. Information social networks supported with open-architecture communications can become a vehicle to promote learning and improve business effectiveness. However, this can run counter to existing norms of behavior. We are aware of one example of actually doing this that ran afoul of corporate guidelines for interorganizational communication. This case involved several research scientists who were employed in several divisions of a large computer company. Informally, these people belonged to the same professional societies, went to graduate school in the same places, and generally owed a loyalty to a profession that transcended corporate structure. As the people began to build up an informal electronic communication system that cut laterally across the several divisions they were employed by, management became concerned. Finally, their electronically supported "community of practice" was dismantled under severe pressure to decrease interorganizational communication.

The last point made by Brown and Duguid gets to the heart of the argument. If the pace of innovation and organizational effectiveness can be improved through individual and group learning, how do we promote this? Their answer lies in a closer integration of working, learning, and innovation. The counter-intuitive appeal of their argument is that large organizations, which traditionally are viewed as barriers to learning, may well possess the critical mass necessary to build very complex communities of practice as a basis for learning.

We would like to suggest that this idea of integration needs to be extended further. First, it needs to be consciously supported as part of a strategic vision of the enterprise. Appropriate technology can be used to provide system support.[25] Also, we believe that as the electronically distributed workplace becomes a reality, integration of work and learning should extend to the wider social community people live in. In a sense, economic development becomes community development. The ideas of Brown and Duguid support this contention—with which we began the book—in the sense that they support the concept that learning is, indeed, something that takes place in a spontaneous fashion and often extends to venues constructed by learners themselves as communities of practice.

Absorptive Capacity

Absorptive capacity is "the ability of a firm to recognize the value of new, external information, assimilate it, and apply it to commercial ends.[26] Cohen and Levinthal argue that this capacity is in large part determined by the level of prior knowledge. That is, your ability to find and use new external information is a function of how much you already know. This seems to be in keeping with Reich's idea that symbolic analysts learn at ever-increasing rates. [27] The authors go on to extend this model from the individual level to that of the organization. Again, these ideas fit well with the school of organizational learning that stresses collecting external information and using it as a basis for business decisions.

If this variable of absorptive capacity is critical to the continued growth and flexibility of the organization, how do we increase it? Cohen and Levinthal suggest that promoting the diversity of expertise within the organization can help. Obviously, promoting, and funding, basic research-and-development efforts is another way. Let's take a moment here and examine the implications of these relatively straightforward findings.

Increasing the diversity of ideas, perspectives, and problem-solving approaches within an organization can also create much tension and increase the cost of decision making. When a business entity deliberately creates differences, it develops a situation in which creative tension must be resolved. [28] This increases the cost of decision making. It takes more time to reconcile different assumptions and sort out the priorities of action that occur from differences of opinion based on an increased number of perspectives. The implication, we believe, is that when you increase diversity of ideas (or in cybernetics terms, the requisite variety), you need concomitantly to put in place a capability of reconciling these differences. The added cost in terms of money and time will be rewarded. The basic issue is whether or not diversity is valued for its creative potential or seen as an unwarranted additional cost. The Cohen and Levinthal data suggest that the cost is well worth the investment.

The second implication of their work concerns dealing with external information. External information often causes people to question what previously appeared to be a valid interpretation of the environment. Our experience is that this information is often attenuated as a function of its likelihood of raising questions concerning the wisdom of current organizational purpose and direction. That is, there is an organizational inertia behind product development, marketing strategy, and customer satisfaction. When externally gathered data begins to cast doubt on these areas, the data becomes suspect and discounted in value. This is exactly the point of creative tension at the organizational level.

What Cohen and Levinthal are telling us is that we must deliberately create these situations at the individual and work-group level through diversity, and at the organizational level through collection, examination, and dissemination of external data. Without these informational gaps of "what is and what could be," there is no energy toward improvement. The system tends toward entropy as it becomes more and more insular. [29] Again, the practical implication of creating more absorptive capacity is recognizing the need to design technical and social systems that value diversity of ideas and actively seek to import challenging information into the business enterprise. The converse implication is that enterprises that fail to do so are destined for decreasing market share and severe cost pressures.

From New Ideas to New Practices

These new ideas of learning have implications for how we help managers integrate new technologies into the workplace. We believe that the missing component today is a shift in perspective away from seeing work and learning as separated activities and toward a more systemic perspective. Moving from thinking to doing is not easy. There are many structural impediments in our society today. While the advent of new technologies certainly present us with opportunity, they also present a challenge to our creativity, patients, and will toward more effective business organizations. We now turn to a more practical discussion of how to more forward with these ideas of organizational learning.

LEARNING AS WORK AND WORK AS LEARNING

The Brown and Duguid article points the way toward the future. Technology is allowing us to foster a closer relationship among work, community, and learning. We believe that the distinction among these activities will blur over time, young adults will begin their professional lives earlier, and learning will become a lifelong activity that is incorporated into other spheres of our lives.

It is our contention that white-collar people will need to spend 20 percent of their work lifetime learning new skills and thinking abilities. That's 20 percent out of the normal work schedule. This might not be a steady one day a week, but over the space of several years, this figure will prove accurate. We have begun to witness the use of sabbaticals in corporate America as a way of re-educating the professional workforce. We believe that this will extend to other ranks and positions over the next decade as we respond to the need to re-educate our workforce. Our 20 percent is not much of an extension of the traditional academic sabbatical of one year out of seven spent devoted to increasing capability.

What kinds of things will people be learning? What specific abilities will corporations need to develop? Aside from the general ideas we have presented from the organizational learning literature, other areas are becoming apparent. Returning to our original theme of Chapter 1 about what's driving the need to integrate technology diffusion and organizational development, we can isolate four specific abilities that demand greater development.[30]

The increase of symbolic analysts as a key component of the workforce of the future requires four basic abilities as follows:

1. *Abstraction.* Most Western education is built on a reductionistic method of analysis. In fact, analysis is the cornerstone of most educational programs. The global environment demands an ability to put parts into wholes—to synthesize information. Merely regurgitating facts and figures is insufficient to develop an understanding. We need people and organizations that can pull, from the mass of information floating around them, the abstract pattern and utilize that pattern in a self-generated process that allows understanding and prediction.
2. *Systems thinking.* We hardly need to say more about this ability. This entire book is based on the premise that the only reliable way to analyze organizations is to adopt a systems perspective. Further, we suggest that Reich's ideas extend to the use of more formal frameworks of thought brought from the Eastern traditions of increasing understanding. We are reminded of a story where two engineers are brought into a room and shown a complex machine in pieces on a table. One

engineer is Asian; the other, North American. When asked to describe the machine, the North American begins with minute descriptions of each piece. The Asian begins with describing the function of the assembled machine. This ability to see whole systems will be critical to workers in an information-intense environment. What is the pattern that connects the pieces?

3. *Experimentation*. This is a methodological as well as a social skill. The method of experimentation is a kind of knowledge embedded in the sciences but not well practiced in most secondary schools. For example, lecture courses predominate over laboratory courses in most schools. However, the social skill of learning from mistakes is the critical element. Experimenting with business processes needs to incorporate techniques such as simulation, discussed earlier. The bottom line requires allowing people to use this technique outside of the tightly controlled laboratory.

4. *Collaboration*. This ability above all others requires the design and use of new technologies. We have seen the advent of groupware and collaborative technologies during the past decade. However, as we noted in Chapter 2, they have been unsuccessful because they often ignore the fundamentals of interpersonal behavior. Knowing how to work in a relatively statusless team is becoming a business necessity—not a nicety. This is the *key* problem facing systems designers. How do we design communication technologies that support people working in a collaborative fashion? True collaboration—not just cooperation.

These are the skills that will form the foundation for individuals and organizational learning in the coming decade. They are as much technical as they are social—an important point. Our educational systems, as well as our business enterprises, must respond to redress the traditional imbalance in capability development. The work world of the future demands a co-evolution of technical and social skills.

CASE STUDY

We now conclude this chapter with a presentation of an extended case study of the factors related to developing a learning organization. This study focuses on a practical problem of integrating the continuing-education function into strategic management of businesses. (The case study was prepared originally by Carolyn Schultz as a master's thesis project with the University of San Francisco).

Integrating Continuous Engineering Education and Human-Resource Development with Business Strategy

Due to the accelerating pace of change, demographic realities, and the competitive demands of a global, market-driven economy, continuous education is necessary for individual and corporate survival. The challenge of pursuing economic leadership in world markets has been studied at length, and specific recommendations regarding employees in high-technology industries have been advanced by the National Academy of Engineering,[31] the National Research Council, and the American Society for Training and Development, in conjunction with the U.S. Department of Labor. All reports are consistent in their conclusions: Continuing engineering education and professional development are seen as critical for U.S. industry to embrace in order to maintain a competitive advantage, and for the country to achieve economic leadership in the world market.

Training and education in corporations are generally ad hoc exercises, used to prevent what is broken or to prevent immediate difficulties; rarely are they used to prepare for the long term.[32] Figure 8-2 addresses these issues by contrasting education and training characteristics. The purpose of this study was to explore the utilization of continuing education as a strategic human-resource effort, and to examine the nature of the linkages between human-resource management and the strategic business-planning process.

The premise of the study was that if continuing education was considered to be a key human-resource effort, the human-resource management was closely linked to the strategic business-planning process, then continuing education would also be linked to an organization's strategy. The study attempted to verify this hypothesis by surveying policy makers and senior managers of organizations in high-tech industries in order to verify characteristics, suggested in earlier research, of organizations that consider human resources and continuing education strategically.

It was also hypothesized that the higher the level of integration of human-resource management (HRM) with strategic business planning (SBP), the more continuing education will be institutionalized. This study looked closely at senior management's perceptions of continuing education's value as a key human-resource-management effort, perceptions of the human-resource function, organizational characteristics, and the links that exist between human-resource management and the strategic planning process.

The significance of identifying the characteristics of linkages of human resources to the strategic business-planning process lies in the potential for developing a model to answer the questions: What types of linkages between HRM, the SBP, and continuing

EDUCATION	TRAINING
Learning as an end in itself	Learning as a means to an end
Future Utility	Present Utility
Understanding	Results
Subject-oriented	Problem-oriented
Concepts emphasized	Skills emphasized
Broad perspective	Focus on internal issues

Adapted from W. R. Scott and J. W. Meyer (1991), "The Rise of Training Programs in Firms and Agencies: An Institutional Perspecitve," *Research in Organizational Behavior*, vol. 13 pp. 297–326, Greenwich, CT.: JAI Press.

Figure 8-2. *Contrasting Education and Training*[33]

education exist? What are the organizational characteristics that fit with these linkages? and ultimately, Which linkages should be developed for various organizational development stages? This research was considered a pilot study for a larger (in scale) study, and focused on the process of integration of the human-resource function rather than the content of strategic plans.

Methodology

The subjects of this study were companies in high-tech industries that employ large numbers of technical professionals, and were determined, through the use of secondary information, to be companies where continuing engineering education is utilized. Five companies were initially contacted, and three accepted the invitation to participate. An administrative contact in the human-resources funcational area served as primary liaison. This person in all three organizations chose the company-specific subject list with the following list of general, functional titles:

- V.P., Human Resources
- Director, Human Resources
- V.P., Research and Development
- Director, Research and Development
- V.P., Manufacturing
- V.P., Engineering
- Director, Engineering
- Engineering Management

Other functional titles, such as marketing, finance, etc., were discussed with each administrative contact. It was urged that the functional area be related to technology and the management of technical professionals, and that respondents would have senior policy-making responsibility.

The logic of the research approach is shown in Figure 8-3. Questions at both levels attempted to determine: (1) the role of continuing education for technical professionals and its perceived value; (2) the role HR currently plays in the strategic business-planning process. Finally, questions about the critical elements identified as influencing the degree and speed of strategic integration were verified.[34]

The critical elements explored were:

- Perceived importance of technical employees as a key success factor
- Abilities of the technical workforce
- Abilities of the technical workforce in comparison to the firm's competition
- Environmental factors
- Degree of people-orientation in the corporate culture
- Structure, by exploring the role of the HR executive
- Perceived business capabilities of the HR staff
- Management systems by identifying the degree of communication

Frequency distributions were calculated for each question, and cross-tabulations were calculated in order to examine the relationships between different response categories.

Determine perceived value of continuing education as a key HR effort	♦	Determine role HR plays in strategic business planning process	♦	Identify/verify linkage characteristics in order to determine linkage category of HR and SBP

Figure 8-3. Research Approach

Chi-square was used to test significance. Tests of significance at the 0.05 level were used, and cross-tabulations that did not meet this test were discarded. Gamma is an appropriate measure of association for ordinal data and was only calculated on those Chi-square calculations that were determined to be significant.

Respondent Demographics

This display of Respondent Demographics shows the areas of functional responsibility for respondents. As you can see, the majority were functional administrators or tactical human resource experts.

Number of Respondents	36 of 45	(80%)
Functional Responsibility		
• Engineering and other technical areas	12	(36%)
• Human resources	13	(36%)
• Administrative	4	(11%)
• Not available	7	(21%)
Technical Degree	21	(64%)
Hold an Advanced Degree	25	(76%)

Questions and Responses

Question 1
"How would you characterize the external business environment your company operates in?"

Don't know	2	**
Declining	5	*****
Weak	1	*
Stable	5	*****
Dynamic	23	***********************

Question 2
"How would you rate the degree of 'people-orientation' in your company culture?"

Very low	0	
Low	8	********
Average	17	*****************
High	9	*********
Very high	2	**

Question 3
"How would you rate the level of importance that the chief executive officer of your firm places in developing the value of human resources in your firm?"

Don't know	0	
Very low	3	***
Low	4	****
Average	11	***********
High	13	*************
Very high	5	*****

Question 4
"What is your view of the role of the chief human-resource executive at your firm?"

Functional administrator	14	**************
Tactical human-resource expert	13	*************
Strategic partner regarding human-resource issues organization-wide	8	********
Senior planning executive for all issues affecting the firm	0	
Other	1	*

Question 5
"How would you rate the value of the human-resource executive's input into the strategic business planning process?"

Very low	7	*******
Low	13	*************
Average	12	************
High	4	****
Very high	0	

Question 6
"What do you think other senior managers in your firm think of the human-resource function?"

View as a cost-center	22	*********************
Resource for implementation of strategic business plan	13	*************
Key success factor for competitive advantage	1	*

Question 7
"How would you rate your understanding of how human-resource development efforts for technical staff in your firm can contribute to the firm's overall business performance?"

Very low	0	
Low	2	**
Average	4	****
High	20	********************
Very high	10	**********

Question 8
"Rate the importance of technical employees (engineers, scientists, R&D staff) as a key success factor to building your company's competitive advantage."

Very low	0	
Low	0	
Average	0	
High	7	*******
Very high	29	*****************************

Question 9
"Overall, how would you rate the knowledge, skills, and abilities of the technical staff at your firm in comparison to your competitors?"

No opinion	0	
Low	0	
Average	4	****
High	20	********************
Very high	12	************

Question 10
"In considering the following human-resource efforts in the development of your organization's technical staff, please rank the contributions to competitiveness of the following human-resource development efforts." (See Figure 8-4.)
"How would you rate the effort of your company to communicate, both formally and informally, to the firm's stakeholders the organization's strategic business plans?"

| Very low | 3 | *** |
| Low | 7 | ******* |

	1	2	3	4	5	6	wtd factor	Rank
Recruiting	4	2	3	7	4	15	155	1
Compensation	2	8	10	4	8	3	122	4
Continuing Ed.	2	2	5	10	11	5	146	2
Training	2	7	5	7	7	7	136	3
Mentoring	4	8	8	6	8	1	114	5
Other	17	2	0	2	0	7	71	6

Figure 8-4. Weighted Factor Scores[35]

Average	16	****************
High	9	*********
Very high	1	*

Analysis of the Findings

Continuing Education's Value as a Key Human-Resource Effort

When asked to rank five human-resource efforts in order of importance for the development of a technical staff that would strongly contribute to the competitiveness of the organization, recruiting was ranked first, with continuing education ranked next. The rankings were summarized using a weighted factor that revealed a cumulative score for each category. Each category was then ranked from largest response to smallest. Training ranked third, compensation (of technical staff) fourth, and mentoring fifth. The "other" category was a distant sixth. The CEO-designate interviews revealed a bias toward recruitment of engineers with advanced degrees. In one organization, the interviewee stated that continuing education had become a dominant theme as the organization retooled for the future.

These findings generally correlate with Burack's (1991) other findings: the human-resource application areas receiving the greatest attention and resources were recruitment and development of upper management and technical professional staff.

This ranking of continuing education as a critical human-resource effort, second after recruiting, was not shown to have a statistical relationship with any of the other survey questions, but when the responses to the question regarding their understanding of how human-resource development efforts were applied to technical staff were considered, 83 percent answered that they had a high or very high understanding. It is likely that due to the small sample size, a statistical relationship was not found, although it appears through examination of the data that there is a perception by senior management of the value of continuing education as a key human-resource effort, as assumption supported by the qualitative data collected in this study's interviews of CEO-designated executives.

Perceived Value of Human Resources and Its Role in the S-BP

Several questions explored perceptions of the human-resource function, the perceived value of the chief human-resource executive's input into the strategic business-planning process, as well as the view the CEO takes of developing human resources in the firm. Results from the survey, as well as from the interviews, indicate that the CEO has stated in these organizations that building competitive advantage through the development of the staff, and technical staff in particular, is critical. However, respondents generally viewed the chief human-resource executive either as a "functional administrator" (39 percent), or as a "tactical human-resource expert" (36 percent), with only 22 percent of the respondents indicating a more strategic role for the top HR executive in the firm. Since 36 percent of the respondents came from the HR function, these findings could be slightly biased.

There is a moderate statistical relationship between the perceived role of the chief HR executive and the senior manager's view of the HR function. The more the HR executive is viewed as a strategic partner, the more the HR function is viewed as a key success factor to the organization, and less as a cost-center. These findings correlate with work by Spector (1988) that found HR efforts were valued by the firm when HR was widely considered to be critical in developing and sustaining workforce competencies, and ultimately organizational competitive advantage.

One CEO-designate interviewed responded to the question regarding the role of the chief HR executive in the S-BP as follows: "The position is not formally designated, but probably should be." Another said the HR function is generally perceived as a "partner" in the S-BP, or internal consultant.

Analysis of the data showed a moderately strong relationship between those respondents who rated a high value of the top HR executive's input into S-BP and the view senior managers have of the HR function as being more than a cost-center. These findings indicate a lack of systems thinking. If these respondents felt the organization was being viewed as a "system," then the value of human resources would have been evident. Seeing the organization as a whole would also have led to the development of shared values and goals. When organizations are unable to develop and communicate a shared vision, paradoxes such as this are likely to exist.

Deeply ingrained assumptions and beliefs that middle management hold about the validity of human resources will prevent these organizations from truly changing and improving, and ultimately could prevent the organization from achieving full effectiveness because goals and objectives will be accomplished with great difficulty, if at all. Previous work in the area of strategic human-resource management revealed key organizational characteristics that either facilitated the integration of HRM with the strategic business-planning process, or provided barriers. This research explored these elements in order to confirm or deny earlier findings.

Environmental Factors

It was revealed in the literature that environments in transition due to increased competition, changes in key technologies, and/or changing labor demographics would create a more important role for human-resource development, and increase the need for continuing education as a key human-resource effort. Sixty-four percent of the respondents indicated that they operate in a dynamic environment. The dynamics of the environment also revealed a moderately-related increase in the ability of the organization to widely communicate its strategic business plan, another factor identified in earlier research as a critical element to S-HRM.

Two of the three CEO-designates interviewed indicated that the turbulent external environment was causing a re-evaluation of all previously held assumptions, including those about human resources, education, and training. In one organization, the evolution of a new mission was causing a reprioritization of technology research and development, and the executive felt that continuing education, among other human-resource efforts, would facilitate the continuous skill enhancement of technical employees. Dynamics such as these respondents described also provide an environment in which learning can more easily take place.

Degree of People-Orientation

Organizations studied in earlier research, which displayed characteristics of two-way linkages or highly integrated linkages between HR and strategic business-planning processes, identified widely held views of people as key success factors for competitive advantage, and as a result invested in their people for future growth, often through continuing education. In this study, 69 percent of the respondents indicated the degree of people-orientation in their company was low or average, yet response to the question of the importance of technical employees as key success factors to building competitive advantage was overwhelmingly strong, with 100 percent rating this importance high or very high. The response to this last question indicates the possibility of response bias, and therefore should not be considered as a significant finding.

This calls for recognition of the contribution of the human resources of the organization. Such a shift in orientation away from the technology of the organization to the human resources of the organization could focus on the staff and their knowledge as ultimate sources of the technology, and facilitate better development and utilization of these resources. Organizations cannot change unless they engage in a basic reorientation of the shared values and beliefs of the organization.

Ability to Communicate Strategic Plans Organization-wide

A moderately strong relationship exists between an organization's ability to communicate its plans organization-wide with its degree of people-orientation and the perceived value of the HR executive's input into the S-BP. These findings correlate with Buller's earlier research indicating that an organization that values its people will extensively communicate its strategic plans. The organizations in Buller's study that widely communicated their strategic plans also had two-way and integrative S-HRM linkages.

Communicating strategic plans can be difficult, but are made even more difficult if a vision of the organization's purpose is not developed or communicated. A truly shared vision enhances communication, facilitates focus, and provides the energy for learning. It also prevents a strategic plan from being shoved in a drawer.

Conclusion

Of the many factors defined in the literature that impact the integration of human-resource management and the strategic business planning process of S-HRM, five were studied in this research, found to be significant, and have some degree of association with the identified variables. These five were: the degree of people-orientation found in an organization's culture; a turbulent environment; the role of the chief human-resources executive; perception of the human-resources function; and the effort of the organization to communicate its strategic plans.

Findings from the CEO-designate interviews indicate a growing recognition of the need for stronger ties between the human-resource development function and the strategic business-planning process. This is likely to be more true in high-technology industries that have a high concentration of technical professionals working in a rapidly changing technological environment. Given the indicated value of continuing education as a key human-resource effort, continuing education as a critical component of the strategic plan is likely to become more widely recognized.

The nature of strategic planning is evolving, and the traditional "strategic plan" is being replaced by "strategic decision making" in order to speedily respond to changes in the marketplace.[36] Implementation of strategic plans will call for key components to be in place, such as technical professionals familiar with leading edge technology developments, as well as the organizational capability for learning. This development will call for human-resource leaders to have highly integrated linkages with the organization's needs and plans, so that the critical human-resource needs of the firm will be in place and prepared to contribute to the organization's competitive advantage.

NOTES

1. Robert Reich (1992). *The Work of Nations*, New York: Vintage Books, identifies "collaboration" as a key skill for the symbolic analyst of the future.
2. An excellent overview is given by Johansen et al. (1991), *Leading Business Teams*, New York: Addison-Wesley.
3. Ray Stata, "Organizational Learning—The Key to Management Innovation," *Sloan Management Review*, vol. 30 (3), Spring 1989, pp. 63–74.
4. This is an instance in which technology can be very helpful by capturing these insights and facts as they are talked about. For example, automated meeting-room technologies seem to enhance group effectiveness in this fashion.
5. See chapters 18 and 19 ("Education of the Symbolic Analyst"), op. cit.
6. The process of Strategic Customer Service discussed in Chapter 4 is built upon this premise.
7. Chris Argyris and Donald Schon (1978), *Organizational Learning: A Theory of Action Perspective*, New York: Addison-Wesley.
8. See Chapter 4, "Strategic Customer Service," Stage 3, Step 3.
9. Alexia Martin (1990), *1990 Ten Year Forecast*, Institute for the Future, San Jose, California: Hamlin Harkins.
10. See McWhinney (1992), op. cit. Bateson first used the term deutero-learning to make this same distinction.
11. Chris Argyris and Donald Schon (1978), *Organizational Learning: A Theory of Action Perspective*, New York: Addison-Wesley.
12. Gregory Bateson (1971), *Steps to an Ecology of Mind*, New York: Ballantine.
13. Chris Argyris, "Double Loop Learning in Organizations," *Harvard Business Review*, Sept.–Oct., 1977, pp. 115–25.
14. Gregory Bateson formulated the concept of double-bind situations. See his essay on the development of schizophrenia in *Steps to an Ecology of Mind* for greater detail.
15. Mark Easterby-Smith (1990), "Creating a Learning Organization," *Personnel Review*, vol. 19 (5), pp. 24–28.

16. Will McWhinney (1992), *Paths of Change,* Beverly Hills: Sage Publications.
17. See H. Wilensky (1967), *Organizational Intelligence,* New York: Basic Books.
18. Peter Senge and Colleen Lannon, "Managerial Microworlds," *Technology Review,* vol. 93 (5), July 1990, pp. 62–68.
19. Senge and Lannon, op. cit.
20. This product is marketed by the Center for Creative Leadership and comes in a University Edition for use in the classroom.
21. This diagram is based on our own experiences. It lacks significant empirical validation at this time. We feel that the overall shape of the curve is valid—but necessarily reliable in a range of change settings. Sometimes it could be shorter, sometimes longer.
22. Jonathan Klein, "Parenthetic Learning in Organizations: Toward the Unlearning of the Unlearning Model," *Journal of Management Studies,* vol. 26(3), May 1989.
23. See citation in References.
24. It is for precisely this reason that we promote the use of Business Process Analysis before attempting to institutionalize learning systems.
25. However, we would again caution that this support does not come without planning, implementation, and change-management costs.
26. Cohen and Levinthal (1990), p. 128.
27. Refer to Chapter 1 and the discussion of the education of symbolic analysts in the global marketplace.
28. Senge, op. cit. (pp. 150–155), argues strongly that this creative tension is a necessary step towards creating novel solutions for business problems. We also practice this in our own intervention work. See the following chapter on individual development for more details about making differences work.
29. In Chapter 4, we discussed the creation of "permeable boundaries" in organizations. The purpose of opening these boundaries is to decrease the resistance to flow of external information.
30. Reich, op. cit.
31. "Continuing Education of Engineers" (1985), Washington, D.C.: National Academy Press.
32. Olson, L. (1986), "Training Trends: The Corporate View," 40(9), pp. 32–35.
33. Adapted from W. R. Scott and J. W. Meyer (1991), "The Rise of Training Programs in Firms and Agencies: An Institutional Perspective," *Research in Organizational Behavior,* vol. 13, pp. 297–326, Greenwich, Connecticut: JAI Press.
34. See Buller (1988), and Golden and Ramanujam (1985).
35. Factor scores were calculated by simple addition of individual element rankings.
36. See Eisenhardt (1990).

REFERENCES

Argyris, C. (1977) "Double Loop Learning in Organizations." *Harvard Business Review.* (Sept.–Oct.):115–125.
Argyris, C. and D. Schon. (1978) *Organizational Learning: A Theory of Action Perspective.* New York: Addison-Wesley.
Bateson, Gregory. (1971) *Steps to an Ecology of Mind.* New York: Ballantine.
Brown, J. S. and P. Duguid. (1991) "Organizational Learning and Communities of Practice." *Organization Science.* 2(1):40–57.
Buller, P. F. (1988) "Successful Partnerships: HR and Strategic Planning at Eight Top Firms." *Organizational Dynamics.* 17(2):73–87.

Burack, E. H. (1986) "Corporate Business and Human Resources Planning Practices: Strategic Issues and Concerns. *Organizational Dynamics*. 15(1):73–87.

Burack, E. H. (1991), Changing the Company Culture—The Role of Human Resource Development. *Long Range Planning* (UK) 24(1):88–95.

Cohen, W. and D. Levinthal (1990), "Absorptive Capacity: A New Perspective on Learning and Innovation." *Administrative Science Quarterly*. 35:128–152.

Dixon, N. (1990) "Action Learning, Action Science and Learning New Skills." *Industrial & Commercial Training*. 22(4):10–16.

Easterby-Smith, M. (1990) "Creating a Learning Organisation." *Personnel Review*. 19 (5):24–28.

Eisenhardt, K. M. (1990) "Speed and Strategic Choice: How Managers Accelerate Decision Making." *California Management Review*. 32(3):39–54.

Fulmer, W. E. (1990) "Human Resource Management: The Right Hand of Strategy Implementation." *Human Resource Planning*. 13(1):1–11.

Golden, K. A. and V. Ramanujam. (1985) "Between a Dream and a Nightmare: On the Interaction of the Human Resource Management and Strategic Business Planning Process." *Human Resource Management*. 24(4):429–452.

Johansen, R. et al. (1991) *Leading Business Teams*. New York: Addison-Wesley.

Klein, J. I. "Parenthetic Learning in Organizations: Toward the Unlearning of the Unlearning Model." *Journal of Management Studies*. 26 (3):291–308.

Manz, C., D. E. Keating, and A. Donnellon. (1990) "Preparing for an Organizational Change to Employee Self-Management: The Managerial Transition." *Organizational Dynamics*. 19 (2):15–26.

Martin, A. *1990 Ten Year Forecast*. Institute for the Future. San Jose, CA: Hamlin Harkins.

McWhinney, W. (1992) *Paths of Change*. Beverly Hills, CA: Sage Publications.

Paoness, C. (1991) "Managing Change." *Discount Merchandiser* 31(6):66, 68.

Reich, R. *The Work of Nations*. (1992) New York: Vintage Books.

Senge, P. (1990), *The Fifth Discipline: The Art and Practice of the Learning Organization*. New York: Doubleday.

Senge, P. and C. Lannon. (1990) "Managerial Microworlds." *Technology Review*. 93(5):62–68.

Stata, Ray. (1989) "Organizational Learning—The Key to Management Innovation." *Sloan Management Review*. 30 (3):63–74.

Spector, A. K. (1988 "Strategic Steps to Management Support." *Training and Development Journal*. (Feb.):42–43.

Wilensky, Harold. (1967) *Organizational Intelligence*. New York: Basic Books.

9

Self-Development

This final chapter brings you full circle in the exploration of technology and organizational change. In a sense, it is a return to the first step in the Enneagram. Aspects of function, being, and will have been followed throughout the book so far. This concluding chapter deals with the point that *fundamental organizational change cannot come about without a preceding, or concurrent, change in self.*

This chapter presents you with several ways to look at yourself, your workgroup, and your organization. At the individual level, the Enneagram is outlined as a way to deepen understanding of self.[1] At the organizational level, this chapter presents practical advice on how to audit and analyze interaction you have with your organization as a way to improve your individual capability. Our underlying belief in presenting this chapter is that organizations can only improve and develop if their leaders improve and develop themselves.

It is our experience that looking at development can open the doors to an exciting and improved future where people realize the wonderful potential of self-directed change. Often this process starts with a concern for use of technology (where we began); moves through very functional concerns, such as Business Process Analysis; and returns to education, which in turn produces significant shifts in personal values. The intention of this chapter is to leave you with an awareness of choices—your choices—and knowledge that you can control and master, beginning with your own development. We present some tools for managing change, and, it is hoped, some degree of confidence in the face of the difficult work entailed.

230

Plan of the Chapter

This chapter is structured in a slightly different fashion from the preceding ones. We begin with our usual approach of specifying where we are in the Enneagram process and laying out the learning objectives of the chapter. After a brief introduction of why self-development is important, we delineate the role of self-development for executives and the individual. Next, we explain a number of principles of self-development we have found helpful in our executive-coaching work. The major part of this chapter is then devoted to outlining a specific process of self-development that you can begin using. The chapter concludes with an explanation of how self-development relates to organizational process and some hints for you to develop your own path toward becoming better at observing yourself and remembering yourself.

This chapter does not contain a case study. Our own experiences in using these techniques of self-development are probably the best case-study material available. The experience of moving through the material in this book and seeing the pattern of the Enneagram that connects thinking and doing has been your own case study.

Where We Are

This chapter represents Point 8 on the Enneagram. This chapter is intended to look at the process of self-development as a cornerstone of the organizational-change process brought about by the introduction of technology. We are moving from Point 7, which looked at developing organizational learning strategies, toward Point 9—a second look at establishing meaningful purpose in the enterprise. This chapter may initially look as though it represents an end to a process. However, we feel that it is merely the closing of one loop, or cycle, of development—and the beginning of another cycle. The wheel continues to move.

In terms of the Enneagram thinking process, this chapter connects self-improvement with structure and technology. You may want to refer back to Figure 1-4 at this time to check where we are in the thinking and doing processes of development. This chapter is also the link between design and structure. What this means is that design can not meaningfully proceed without taking into account how self-development can enhance the design and structure of organizations.

Learning Objectives

The learning objectives for this chapter are:

- Introduce the concept of self-development as an integral part of organizational design
- Specify the key principles of self-development
- Present a method of self-development for use
- Demonstrate the equivalency between self- and organizational-development
- Complete the learning cycle of the Enneagram as a model

This chapter concludes your journey through our methods of linking technology and organizational change. This is the last step in that journey. We would ask you to reflect back on what you already read and seek to put self-development into the context of what you, the reader, will now do with this material. It is our hope that you move forward by adapting your own self-development plan and using that as a platform to help your clients, co-workers, and associates learn how to better use technology in work organizations.

SELF-DEVELOPMENT

Why should we talk about self-development in a book such as this? Because self-development is the primary job of organizations. Rarely is the job of senior management described in these terms, but there is a general understanding of this obligation. Self-development is an ever-present job of all employees. In good times, employees and companies tend to forget this responsibility. When things begin to go bad, when company performance deteriorates, employees and company management seem to remember with great clarity the self-development obligation of others and blame troubles on the lack of commitment. We start asking how do we get people to buy-in and forget we allowed them to buy-out.

Laid-off workers tossed out of the company as a result of its poor performance, have been told it was due to "changing market conditions." They ask whether all these changes were a surprise. They look incredulously at their bosses, so filled with sure answers for the last several years, and ask weakly, "Wasn't it your job to know? Wasn't it your job to look out for the future of the company?" Managers and executives turn philosophic in response. They disavow any responsibility for the employee's own marketability and point the finger of responsibility back at the employee and to regulators and policy makers.

Of course, we would not argue that every change can be accurately anticipated. But, in many cases, senior management has been working at jobs that they defined as managing other people, as managing products, and even as survival of the company. All of these definitions of the job are too narrow in scope and too easy. The key job of executives is the development of the organization.[2]

Self-development for an organization is the responsibility of the senior management and is almost always lost in managing the doing of the various works of the departments. Instead of paying attention to developing and development, top people all too often spend their time embroiled in the day-to-day activities of the organization. Occasionally, management notices that things are a little flat, creativity is gone from product development, problem solving, and customer service. They usually find the employees short of the kind of thinking and motivation needed and so start efforts aimed at regenerating these lost attributes.

Finding great weaknesses in the very people who have looked to corporate leaders for guidance and development each day, management launches a long progression of task forces, study groups, committees, etc., aimed at reinvigorating the organization. Often, frustration with these activities opens the door for consultants promising to be able to deliver the missing thinking and motivation.

Excellence is proclaimed from posters everywhere. Bosses with a fresh tan talk of their experience at camp and testify with camp-meeting fervor that they have found a new, unquestionable goal. Learning forays are attempted at an organizational level. Quality is pursued with a vengeance and with hordes of committees, consultants, and charts. Management misses the goal of organizational development when it misses the lessons of personal development and cannot, even with good intentions, translate for the organization.

Key Principle of Self-Development

Self-development for the organization is the act of continuous redefinition of itself via interaction with its customers. A management focused strictly on directing what the organization is doing cannot work on organizational self-development.

This is not management-bashing. We merely point out that the most senior levels of a company, or any organization, have the responsibility for the "self-development" of the company. The neglect of this responsibility is matched by employees at all levels who neglect their own self-development. Let's look at this side of things.

The Individual

Self-development is likewise the primary job of each individual. This, too, is generally understood but not often expected or demanded in the usual job description. The employee who is not developing himself is the whining sloth that wonders why everything is happening to him. He feels that he is blown about by the whims of the manager to whom he reports. He lives in fear of co-workers, bosses, and subordinates and feels trapped in his job.

This person has the obligation to work daily on self-development of the inner person. People who ignore this responsibility are stuck in a reactive mode, unhappy and always at the effect of things, unable to take charge of life and move forward toward increasingly positive experiences. We know from the psychology literature that working on self-development is a key characteristic of successful business managers.[3]

Hundreds of self-help books, talk shows, gurus, recorded tapes, videos, and a thousand therapists suggest that we are not the only ones holding this opinion. At least, we are not the only ones feeling the need for such work. Self-development is the motivation behind hobbies, exercise, reading, spiritual work, picnics, and everything else we start on with *intention, interest, and personal effort.*[4] Ignoring the responsibility to work on self-development is a shirking of even greater magnitude than that of the executive who similarly neglects his paid responsibility for the organization's development.

Neglect of self-development leaves the individual as hollow and uninspired as the company that is not developing itself. In an almost endless stream of books, articles, and speeches, we hear over and over that people make the difference; that people are the foundation of meaningful change and improvement. Some truth is underneath all the simple homilies about people, even the one that says single individuals are capable of making a significant difference in an organization.

Just as for companies, self-development work for an individual is the hardest work. It isn't an isolated concept that has no relationship to other things; we think it is somewhere on a spectrum of kinds of work. There are many methods that have been offered for people to work on self-improvement. Self-development is the most neglected area of important work in the corporate world. If it is proper to want to have a world full of companies that are growth-full and developing potential for their employees and customers, then we must fill them with employees who match those characteristics.

Ideally, the individual's work on self-development should be an ordinary part of daily work. It should be enabled, or at least allowed, by the normal function and systems interactions made in the course of carrying out assigned jobs.

What we are suggesting here is very active. We suggest starting the race *and* running in it. Giving one's self over to a process that one is in charge of, but in which one has an abundance of choice. What if we were special, more special than we ever thought? What if there is a unique role for us to play? We believe that there is and, almost like a play that we watch unravel, that unique role is just waiting for us to discover it. That is to say, develop it. It is the responsibility of every individual to be all that he or she can be, and to do that by developing his or her essential characteristics in the interests of that very ideal.

The matching goal between people and organizations is that of resource utilization. A company that can get more out of its resources than competitors is way ahead. A person who can get more out of him/herself is way ahead of competitors and the old self that was less effective on the job and with life in general.

Principles of Self-Development

How do we need to think about self-development, once we decide to work on it? We believe that this is an important and serious undertaking and, like any such undertaking tackled by a company, the doing of it needs to be governed by strong guiding principles. These are the principles that we think need to run throughout anyone's work on self-development.

1. *If it isn't hard to do, it isn't developmental.* People have discovered the truth of this principle in many fields of development. One must push against the natural tendency of the moment in order to develop the desired attribute. For an easy physical example, to build muscles one must combat the natural tendency to relax and take it easy in order to make the trip to the gym and work hard against the weights.
   To think about a company equivalent of this process, consider a company trying to change and make major improvements in its normal processes. At the very minimum, the company must take on the added burden of new initiatives while it still has the normal job to get done.[5]
2. *Help is required.* Trying to pull yourself up by your bootstraps is admirable but damned difficult! Meditation, as an example, is almost universally recommended for self-development but, without help, is not easy to undertake and sustain. We

recommend that a person find a source of help—help that is honest and nonaddictive.[6]

Again, in an organization, we see parallels that make sense: new books that the boss reads, consultants, and external threats often provide a needed source of help. This example shows that "help" is, perhaps, a little different from what is usually described. As used here, help is clear, honest comparison of value needed with value provided by you to those around you.

3. *Your role in the bigger scheme of things must get clearer, and the bigger scheme of things must become more important.* Life should get better and you should have more fun. Time, family, and neighborhood begin to push aside immediate gratification of small goals.

How many executives have we heard say, "This company forgot what it is here for." Or, "We are getting back to providing what our customers have wanted all along." Self-development for a company means the same as for a person: Find the real you that is needed by the "neighborhood," find out why that is needed, and supply it as only you can.

It is helpful to think about the individual's mental organization in a manner similar to the way we think about the organization of a company. Single individuals are not really one person. We are not the same person from moment to moment. Always speaking about myself as "I" gives the impression that there is one I. Not true, however, if judged by behavior. Sometimes I am the helpful consultant, not judging or denouncing incorrect thinking or actions; the next minute I (the same I?) is yelling at the driver in the car in front of me because it is obvious that he doesn't think like *me* or else he wouldn't drive like that!

It is our contention that each of us is made up of several individuals, each of whom has different aims and personalities as well as values and abilities. We are not the first to suggest this theory, we just believe it and offer it as a beneficial way to think about the relationship of self-development and organizational learning.[7]

Metaphysical literature describes different attributes of the person as being made up of situational mixtures of aspects of our being. Daniel Dennett offers the "multiple drafts theory" to explain parallel brain processing.[8] While this theory is not entirely accepted, we think Dennett is on the right track and supports others who have gone before in metaphysical literature.

Our way of saying it is that there are a lot of little Larrys inside Larry and a lot of little Charlies inside Charlie. This idea is not so strange as it might seem. We can see ourselves at certain times behaving as we did at age 10, or behaving as our father or mother did in some situation. An oft-heard question is, why did "I" do that? In a not very scientific way, this is proof that it is at least worth asking the question, which I did you identify?

In our view, the organizational metaphor is exactly the same. Organizations behave according to the wishes of those in power based on their temperament and inclinations at any moment. They tend to go this way and that, often losing their direction. If you don't believe that, just look at the number of consultants and professors employed to help with direction, both strategic and otherwise. "Why did the boss do that?" "Well, I don't know, but Bob had just told him about what has been going on in the other company up North." In this situation, we can't tell whether the boss has acted from clear strategy or the little boy in him has acted from anger at some "bully" who stole his glove on the playground.

Further than the individual in the organization, departments gain and lose favor from time to time: we all watch for the light of favor to come down the hall and we all notice when it dims in the office over there. As gains are made and losses suffered, the organization sways and turns, distracted from its original goals. In some families, it is important to check right away and see who is in front in the family photo this year. Corporate picnic photos are often treated the same way.

Having watched our own behavior with incredulity too many times, we say that the metaphor holds for us. We generalize to all and say that the same is true for all people. There is too much evidence that we are not in strategic control of the small people inside us. They often lead us by the whim of whichever one of them is in charge (in favor) at the moment. To test this idea, try this little gedanken experiment. For the next week, do not let yourself think about self-development. We think you will find that one of those little yous in your head will exert its independent influence on your thinking. The question is, "Who is in charge of your thinking, you or your mind?"

Technology and Self-Development

Perhaps it would be good to review the reason for this chapter and why we feel it is important. Technology is developing all the time. Each introduction of technology into the workplace creates an organizational change. To develop technology, we must push it past its old truths. New breakthroughs are hailed as great progress. Yet the world is getting worse all the time. Our belief is that the organization must go through similar breakthroughs. Not anti-technology, but pro-people, development is needed. Albert Einstein once said that he felt humanity was beginning to create problems with technology that would require entirely new ways of thinking to solve. In other words, one level of thinking can create situations that cannot be understood without significantly shifting our mental perspective. Shifting this perspective is a central task of self-development—learning to see the world in new ways.

A new, powerful technology in the hands of a person or organization who doesn't understand its power is dangerous. In an organization that doesn't see that it must walk forward with both feet, technology and organizational development is bound to go forward in a jolting hop-along way, jerking itself into its future in a condition of imbalance. A person who is going into his or her future without working on (internal) organization, we think, will have essentially the same experience. All the attributes that we admire so much in our role models are to be had as the natural output of the process of developing self. Constancy of purpose and direction, reliability and strength of conviction, predictability, calmness are all to be had with work on internal organization.

If we could put these internal little people to work, or out of the picture, we could be much more effective in ways we work and interact with others. At the core of self-development is the remolding of all the little people in each of us. So, just as with a company, the issue is one of alignment and clarity—*clarity of our own personal motives, plans, and actions*.

THE PROCESS OF DEVELOPMENT

What would we suggest to a company that is wondering whether it should undertake some developmental process? We would probably start with suggesting an assessment of some kind.[9] Commonly used, cultural assessments are most helpful in discovering and clarifying the internal state of an organization.

Those assessments often start off with questions about what the organization does well and not so well. They look at attitudes and habits, trends, etc. These assessments are usually done by outsiders or someone within the organization that everyone will talk to. It is usually explained that the information developed in the one-on-one and focus groups will be delivered to those in charge so that it can be acted on with good effect. *We suggest the same for an individual*.

How do you do this with yourself? How do you step outside and begin to get a clearer view of the real you? How do you notice the trends and habits? How do you talk to yourself and get meaningful answers? How do you move that information to some other part of you that enables change, by you? What is good for the organization is good for the individual. We need a strategic plan for our self-development. We suggest that you have meetings with yourself. This isn't as schizophrenic as it may sound. We all have little conversations with the little Larrys and Charlies inside our heads. Make these conversations more formal, regular, and maybe even have an agenda.

Whenever a company or business unit has had a performance that was less than satisfactory, it wants to improve it. More times than not, however, a clear review of the performance would mean confrontation. In many situations, confrontation is avoided in the false belief that harmony will be found in the avoidance of the issue. Performance reviews are one of the hardest tasks that managers have and are often perfunctory or ignored because of the confrontational nature.[10]

Just the opposite is needed. The organization that does not build its capacity for objective "self"-observation is destined to not develop its potential and just stay in its usual groove, producing product until the market steps in with its wake-up call.[11] When the wake-up call comes, it is not pleasant. Managers appear from everywhere, especially from headquarters, with the message that "This is not us!" We are the best in the world and we make better blivitts than anyone." Inside the individual, the same is apt to happen. Upon reflection, we may say "Whoa! That was not like me. I am much better than that."

The starting point of it all is looking at ourselves. The next quality that is needed is *objectivity*. With objectivity, we can begin to understand the meaning of our observations and develop some skill in using processes of choosing, changing, and maintaining motivation.

What does the company do when it finds itself ready to change? Any number of approaches will serve, but let's take something typical. An initiative is begun and placed in the charge of a respected sponsor. Some organizational lines are often forgiven and cut through due to the criticality of the issue and the need for the messages from the effort to be heard clearly at the highest level(s). We suggest that this method is also probably a wise path for the individual.

Does it sound strange? No, we do it all the time but, often, not too thoughtfully. When we finally come up against our own determination to change, we sit down and ask ourselves what is wrong. We think about how we should view the things we are noticing. We think about changing. Churches and schools all suggest that we can be better. But how? Fortunately, we each have the skill set needed to change for the better and to develop ourselves.

Start with a process similar to that started by the company: put one of your selves in charge of the initiative and design a way to respect the work and learnings of the task ahead. Provide a way and time for the information to get through to the real you who is in charge of the whole. Have a little fun with this and select the best of you to be in charge of the change-initiative. Okay, great, you say, just how is that done? Again, let's take the company example and see how easy it can be to start.

Journals

The scattered interviews and observations from the company's assessment are recorded with as much precision, detail, and comprehensiveness as the observer can bring to the task. At the end of the gathering of the data, there is some kind of summation process.

The notes are amalgamated and sifted to find the essentials; examples are sorted and selected to add clarity to the learnings derived. Great effort is made to stay objective during the whole process. When we do these surveys, we check with each other to be sure we don't include any personal biases. Many of our country's early leaders kept immaculate records of their actions, thoughts, and business dealings. These records contain interesting data, but the data is not the thing that caused these people to be the successful people we now revere.

What is important is the process engaged in by the act of keeping a journal in a thoughtful and routine way. What we could learn about ourselves if we looked in a day's mirror each evening and contemplated the things we did, the thoughts we had, and the things we caused that day! The tools needed are paper and pen along with some private time. This meets the first principle: *It must be difficult.* Actually taking time to spend in daily reflection is thought an almost insane idea in the increasingly busy and hectic world of today. We think it should be seen as a true piece of sanity in a healthy daily routine.

Every day, spend some time with a log in which you assess the quality of thought and action you have brought to the many situations you found yourself in during the day. Note the actions and thoughts, both positive and negative, that were not of the quality you would have chosen were you thinking differently at the time. The development plan starts immediately. In the beginning, you can observe how accurately you report the events and in what degree of clarity. After a few days of this recording, you may even find "yourself," in situations, thinking about how you will record something in your journal later that evening.

Therefore, the first step is simply building the ability to objectively observe yourself. The business parallel is the use of audit or test steps in the course of any plan implementation. How many times have we read that "The company representative stated that the company lost sight of the market." Or, "They failed to notice that their customers wanted different features," etc.

Now, what goes in the journal? Do I make a list of all that I thought, did, spoke? No, instead, try writing down the events of the day in some structured way. For example, briefly state the event, why it happened or was necessary. Note your feelings about the event and how they influence the behavior you exhibited. If you struggled with emotional responses, when calm reasoning was needed or rational thoughts when emotion was needed, note what you struggled with and why. Figure 9-1 is an example of a journal design we have used.

Observe whether you or some whims were in charge at various times of the day. Can you name these whims, the small yous? This is hard to do and may seem silly at first. Recently, my mother told me she was eating too much ice cream, and Dad wasn't. I asked her, "Which you is it that wants so much of that ice cream?" She said, "That little girl who couldn't get ice cream during the Depression."

Quickly, you are confronted with the need to judge the person you are reporting on instead of simply noticing. Try to avoid that judging. The focus here is to build the skill to observe in the interest of being ever more able to judge the appropriateness of an action or thought.

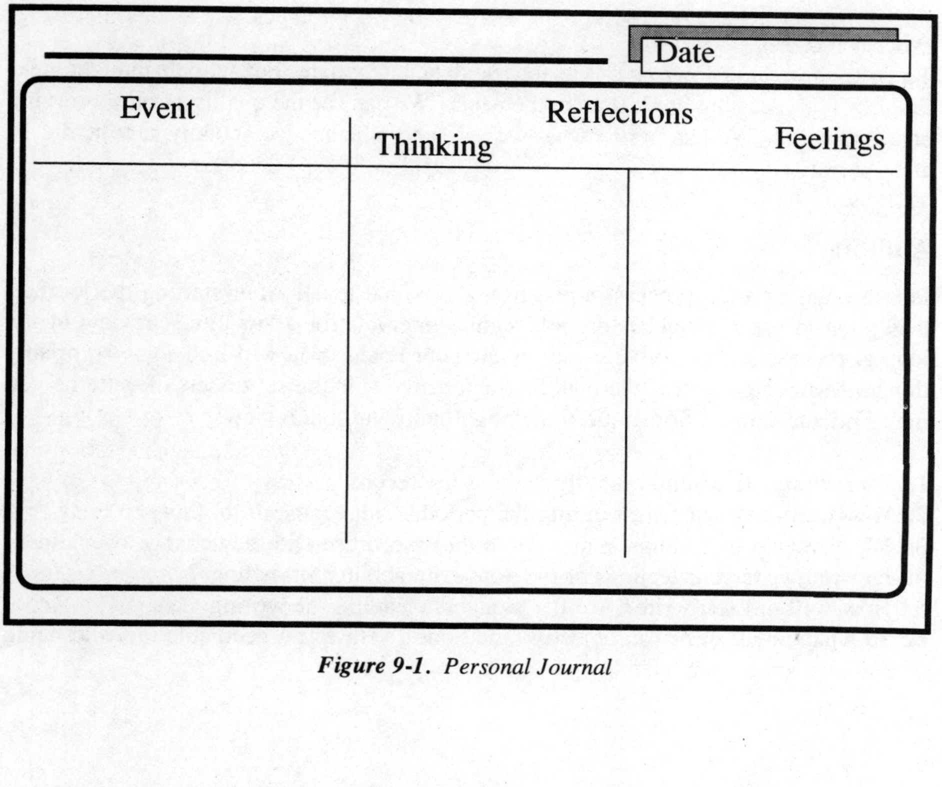

	Date

Event	Reflections	
	Thinking	Feelings

Figure 9-1. *Personal Journal*

Some Hints for Staying in Control

1. First, *trust your feelings* and acknowledge them for the power they have for alerting you to danger.
2. Second, *put* **you** *in charge of your feelings.* Acknowledgment does not imply giving in, but means that when feelings reach the level of awareness they are worth some consideration and assessment.
3. Third, keep in mind that self-development, like the development of a photograph, means making the real picture of you clear and sharp; *it is not becoming a different you.*

Each step of the development process gets to be more difficult. The next step is to begin to look carefully at the patterns of the situations in which you have been less than pleased. Let's look at the processes involved in keeping a journal.

Processes

Process No. 1
In order to write any report of the day, one must have observed the day. This means that the normal, habitual way we go through the day will now have to be experienced another way. We must notice. "Noticing" is different in nature from the ordinary process of seeing—evaluating—doing. It introduces a step in the process that is added and is different in nature. The difference is the absence of judging. Noticing gives us a chance to "read only" and just record the subject without the evaluating that normally (and naturally) goes on.

Process No. 2.
To write something down causes us to articulate the thought. Fuzzy, half-thought ideas feel like real ideas but don't flow to the paper. We can see the quality of our observing and evaluating. We can notice what we saw and whether we actually saw it, did it, etc., or not.

Auditing

Put an ongoing audit process in place on a personal level. After starting the journal, it is good to use a calendar to mark regular intervals for a "required" review of the journal process itself. Go back and review your notes. You will find some surprising things. Most important of the material under review is the set or sets of patterns you may find and note.[12] Some questions might help with the review:

1. What things were important throughout the record?
2. How did importance shift during the period? Did it move from thing to thing?
3. What were your feelings as you wrote these records? Did they change over time?
4. Did you write your feelings or did you write about your feelings?
5. How well did you write? Are the thoughts clear? Is the writing clear?
6. To what extent were you objective and honest? Have you been able to avoid being negative about yourself?

Record the answers to your questions and make them part of the next review when you repeat the process.

A version of this in a workgroup can provide amazingly quick results and begin the process of building group memory and planning capability.[13] It helps to keep the workgroup moving forward, as it reminds it of undone plans and original intentions and goals.

Find some help when you need it. Much of the early leaders' reflection was in private and only bits of it were shared with the closest friends. Anyone undertaking this process and the work it entails is quite capable of reflecting on the thoughts and actions of a day and to draw meaning from them. Sometimes a friend can help and sometimes they just like to join you in emotional log-rolling. Find help when you need it.

Helping Behavior

An old Webster's dictionary we have defines help (in part) as: "strength or means furnished toward promoting an object, or deliverance from difficulty or distress." To give strength is the definition we would emphasize. There are many who claim to be able to help you. Many are not working on their own self-development and, as a result, need strength but don't help you build yours.

So, how do you know if you are being helped? First of all, help doesn't make you dependent, or more dependent, on someone else. Second, it may scare you because of the suggestion that your future and all the good you could purposefully desire is available. Third, it seems to appeal to the largest person, as opposed to the meanest person, in you.

Help is respectful and encouraging of the *you* that is trying to develop.

We are able to safely look again at our day and decide the wisdom of some of our judgments and actions. The actions of others can come under scrutiny and allow us to appreciate without losing ground the adequacy of their actions.

BENEFITS OF SELF-DEVELOPMENT

At this point we have created three very important benefits:

1. The chance to improve what we think and what we do, and to catch up to some of the things we left undone, left by the way.
2. The chance to improve our observing.
3. The opportunity to look at the adequacy of the scope of our own interests.

There are other ancillary benefits. Dating the journal reminds us of the passing of time and provides, thereby, a chance to review our goals and progress toward them. We can notice how well or how poorly we write and go to work on that. We get to sit down and look back at the day instead of anxiously anticipating the next thing we are going to do.

SELF-OBSERVING COMPANIES

Let's switch back to the company again. How much sense would it make for the organization to have some periodic, systematic process for doing this kind of self-observing? We think it is the heart of the learning organization processes. And the remembering and observing aren't just about people-things. Some chemical companies are discovering that much of their data has gone out the door with retiring employees. Actual discoveries are having to be rediscovered!

At this point, it might be good to ask the "so what?" question. So what? Isn't this all common sense and don't we all reflect on the day on the drive or flight home? No, we don't; and no, it isn't the same. What we usually do on a daily basis is repeat some fuzzy thoughts and feelings, aimed, for the most part, at self-comfort and self-justification.

Caution: the little person who asks this "so what?" question will be the version of you *most threatened by the self-observation*. He, or she, will remind you that you have no time for this and it is stealing time from your family, job, etc. The little person will also find a thousand other things to take you away. This is why it is hard to do. Constancy is the first lesson. Isn't this the same as in organizations? Don't we often see it? When an initiative starts, many jump on—the usual ones. Shortly after the announcement of the initiative is made, all these people let it be known that they were part of the original breakthrough that brought it all about and made it what it is.

Soon, they make an assessment of the potential the project has for success. If the prospect is in difficulty, they grab some bonus points from the boss for being involved in the important new activity and jump ship, disassociating themselves from any further involvement. It is said that in some companies, you can see them sneak back into the conference room after the announcement is made to wipe their fingerprints off the whiteboard, then scurry down the hall to denounce the project in favor of its successor.

There is another caution to be given here. That is to notice the way you are looking at yourself and whether you are judging good versus bad. One of the reasons that companies and people don't usually do this detailed observing and remembering is the negative assessments that tempt one. There are no end of references to the harshness of the mirror. This process is one of holding up a mirror and getting better at seeing what is in the mirror. We are seldom pleased by the vision. That is the way our mind works and it is the secret weapon hidden in the activity.

When we look objectively, we see. When we see, we can't help but want to improve what we look at. The little people inside know this instinctively and will try almost anything to keep us from looking. Is the same true of companies? You bet! In companies, we put audit departments in place and require them to periodically investigate, to see objectively, whether we look like we think we do. This helps us get around the rather normal tendency to avoid looking—or being looked at. We work hard at trying to "pass reviews" and "pass audits."

Companies usually hire outside help when they undertake a project or plan that is beyond their capability to do a cost-effective job of whatever is being considered. They also hire out help when they feel they are in desperate need and are in an unstable condition. The method that we are suggesting for self-development is aimed at keeping you in charge of every step of the developmental process. It may be hard to believe for those who have not used this technique, but the benefits of this method are empowering and rewarding.

The most important learning is that your "self-observing" gives you power. It makes self-directed change possible and puts the decision about how, and how much, in your hands. If you get to a point where you want to tackle a particular change that seems bigger than you can handle, then, as with the company, it seems reasonable to get outside help.

The periodic review of the way you are working with your journal should be followed by a judgment of the quality of work you are doing: how steadily you attend to the recording, whether your thoughts are large in scope or small and mean. You should ask yourself whether the practice of entering these observations in the journal is causing any change, what kind, and if not, why not? Ask whether you are gaining control of some of the little people who are less than helpful. Ask whether you are making more right decisions for better (and bigger) reasons.

Over time, as progress is made, the relevancy of external factors begins to shift and new factors are given importance. Another way of saying this is that the strategic process for both the company and the person is one of *developing the ability to choose the challenges to be encountered*. Go far enough down this road and self-determination becomes more and more a predictable reality. Take a look at how you go through your days. Are you "catching yourself" and changing the way you usually respond to situations? Are you more proactive and less reactive?

The answers to these questions, we believe, will come up positive. In any event, they can be useful in motivating further work and keeping the self-observing alive and important. This is an invigorating and deeply rewarding process especially beneficial if the development of self is undertaken with a balance of family, business, and community interests. Is self-development that big a deal? We believe it is. The cry for ethical management, the astonishment of employees who suddenly become aware of the turns life has taken, the loss of competitiveness of both companies and individuals point to a gap in the development of both organizations and individuals. Companies start and, if they grow successfully, become comfortable, bloat, go to sleep, fall behind competition, and suffer. People can, and do, follow the same path unless the responsibility for self-development is acted on.

YOUR PATH FORWARD

The path that you choose to move forward on your own self-development journey is *yours* to choose. All of those little people inside your head need to have a meeting and decide who is in charge. The material we have presented here is just a start. Self-development is a neverending journey. You have gone through one very quick cycle of the framework we use to guide planning and action.

You need to go through this cycle several times; it must become almost second nature to think in these patterns before you really begin to discover their value. We hope you have found the journey we have led you on to be helpful. Some final advice:

- Always seek the truth.
- Live in the experience.
- Serve a purpose larger than yourself.

We hope that you continue to develop respect for the possible, and realize the power of your potential in the difficult journey ahead.

NOTES

1. Helen Palmer (1988), *The Enneagram,* New York: Harper and Row.
2. See Chapter 6, Figure 6-1, which identifies the distinct organizational levels and core concerns.
3. Julie Hay, (1990), "Managerial Competencies or Managerial Characteristics." *Management Education and Development.* Vol 2. (4) pp. 305–315.
4. These activities of development are not all bad. However, one should be careful not to mistake activity for true self-development.
5. A good rule of thumb is that companies should be spending between 2 and 5 percent of their total budgets for development. This needs to be split between organizational and individual programs.
6. Anne Schaef and D. Fassel (1988), *The Addictive Organization,* New York: Harper and Row.
7. Peter Berger, B. Berger, and H. Kellner (1974), *The Homeless Mind,* New York: Vintage.
8. Daniel Dennett (1991), *Consciousness Explained,* Boston: Little Brown and Co.
9. Refer back to our six step model of process in Chapter 3, Figure 3-3.
10. Imposition of external standards is resisted everywhere—both in organizations and in individuals. Earlier in Chapter 3, we talked about how when external standards are seen as harmful—the self feels that it doesn't have enough power and inward-directed hostility results.
11. Charlie Tart, *Waking Up,* Shambala, 1987.
12. Gregory Bateson used to say that one of the most important things we can do is to notice the "pattern that connects" events in our lives and the world around us—synthetic thinking as opposed to analytic thinking.
13. See our discussion of organizational learning in the previous chapter.

REFERENCES

Bateson, G. (1991), *Sacred Unity.* R. E. Donaldson, Ed. New York: Harper-Collins.

Berger, P., B. Berger and H. Kellner. (1974) *The Homeless Mind,* New York: Vintage.

Dennett, D. (1991) *Consciousness Explained.* New York: Little Brown.

Hay, J. (1990) "Managerial Competencies or Managerial Characteristics." *Management Education and Development.* 21(4): 305–315.

Palmer, H. (1988) *The Enneagram,* New York: Harper and Row.

Schaef, A. and D. Fassel. (1988) *The Addictive Organization,* New York: Harper and Row.

Tart, C. (1987) *Walking Up,* Boston: Shambala.

Index

245